Lobbying for Social Change, Second Edition

Errata

Page	*For*	*Read*
vi	ABOUT THE EDITOR	ABOUT THE AUTHOR
49, line 13	countinued	counted
56, line 14	your	his or her
339, lines 20 & 22	Bartlett	Barlett

Willard C. Richan

Lobbying for Social Change
Second Edition

Noteworthy
REVIEWS
OF THE FIRST EDITION . . .

"In *Lobbying for Social Change*, Willard C. Richan, writing from a social work background, offers an in-depth description of what it takes to successfully lobby or advocate change in the absence of significant economic resources.

Various chapters cover assessing strengths and weaknesses, setting the action agenda, understanding policy makers, gathering evidence, lobbying one-on-one, speaking to an audience, testifying at hearings, using the mass media, and adapting one's approach to the particular issue content. While obviously written from a particular perspective, this book could be read profitably by anyone interested in lobbying."

Government & Politics Alert

More pre-publication
REVIEWS, COMMENTARIES, EVALUATIONS . . .

"Willard C. Richan's *Lobbying for Social Change* is a step-by-step handbook for entering the political arena. The book is thorough enough to be useful to someone launching a full-blown lobbying effort. It will also be useful as an occasional reference tool for those who find themselves involved in the public policy arena periodically, as is often the case with community psychologists."

The Community Psychologist

"Richan's highly readable book on lobbying is a must for any concerned professional or citizen seeking to affect social change. He covers all the bases, bringing together principles, examples, experiences, and 'how to do it' advice. The book is ideally suited as a text as well as a handbook for organizations and individuals."

Marvin Rosenberg, PhD
Associate Professor
of Applied Social Sciences,
Case Western Reserve University,
Cleveland, Ohio

"This is a useful volume for social workers functioning in the political arena and for teaching social work students the nuts and bolts of community organization or policy practice."

Dr. Edward Allan Brawley
Social Work Program,
Penn State University

"Using his hands-on experience with city and state legislators, Richan has fashioned a first-rate book that provides invaluable and practical information to those who wish to shape the development of public policy. An important contribution to the emerging policy practice literature."

Bruce S. Jansson, PhD
Professor,
School of Social Work,
University of Southern California
at Los Angeles

The Haworth Press, Inc.

NOTES FOR PROFESSIONAL LIBRARIANS AND LIBRARY USERS

This is an original book title published by The Haworth Press, Inc. Unless otherwise noted in specific chapters with attribution, materials in this book have not been previously published elsewhere in any format or language.

CONSERVATION AND PRESERVATION NOTES

All books published by The Haworth Press, Inc. and its imprints are printed on certified ph neutral, acid free book grade paper. This paper meets the minimum requirements of American National Standard for Information Sciences–Permanence of Paper for Printed Material, ANSI Z39.48-1984.

Lobbying for Social Change
Second Edition

HAWORTH Social Administration
Simon Slavin, EdD, ACSW, Senior Editor

New, Recent, and Forthcoming Titles:

Social Administration, 2nd Edition by Simon Slavin
Part I: An Introduction to Human Services Management
Part II: Managing Finances, Personnel and Information in Human Services

Beyond Altruism: Social Welfare Policy in American Society by Willard C. Richan

Human Services Computing: Concepts and Applications by Dick Schoech

Research Utilization in the Social Services: Innovations for Practice and Administration edited by Anthony J. Grasso and Irwin Epstein

Social Work Ethics on the Line by Charles S. Levy

Community Organization and Social Administration: Advances, Trends, and Emerging Principles by Terry Mizrahi and John D. Morrison

Performance Evaluation in the Human Services by Wayne Matheson, Cornelius Van Dyk, and Kenneth Millar

Lobbying for Social Change, 2nd Edition by Willard C. Richan

Lobbying for Social Change
Second Edition

Willard C. Richan

The Haworth Press
New York • London

The Haworth Press, Inc., 10 Alice Street, Binghamton, NY 13904-1580

Library of Congress Cataloging-in-Publication Data

Richan, Willard C.
Lobbying for social change / Willard C. Richan.–2nd ed.
p. cm.
Includes bibliographical references and index.
ISBN 0-7890-6003-5 (alk. paper).
1. Lobbying–United States. 2. United States–Social policy. I. Title.
JK1118.R53 1995
324'.4'0973–dc20 95-35019
CIP

Eudice Tontak Glassberg
1925-1988

Beloved friend and colleague,
and advocate for children to the end.

ABOUT THE ~~EDITOR~~ Author

Willard C. Richan, DSW, is Professor Emeritus at Temple University. He taught social welfare policy and lobbying for more than three decades prior to becoming "full-time retired" in 1993. He is currently actively involved with issues of welfare reform and childhood lead poisoning and continues to give workshops on lobbying. Dr. Richan was chosen "Social Worker of the Year" by the Pennsylvania Chapter of the National Association of Social Workers, mainly for his advocacy work. The former Chair of the Pennsylvania Political Action for Candidate Election (PACE), he is the author of several books on social welfare policy and practice, including *Beyond Altruism: Social Welfare Policy in American Society* (The Haworth Press, 1988). He is also the editor of *Human Services and Social Work Responsibility.* Dr. Richan is a member of the National Association of Social Workers, the Council of Social Work Education, and the American Association of University Professors.

CONTENTS

Preface to the Second Edition

When *Lobbying for Social Change* first appeared in 1991, George Bush was anticipating an easy reelection, buoyed by widespread support for Operation Desert Storm, the quick and easy victory over the forces of Iraqi strongman Saddam Hussein. Despite an apparent lock on the White House on the part of the Republicans, Congress remained firmly under the control of the Democrats, as did a majority of governorships in the country. It would ever be thus. Or so it seemed.

The second edition of this book arrives on a vastly different political landscape. Bush's Democratic successor, Bill Clinton, was in political hot water even before he took office, and his presidency has been wracked by conflict ever since. More important, both houses of Congress are now under Republican control, as are a majority of governorships, and the GOP is pushing a legislative agenda that threatens policies that were assumed to be solidly in place for the foreseeable future.

The nature of the political process itself is going through major changes, driven by a revolution in the technology of communications. Yet the underlying principles that have guided lobbying activity in the past continue to prevail. Politicians' attention spans are still closely tied to the intervals between elections. The ability to network with allies, stay focused on one's agenda, understand the policymaker's mindset, bone up on the issues, mobilize constituencies, and utilize the media of mass communications is still at the core of what it takes to be an effective advocate.

The first edition of *Lobbying for Social Change* profiled three members of the Pennsylvania State Legislature, to give insight into how things look through the eyes of the people charged with enacting policy. Senators John Peterson and Roxanne Jones and Representative Allen Kukovich are still there. Republican Peterson is back as chair of the Senate Public Health and Welfare Committee, after a brief hiatus when his party lost control of the chamber. Senator Jones is now the ranking Democrat on that committee. Many lobbyists whom we met in the first edition are still patrolling the corridors of the state and national capitols, getting a friendly legislator to insert a word or a comma in a bill, feeding policymakers strategic information, and, increasingly, mobilizing the folks back in the district to apply pressure to their representatives.

A new section has been added to the book, one reflecting the changing political scene. It contains a chapter on the increasing frustration of middle- and working-class Americans as they see their position in society erode and try to cope with a revolution in social relations and lifestyles. A second chapter looks at the revolutionary changes in technology and how they are transforming the political process. But the principles of lobbying originally outlined in *Lobbying for Social Change* continue to apply. Officeholders will come and go in future years, but the work of persuading them to act or not to act will be at heart the same.

Willard C. Richan, DSW

Acknowledgments

I owe a debt of gratitude to several people who helped to make this book possible. To David Austin and Bruce Jansson for reviewing major portions of the manuscript and making valuable suggestions. To Adeline and Murray Levine, who were most helpful in their comments on the sections dealing with mental health and abortion policy and the Love Canal crisis. Adeline was also instrumental in tracking down some critical material on Love Canal. To Ned Potter for his suggestions regarding the content on the mass media. To Richard Weisshaupt, Esq., and Susan Rogers for help in locating amicus briefs. Deborah Beck, my former student and now a professional lobbyist, not only arranged for contacts with state legislators and their staffs, but gave helpful feedback on the chapter on lobbying. More generally, her insights into that mysterious art form were invaluable. To Pennsylvania Senators Roxanne H. Jones and John E. Peterson, State Representative Allen G. Kukovich, and Barbara J. Gleim, former Executive Director of the Senate Public Health and Welfare Committee, I am especially grateful for being so open in sharing their experiences. Simon Slavin, my editor and respected colleague, was supportive throughout the enterprise. Finally, special thanks to those legions of students who helped me hone this material over more than a dozen years.

Introduction

This book is a guide to that mysterious world where our state and national policies are made. These policies determine the kind of air we breathe, the sort of treatment we and our loved ones can expect from the state if we get into trouble, the many ways government impinges on our lives every day–in short the very quality of life itself. I do not assume the reader has any prior knowledge of the world of public policy, only that he or she would like to be able to affect it.

They say a book should be written with *a* reader in mind. My imaginary reader is somebody who cares about what happens to people and wants to make a difference in the world but is not sure how to go about it. I have used as my model the hundreds of social work students I have taught these principles to and other professional and lay persons who have taken part in short-term workshops. Many of these people were at first intimidated by the whole process, certain they could never persuade policymakers to do what they wanted them to. It has been exciting to watch their confidence grow and with it their actual ability to make a difference.

My imaginary reader knows those are real people in Washington and the state capital making the decisions that rule our lives. The public policy arena, however, is seen as another world, far removed from the mundane existence most of us know on a daily basis. In that other world there is money–a lot of it. Power brokers can summon huge pressure groups, and famous names and faces that dominate the news media. While you and I rush around trying to meet deadlines in our unglamorous jobs and studies, wonder why we keep getting into stupid arguments with loved ones, and worry about an aging family member, *they,* that mysterious they, are out there pulling the strings. If this sounds at all like the way you see things, then you are the reader I had in mind.

First you must get rid of that vision of two separate worlds–one world inhabited by people like you and me and the other by those larger-than-life public figures. They, too, sometimes get bored and restless in their jobs, have pointless quarrels with loved ones, and feel the frustration of their own powerlessness in the hands of some other *they.* There is always another *they* to taunt us. Were that not so, the rate of alcoholism among members of Congress would not be so high, and promising politicians would not jeopardize their whole careers with a fleeting adventure in a motel room. They are human like the rest of us–a bit frightening when one stops to think of the power they wield.

Powerful they are. This is not, however, because they are smarter than we are. There are ways in which they *do* differ from the average American. One way is the driving ambition that got them where they are. That ambition–call it by its more attractive name, commitment–leads them to use their time in acquiring the knowledge and skill which is the true key to gaining influence in the policy arena. To a great extent this kind of information is free of charge. This means you and I can begin to wield more influence. We may never achieve major public office, but we do not have to in order to affect public policy.

It is my firm belief that the major reason more people do not become actively involved in advocating social change is *not* a lack of interest. How could anybody not care what happens to their tax money, the air they breathe, and the quality of life they bequeath to future generations? What deters most of us is a belief that what we say or do will make little difference. This is part of a general lack of confidence in our abilities; we do not want to look foolish. Understand that this set of beliefs did not just happen. It is drummed into us from our first breath to trust people more powerful and wise than we are. If this book teaches you to be less trusting in the wisdom of people in that other world, and more trusting in your own ability to think and to use basic good sense, it will have gone a long way in achieving its objectives.

If the idea of becoming an advocate in the public policy arena is overwhelming, it may help to know about other people who felt the same way. Lois, for instance, was the last person you would expect to be a lobbyist. She was a shy, retiring housewife until a tragedy transformed her into the leader of a national crusade that took her into the offices of mayors, governors, and members of Congress. In the process, this young woman with a high school education learned two cardinal principles of advocacy: you have to do your homework and know what you are talking about, and you can take on the so-called "experts" on their own ground without being one of them.

Jennie was a more typical first-time advocate. Her first taste of lobbying was as a student in a social work course. She had spent months studying the problem of truancy and was ready to "educate" a state senator. Her goal was to get a state education system to keep statistics on truancy in its local school districts. While not an earthshaking issue, perhaps, it is important if one considers the critical role of public education in preparing future citizens.

During her meeting with the senator, Jennie made a significant discovery: his 16-year-old son was a chronic truant. Drawing on her social work skills, Jennie helped the senator think about strategies for improving the chemistry between his son and the school. Yet she knew enough not to get permanently sidetracked from her original mission. Before she left she had exacted a promise from the senator that he would talk to the chair of the Senate Education Committee.

Don has no vision in either eye and gets around with the help of a white cane. He came to me in a panic when he learned that one of his assignments was to write an extensive policy brief laying out the arguments on both sides of an issue. The other assigned task was to do some lobbying. "I'll have to do an alternative assignment," he told me after the first class session. "No you won't," I responded, "though you and I may have to spend a lot of time together and it may take more than the regular semester." Later, I was glad I insisted, because Don ended up collaborating with the staff of a U.S. senator on policies concerning employment of the disabled.

Marty was once told he would spend the rest of his life in and out of mental hospitals. Now, as head of an organization of mental health consumers, he frequently lobbies public officials and teaches other "mentally ill" persons how to be advocates. There are people we label as "mentally retarded" who tell state legislators about the plight of the developmentally disabled in a way that you and I could not. They get a respectful hearing and, more important, results.

Deb Beck comes closer to fitting our stereotype of lobbyist. She has become a skilled advocate on drug and alcohol abuse issues. A few years ago her local unit of the National Association of Social Workers named her Social Worker of the Year for her lobbying work on behalf of drug and alcohol abuse victims. However, her task is the same as that faced by the neophytes: persuade people with the power to make decisions to make the right decisions.

The title of this book talks about advocating social change. Are advocates always seeking something new? In recent years, under the impetus of attempts to reduce government's social welfare functions, human service advocates have frequently found themselves fighting off changes they considered negative (Richan, 1983).

So you may at times want to lobby against social change, not for it. The principles you will employ in a resistance movement will be the same as those used in promoting affirmative changes. Given the nature of our political system, however, the task of the advocate is typically to call for new approaches, not simply hold onto old ones. At times, our government drags its feet, in the face of a crisis, as in the weak and belated response of both the administration and Congress to AIDS. Moreover, when government does act, it may meet the needs of only certain people. Most of us would probably agree that the problems facing ordinary citizens should take precedence over those of defense contractors, and the plight of the people with very limited means has priority over that of the very affluent. Not that the pain of personal crises is any less wrenching for the rich than the poor, but intuitively we sense that the former have fewer such crises and more alternatives for dealing with them.

THE POLICY CYCLE

There is a logical sequence in thinking about social policy that is different from the *chrono*logical sequence. The logical sequence starts with analysis of a social problem, which leads to formulation of policy, enactment of the policy in modified form, rules for implementing the policy, programs to carry out the intent of the policy, and finally, evaluation of the consequences. In reality, the problem-policy-program sequence is a never-ending series of interlocking cycles, one stage leading to others. It is a little like the old question, which came first, the chicken or the egg?

A social problem is not just adverse circumstances. It must be circumstances which affect a significant segment of the population *and* appear amenable to change. This definition is constantly changing. There was a time when slavery was not defined by the majority of Americans as the evil we know it to be, so for them it was not a "social problem."

There are personal troubles that individuals want to rid themselves of and which they try to resolve, with or without much real planning. Unless the trouble is seen as more than idiosyncratic, however, it is not defined as a social problem. When people began to realize that AIDS is more than a rare disease which happened to befall a few isolated individuals, it became a social problem.

Problems have different histories. When we first became aware that toxic waste disposal posed a massive threat, it was so new that no country had answers for dealing with it. The closest approximation to this kind of human-made disaster had been so-called natural disasters such as floods and tornadoes. As a result, there was a question whether the toxic waste disposal problem fell within the existing legal framework. Contrast that with welfare reform which has almost too rich a history. Old solutions and old debates make it hard to take a fresh look at poverty and chronic unemployment.

Our society is generating new social problems all the time. For example, we are developing a generation of young adults, many of whom will be wearing hearing aids before their parents are. The serious damage to young people's hearing caused by rock concerts, boom boxes, and headphones is predictable. Changing definitions will also create new problems in the coming years. Today, the lack of skill with a computer has not been defined as a social problem the way illiteracy has been. The time is fast approaching though, when computer illiteracy will indeed be looked on as a social problem. As people get older, certain symptoms are so widely shared and appear so inevitable that they are simply accepted as part of life. If science finds ways to maintain people's eyesight, hearing, and gastrointestinal functioning–to say nothing of life itself–far beyond what is now considered "normal," the aging process as we know it will also become a "social problem."

Being strictly tied to a linear conception of problem-policy-program can get in the way of seeing the true nature of the policymaking process. In 1988, some public officials had a problem–namely, getting re-elected. These officials saw welfare reform as a safe issue on which to mount a crusade, around which one could rally conservatives bent on getting the chiselers off the welfare rolls, humanitarians wanting to integrate the very poor into the economic mainstream, and feminists angry that absent fathers were getting away without supporting their families. So, with the help of authors who had achieved prominence writing about welfare dependency, they turned welfare reform into a major issue. The welfare rolls had been declining and the total cost of welfare transfers had been declining even more. Therefore, the problem of getting people off welfare and into jobs was no more urgent at that point than it had been for years. Note two points: there was not a new social problem of welfare dependency, and the policies being debated did not deal with a single social problem, but several.

Food aid policies deal with two quite different problems: increasing the nutrition of needy populations, and aiding agriculture. Some government housing programs have the function of increasing poor people's access to shelter and stimulating the construction industry.

You have a great deal of control over the extent to which you become active in trying to change policy, but little control over where in the cycle you enter the fray. Let us say that you are employed by a community mental health agency that must trim back its services because of federal budget cuts. The problem you and your agency face is salvaging programs that you believe are helping people in need. The etiology of mental disorders is relevant, but you do not have the luxury of stopping to design ideal solutions. The issues in the debate on funding are probably already well defined, and your task is to arm yourself with the best available information with which to argue your point of view.

The state legislature is considering a bill which would restrict access of minors to abortion services. The problem for one faction is abortion itself, which they consider to be murder. The opponents say the problem is denial of freedom of choice to young women and risks to their physical and mental health. During the debate you may find yourself arguing about the cost to the taxpayers caused by either outcome.

On the other hand, you can get involved at the beginning of the cycle and contribute to the thinking about AIDS or toxic waste disposal in new ways. Examining social problems in fundamental terms and opening up the widest possible array of solutions, along with preventing crises instead of always mopping up after them, are desired. Meanwhile, a large number of decisions with impact on many lives will go on being made. You can either have input into those decisions or abdicate the field to others.

This book does not deal with the whole policy cycle. The process of policy formulation may involve months, or even years, of searching for solutions to social problems. We pick up the process at the point that somebody is proposing solutions. A pro and a con are already emerging.

TAKING ONE STEP AT A TIME

Any task which is at first overwhelming becomes less intimidating if it is broken down into specific steps. This is certainly true of lobbying. The book is divided into three parts. The first, The Changing Context of Political Action, is new with this edition. It addresses the forces impinging on the political process in the last decade of the twentieth century. Chapter 1 looks at the political fallout from growing frustration with current social and economic conditions and insecurity about the future. The resulting political unrest has been capitalized on by conservative interests. In Chapter 2, we examine the transformation of the political process itself wrought by the current technological revolution.

Part II, Basic Steps, outlines a series of tasks which the advocate must carry out in preparation for lobbying–regardless of who is to be urged to do what and under what circumstances. While this may sound like a rigid formula-for-all-occasions, the steps are really guidelines which allow one to exercise a great deal of flexibility. The first step is assessing one's strengths and limitations, the subject of Chapter 3. We tend to underestimate our strengths and exaggerate the limits of our power. This chapter should be a useful antidote to that tendency. Next comes setting the agenda for action, the subject of Chapter 4. From the agenda, all else flows. As this chapter points out, it is usually easier to say what one does not want than to decide what one wants. Chapter 5 deals with the analysis of the target of one's lobbying: the policymaker. We must first decide who shall be the target, then try to understand how that person views the world. The definition of the situation is what the advocate seeks to change, as a way of getting the desired action. Chapters 6 and 7 go together. Chapter 6 deals with the gathering of evidence with which to persuade the policymaker. That step can be understood only in the context of putting together one's case, the subject of Chapter 7. In Part III, different kinds of action are discussed, not just lobbying in the narrow sense of direct work with a particular policymaker. We look at several different strategies, including such indirect approaches as speaking to community groups and using the mass media. Taking one's message directly to the policymaker, the topic of Chapter 8, is lobbying in its purest form. We look at ways of adapting one's message to the particular target's definitions. In Chapter 9, we consider ways of carrying one's message to the public as a speaker. As with the visit to the policymaker, the message must be adapted to the specific audience. Testifying in a legislative hearing, the subject of Chapter 10, can be an intimidating task. Knowing the territory and taking the task step-by-step helps to demystify the process. In Chapter 11, the use of the mass media is discussed. Television, radio, and the printed page are playing an increasing role in advocacy for social change, and it behooves us to learn how to get maximum mileage out of them. A critical factor in the way one uses the skills of the lobbyist is the content of the policy about which one is lobbying.

Most people have a general idea of how things work in Washington, DC and a vague sense that state government is basically the same. If one is to engage in lobbying at either level, it is essential to know the territory. Because this is familiar terrain to many readers, I have included this information in an appendix rather than in the main body of the book.

CASE EXAMPLES

To illustrate the general principles in the book, I have chosen four cases of social policy advocacy which involve diverse issues at all levels of government, and in the private sector. Since they are used only to illustrate major points, rather than being case studies in themselves, they are sketched in brief strokes. The references cited in the text will give you a fuller understanding of the cases. They concern the abortion controversy, funding of community mental health services, welfare reform, and toxic waste disposal.

Abortion: Holy War or War of Liberation?

It has been stated that wars based on ideology are among the most difficult to resolve, and this is apparently true of the abortion controversy. It gives us an opportunity to see how the political process evolves when there is virtually no give on either side. Yet here, as in all policy debates, the stakes are different for the respective parties, and there are many third parties seeking accommodation.

The abortion controversy is a good example of "single-issue" politics. Particularly for the core of the right-to-life movement, this is *the* issue. Its adherents have a single litmus test for politicians to deal with. This can give a constituency a real advantage which can outweigh the greater numerical strength of opponents with diverse interests.

There is little disagreement about the nature of the processes by which an ovum is fertilized, the biological changes that occur up to and after birth, or the physiology of abortion. There are different views about the trauma or lack of it for the woman and the fetus, particularly the psychological effects of abortion on women. But these are not the paramount issues in the controversy that has swirled around this question for more than two decades. The question so central to much of the debate–when does life begin?– is asked, not in a medical as much as a philosophical context.

The United States had no policy on abortion until the latter half of the nineteenth century, unless you call the evolving compilation of judicial experience in English and American common law a policy. Life was believed to start at the "quickening," the point in the fifth or sixth month when the woman could feel the fetus stirring inside her. However, even abortions after this stage of the pregnancy were generally considered misdemeanors.

It was after mid-century when most states passed tough laws that treated abortion at any time after conception as a felony except when the woman's life was in danger. The impetus came not from the church but from the medical profession. This fact is reflected in the discretion the statutes gave to doctors in abortion decisions.

Once the medical profession had established its hegemony over abortion, the issue faded into the background and the subject became more or less taboo. But, in practice, abortion was more prevalent than the language of the state laws might have suggested. The real concern was about the "back alley and coat hanger" variety of illegal operation. To the Catholic church, however, abortion under any circumstances was a mortal sin.

California was the first major battleground. A five-year campaign by liberal reformers resulted in a new law in 1967 which broadened the grounds of therapeutic abortions considerably. Instead of ending the abortion controversy, this outcome only served to raise it to a new level of intensity. Feminists decried the continued subordination of women to medical discretion and pushed for a policy of abortion as a right. Even more unhappy were traditional Catholics, especially when the number of therapeutic abortions went from 5,600 to more than three times that number in one year and passed the 100,000 mark by the early 1970s (Luker, 1984:94).

The abortion controversy entered a new phase on January 22, 1973, when the U.S. Supreme Court declared not only that abortion was legal but that a woman could demand one as a matter of right. The decision represented a crushing defeat for the anti-abortionists, who were becoming a significant political force in many states. It also symbolized the same "raw judicial power" that had helped to make school busing and other issues so inflammatory during the 1960s. It thus brought into the abortion controversy two powerful constituencies which had shown little interest in the issue up to that time: ultra-conservatives and Christian fundamentalists. The initial drive was for a Constitutional amendment declaring that life begins at conception and thus the fetus at any stage of gestation must be accorded the same protection as all citizens. When this drive stalled, the strategy became one of tacking anti-abortion riders onto various bills, particularly those dealing with health services. The high point in the campaign at the national level came with passage in 1976 of the Hyde Amendment denying Medicaid funds for abortions. This was upheld by the Supreme Court in what appeared to be a reversal of the stand taken in *Roe v. Wade*.

Throughout most of the 1980s, the anti-abortion coalition continued to hold the initiative, and it took on the aura of an unstoppable movement. But as so often happens in American politics, the winds suddenly shifted at the end of the decade. When the conservative majority on the Supreme Court upheld a particularly restrictive Missouri law, feminists reacted in outrage. The pro-choice forces went on the offensive, staging huge rallies and submitting bills in Congress and state legislatures aimed at liberalizing abortion policies. States rejected several anti-abortion proposals, and the fortunes of avowedly pro-choice candidates for office suddenly improved. The news media began treating this latest turn of the weather vane as a sea change which promised to reverse the previous anti-abortion trend.

Yet, clearly, the right-to-life movement was still a powerful force. The president promised to use the veto to resist efforts to liberalize the laws, and the Supreme Court would continue to interpret them conservatively, perhaps for decades to come. As of the mid-1990s, the war over abortion was looking more and more like a war of attrition.

Community Mental Health: The Unfulfilled Promise

Our second case is in many ways the opposite of the first. The need for quality mental health services is not controversial, although where these services ought to be provided–in hospitals or the general community–is a point of contention. Historically, the only politically active constituency for mental health services was professionals. Recently mental health consumers and their families have joined the effort. This latter constituency is stigmatized by the general public, which is concerned mainly about protection *against* the mentally ill. Not surprisingly, given these cross-currents, there has never been the political support for funding services on the scale commensurate with the conception. Ironically, community mental services were among the first examples of federal tax revenues going to welfare state benefits for the non-poor. Additionally, a major rationale for moving the mentally ill out of state hospitals was the failure of those institutions to provide treatment.

Between 1950 and 1981, the number of mental hospital beds in the United States was cut by two-thirds. In effect, we went from one bed for every 250 Americans to one bed for every 1,100 Americans; this during a time when the proportion of elderly in the population, the heaviest users of mental hospitals, was going up (U.S. Bureau of Census, 1962, 1983). This dramatic shift was not caused by political pressure, but by a revolution in mental health care in which new medications allowed the majority of patients to be released into the community.

The first entry of the federal government into the community mental health field was modest. Under a section of the National Mental Health Act of 1946, the main purpose of which was research and training, grants were made to states to establish community mental health services. Between 1948 and 1958, the federal support crept from $3 million to $4 million. State and local funds during the same period rose from $2.6 million to $50 million (Kurtz, 1960:386).

In 1963, President John F. Kennedy unveiled plans for a massive attack on the scourge of mental illness:

> If we launch a broad new mental health program now, it will be possible within a decade or two to reduce the number of patients now under custodial care by 50 percent or more. Many more mentally ill can be helped to remain in their own homes without hardship to themselves or their families. Those who are hospitalized can be restored to a useful life. (Kennedy, 1963:2)

Congress bought the conception, passing the Community Mental Health Centers Act by comfortable margins. The administration counted on the states to use funds, then being freed by the exodus from state mental hospitals, to take on the financial responsibility of putting flesh on the bones of the policy. This turned out to be a wrong assumption, and by the time of Kennedy's assassination, community mental health services were still an unfulfilled dream (Levine, 1981:52-53).

Kennedy's successor, Lyndon Johnson, and a compliant Congress moved the federal government more directly into the funding of the centers. The National Institute of Mental Health (NIMH), which administered the program, was able to bypass state mental health authorities and deal directly with local sponsors.

In the original conception, community mental health centers were supposed to both pick up the patients being jettisoned by the hospitals, and respond to an expanded demand for preventive services. As it turned out, it was the latter need which received the primary response from the professionals who ran the centers. As a result, most chronically mentally ill were ending up in nursing homes, general hospitals, homeless shelters, or the streets with little or no treatment other than medication to control their behaviors. (See U.S. Senate, 1976.)

It was clear by the late 1970s that the expansion of community-based services was not keeping up with the demand. Then in 1981 came the Reagan "revolution," with some of the sharpest cutbacks coming in community mental health services. The professionals found themselves no longer the unquestioned authority on the problem of mental illness. Meanwhile, new support for community-based mental health services was emerging from a source which had an even greater stake in the issue: consumers and their families.

The advocates for mental health funding faced an interesting dilemma. When these advocates presented the need for mental health care as a crisis, they were likely to alarm the public, thus adding fuel to the drive to rehospitalize the chronically mentally ill. Between the public fear and the pressure to keep down costs, expanded funding for community based services seemed a long way off.

Welfare Reform: Many Solutions, Few Successes

The next case, welfare reform, has been around in one form or another for at least 500 years. The term itself is ambiguous. In the 1960s, it was associated with attempts to expand the role of government in helping the poor. Now it has a different connotation– finding ways of moving the welfare recipients and potential recipients toward self-support.

Over the years, the basic issues have remained the same–is welfare primarily to meet basic survival needs or move people toward self-support? Are the recipients of aid short-changed by a miserly and oppressive system or are they living high off the hog at the expense of hard-working taxpayers? The fact that the problem remains while old solutions are dusted off and tried again in slightly different form suggests there are some underlying problems in the basic societal structure that are not being addressed.

In the first case example, we saw an impasse between two constituencies with sharply contrasting worldviews. In the second, there was a general consensus that mental health services were a good thing, but with uneven commitment to their support. In our third case, there is a set of broadly shared values which is in potential conflict: a belief that we should help the poor *and* that the poor should help themselves. That is one reason the same issues keep coming up, new solutions which look a lot like the old solutions keep being tried, and the problem never goes away.

Ronald Reagan put it this way in laying out his blueprint for America's economic recovery in his first State of the Union message in 1981:

> Those who through no fault of their own must depend on the rest of us . . . can rest assured that the social safety net of programs they depend on are exempt from any cuts. . . . But Government will not continue to subsidize individuals . . . where real need cannot be demonstrated. (Reagan, 1983:254)

Throughout his eight years in office, Reagan made welfare a particular target of his efforts to roll back government spending on social programs. The majority of Americans appeared to share his belief that public assistance, far from helping the poor, actually hurt their chances of escaping poverty by making them dependent.

The federal government first took on a role of providing public assistance to the needy in the depths of the depression of the 1930s. The idea of giving a helping hand to those who were down on their luck was hardly controversial, since most Americans knew victims of the economic crisis personally. But after World War II, when the large welfare caseloads continued despite relative prosperity, the old public belief in self-reliance asserted itself again, and with it a hardening of attitudes toward the welfare recipients. The fact that African Americans were disproportionately represented in welfare caseloads (not surprising, since they were also among the poorest Americans), exacerbated the resentment.

Every American president from John F. Kennedy onward set out to cut back on welfare costs. Each expressed in one way or another the dual agenda–take care of the truly needy but move the truly able into the work force. Ronald Reagan was the only one who made good on that promise. As part of an overall reduction in social programs, he got Congress to tighten up on eligibility standards. In particular they eliminated from the rolls many working people whose incomes fell below the poverty line. Still, there was the perception that welfare was too easy to obtain and, once on, families tended to stay on.

As the 1988 election year approached it looked as if welfare reform would again be a major issue. Several proposals were before Congress, all emphasizing moving recipients of Aid to Families with Dependent Children (AFDC) into the labor force and off welfare. A plan put forth by Senator Daniel P. Moynihan became the vehicle of policy change. In its final version, it stressed responsibility of the absent parent for child support, allowed states to require mothers with children as young as one year old to participate in work and training programs, and took a harder line in other ways to reduce welfare dependency, while building in support for day care and modestly expanding the eligibility of two-parent families.

Welfare reform was barely mentioned by either presidential candidate in the general election campaign of 1988, even though one of them, Michael Dukakis, had initially made the success of his own state's program a major part of his earlier drive for the Democratic nomination. Whereas Ronald Reagan had run against welfare in most of his campaigns, George Bush was more concerned with crime, the environment, and taxes. In the 1992 election, and again in the 1994 off-year elections, welfare reform roared back to center stage.

This apparent paradox–public clamor one moment, loss of interest the next–may be explained by the fact that the American welfare system, as it has evolved over the years, reflects two sharply conflicting, widely shared values: the poor should be helped, but everybody should stand on his or her own two feet. (See Tropman, 1989.) Under the circumstances, it takes little to spark a controversy about a system about which most Americans are unhappy but for different reasons.

Toxic Waste: The Ticking Time Bomb

In her celebrated book, *Silent Spring,* Rachel Carson begins by telling the story of a town in the heart of America, a place of prosperous farms and abundant forests full of birds and animals. Then a strange plague descends on the town and its surroundings, killing everything in its path. Children are stricken at play and die within hours. There are no more animals or birds, and the vegetation becomes brown and withered. Carson goes on to say:

> This town does not actually exist, but it might easily have a thousand counterparts in America or elsewhere in the world. I know of no community that has experienced all the misfortunes I describe. . . . A grim specter has crept upon us almost unnoticed, and this imagined tragedy may easily become a stark reality we all shall know. (Carson, 1962:3)

Fourteen years after Carson wrote her all-too-prophetic parable, a quiet residential area in upstate New York began to experience many of the things she had described. She saw the tragedy coming from the overuse of chemicals in agriculture. In the real-life enactment, a chemical dump was the culprit.

The romantic connotations of the name, Love Canal, are doubly ironic, for it is located in the honeymoon capital of the world: Niagara Falls, New York. It is hard to think of anything more reassuring to Americans than Niagara Falls: the symbol of unspoiled nature, for generations the picture on the Shredded Wheat® box. What few outside the area realize is that the cheap source of water power nature created has made Niagara Falls and the surrounding region a prime center of the chemical industry, and that means chemical waste dumps.

If you were trying to think of a movie script about the little guys against the big guys, you could not do better than the true story of Love Canal. Honest, hardworking folks begin to notice their children developing strange symptoms, and an ugly black ooze spreads over basement walls. Kids' feet and animals' noses are singed when they come in contact with the ground. Rocks explode when thrown against a wall. Out in the nearby playing field, half-decayed drums of noxious substances begin working their way up out of the ground. It is like an invasion from outer space, except that it is really happening (Brown, 1979, 1980; Levine, 1982).

Alarm over the situation spread rapidly. Homeowners living on top of the mess began to organize. Lacking funds, technical knowledge of waste disposal, and political experience, they forced a response from local, state, and national officials and triggered lawsuits involving staggering sums of money against the company that had done the original dumping. Love Canal and its fallout of national publicity helped accelerate action on the federal Superfund bill, charging the federal government with the responsibility for assuring that toxic waste would be cleaned up.

Our interest in this case arises from the fact that it pitted homeowners with limited resources against a multinational corporation and a resistive state bureaucracy. In addition, the residents, none of whom were experts, were dealing with highly technical matters. It thus holds important lessons for the advocate who lacks the obvious sources of political power.

At first, there was a tendency for residents of Love Canal to feel this was somebody else's problem (Gibbs, 1982). As the reality dawned on them they became frightened, then incensed, then politically mobilized. One factor in their success was their ability to keep tightly focused on achievable ends, resisting the temptation to be swept up in other people's causes. For example, they targeted their fire on public officials, passing up the temptation to punish the chemical company which had dumped the evil brew in the first place. Also, they used the national spotlight to gain concessions for themselves, rather than be lured off course by their temporary celebrity status.

In the end, the homeowners won their fight to be moved out of the area at government expense. A kind of victory, but meanwhile lives had been disrupted, people's health irrevocably destroyed, and women had miscarried. And the time bomb continues to tick under countless other neighborhoods.

The story of Love Canal begins in the 1940s, when the Hooker Chemical Company started dumping waste in the abandoned and uncompleted canal excavation. The dump was covered over and the land later deeded to the Niagara Falls School Board for one dollar. Under the pressure of the baby boom, the school board erected a school at the site and homes sprang up around it. Heavy rains later unsealed the chemical stew, precipitating the crisis (Brown, 1980).

Love Canal is an excellent example of advocacy by people who had to learn as they went, and in the face of seemingly overwhelming odds. While the case contributed to the enactment of the Superfund bill, the homeowners' primary concern was protection of their lives, health, and meager financial resources. Litigation against Occidental Petroleum, though perhaps the most significant element from the standpoint of the money involved and precedents for the future, was not the main focus of the citizens' action. The case comes closest to fitting what can be called *administrative* advocacy, efforts to get appointed officials to implement existing policy in a responsive and effective manner.

The administrative arm of government is at once the most immediate and remote branch. We are intensely aware of intrusions into private lives and the bite at tax time. For those living on the edge of desperation, a sudden withdrawal of benefits for arbitrary reasons can be the last straw. Yet the bureaucracy remains shrouded in relative mystery, faceless strangers meting out their own conception of just treatment. Except quadrennial elections, when we must choose between candidates for chief executive, whose stands on a wide range of issues have to be assessed in a lump, we feel powerless to hold anybody accountable. No wonder government bureaucrats have become the favorite whipping boy for cartoonists and politicians. The problem is, no one has come up with a better way to run the complex machinery of government.

Then there are the hopeful notes like Love Canal to tell us that the system does work, however imperfectly, and private citizens can demand redress and get it. As homeowners of Love Canal discovered, the way is not easy. Experienced officials know how to waffle and wait out the most adamant complainant. The answer is simply to learn the rules by which the game is played and be fiercely determined to get satisfaction.

Decisions and regulations coming out of Washington and your state capital are continually affecting you and your family and friends. Even those decisions about the troubles of "somebody else" may well affect you indirectly. If you work in a social agency, your work is impacted every day by public policies. Most of us have elderly family members who are facing dilemmas regarding their living arrangements and their need for adequate medical care. You may know somebody who has AIDS or is hooked on drugs or alcohol. Problems of domestic abuse, mental illness, and economic distress may seem rather remote, but they affect all of us directly or indirectly. Public policies have a major impact on all professions these days, so if you are a professional practitioner or training to be one, you have a stake in the decisions being made in the public sector.

In short, you cannot avoid social policy even if you want to. I hope you will do more than simply "live with it." I hope you will try to have an impact on social policy. In a real sense it means getting a little more control over your own life.

PART I: THE CHANGING CONTEXT OF POLITICAL ACTION

In recent years two trends have had a major impact on every aspect of the political process. One is the growing fear and frustration among middle- and working-class Americans as they watch their economic position erode. The reaction to downward mobility in the economic sphere has been compounded by a crumbling of old status relations among races and genders and rapid changes in lifestyle values. Chapter 1 describes these changes and how they impact electoral politics and the legislative process.

The second is a revolution in the technology of communications. Computers and satellites have both opened up the political process to groups which suddenly are able to send out their message in ways never before dreamed of, and tilted the balance between the haves and have-nots, because of the cost of many communications techniques. These changes and their political ramifications are examined in Chapter 2.

Chapter 1

The Politics of Frustration

In 1935, the most popular radio commentator in America called for rejection of the presidential candidates of both major parties and blamed the ills of the nation on Jewish banking interests. In 1995, the most popular radio commentator in America called for a rejection of mainstream politicians–his contempt for the previous Republican president exceeded only by his contempt for his Democratic successor–and blamed the ills of the country on the activities of feminists ("feminazis"), environmentalists, and civil rights leaders.

Father Charles Coughlin, the Depression-era evangelist, had an estimated weekly listening audience of ten million. An estimated 20 million listeners tune in to Rush Limbaugh each week. This is remarkably consistent in view of the increase in population in the interim. In both cases, their biggest appeal was to white males aged 25 to 50. These were people who thought they had a piece of the American dream only to discover that it was slipping out of their grasp. In the 1930s, the whole system was falling apart. In the 1990s it was less obvious, but for the first time, children from mainstream families were expected to do less well, economically, than their parents.

This is the politics of frustration. It can lead to the formation of armed militias and atrocities such as the bombing of the federal building in Oklahoma City. More typically it is expressed through the mass media and the ballot box. In the 1930s, it ushered in the rise of a militant labor movement and progressive government policies. In the 1990s, it has worked to the benefit of politicians who want to turn back the clock, in some cases all the way back to what existed before the 1930s. We need to understand the politics of frustration in order to devise effective lobbying strategies.

Political analyst Kevin Phillips was writing in the aftermath of the 1992 presidential election, but he could as easily have been describing what happened in the midterm congressional elections in 1994: "The election of 1992 marked the eruption of a powerful new force only beginning to make its mark in American politics: widespread frustration over the decline of middle-class prosperity" (Phillips, 1993:16). Republican President George Bush's popularity rating was the lowest of any president since Herbert Hoover's depressing percentage in the early days of the Great Depression, a harbinger of what was to come for Democrat Bill Clinton. After Ronald Reagan's 1980 victory, public opinion polls revealed that voters trusted Republicans more than Democrats to deal with the problem of unemployment, a margin of 61 percent to 20 percent. At the time of Bill Clinton's victory in 1992, the figures were reversed, with the Democrats viewed as more able to deal with unemployment by a 66 to 20 margin.

Phillips and other commentators blamed the voter reaction to Bush in part on the recession that accompanied the end of his tenure in the White House. But Clinton's low ratings two years later occurred during a surging recovery. Clearly something more fundamental was at work.

DOWN THE SLIPPERY SLOPE

On the surface, Allen Stenhouse and Mollie James would not seem to have a lot in common. Stenhouse was a $50,000-a-year insurance specialist with the CIGNA Corporation, living in a $279,000 condo in West Hartford, Connecticut. At age 48, he was a respected member of his community, served as senior treasurer of the local United Way, and was active in the Greater Hartford Arts Council. Mollie James was a $7.91-an-hour production worker who owned a modest home in a working-class district of Paterson, New Jersey. What unites these two is the fact that both have become victims of changes in corporate America during the 1980s. They have a few other things in common: they were part of the broadly defined sector of American society known as the middle class and dropped out of it. They believed their place in the pecking order was secure. And they played by the rules and lost.

Allen Stenhouse worked his way up, attending night school at Georgia State University while employed full time. He worked in the insurance field for 24 years. But two days before Christmas 1988 he was laid off, along with 2,000 other CIGNA employees. Try as he might he could not find another job. In 1989, his 14-year marriage ended in divorce. In 1990, he was able to get a minimum-wage job in the stockroom of a discount store. In 1991, he lost $13,000 trying to start his own consulting business. In 1992, the condo foreclosed and auctioned off his apartment. He owed $22,000 to the IRS for back taxes and penalties because he had withdrawn his retirement funds prematurely to pay bills. He sold his camcorder, photocopier, and fax machine to pay other bills. Suffering from depression, he ended up on a $1,039 disability pension. He paid for a psychiatrist out of his own pocket. As his economic fortunes declined, so did his place in society (Nussbaum, 1992).

In the 34 years she worked at Universal Manufacturing Company, Mollie James learned to do laminating, testing, machine operating, and press operating. She started at 95 cents an hour. "I could do any job in the plant," she said afterward. But that made no difference to MagneTek, Inc., the Los Angeles investment firm which took control of Universal in 1986. On June 30, 1989, it moved the operation from Paterson, New Jersey, to Matamoros, Mexico. The Paterson plant was turned into a distribution center, and James was offered a job in the shipping department. But she was not able to do the heavy lifting required, so she was let go. "We just always thought we would have a job," she said (Barlett & Steele, 1992:32-34).

In the summer of 1994, the Leslie Fay Company, a manufacturer of women's apparel, announced that it was moving 1000 jobs from its Wilkes-Barre, Pennsylvania, plant to Honduras and Guatemala, where it employs12- and 13- year-old girls to work 54 hours a week at less than 40 cents an hour. The company argued that it was forced into the move by global competition. In the past few decades, there has been a wholesale movement of clothing manufacture from the United States to developing countries.

Time was when cheap labor costs overseas meant cheap goods, but no more. Information-age technology has revolutionized the production of clothing in the past few decades. With the aid of computers and satellites, the manufacture of precision-crafted garments can be broken down into a number of steps that may take place in different countries or different parts of the same country. It is now possible for a company to seek out the locales with the cheapest labor and the most lax workplace regulations for producing parts of the same blouse or coat, with assembly of the final garment taking place in another low-wage area (Kamel, 1990).

U.S. auto firms have parts manufactured in *maquiladoros* just over the Mexican border. Banks in New York now have their accounting work done in the Caribbean. An American toy manufacturer has set up shop in southern China. The global workplace has come into its own in recent years, with devastating results for American workers.

Sometimes the cheapest labor is right here in the United States. Sociologist Elizabeth Petras (1992) used to have her students check the labels on their jackets to see where they were manufactured. She wanted them to see for themselves how jobs once held by Americans were now being performed in faraway places with low wage rates. But then she began getting a different answer: increasing numbers of students reported their clothes were "Made in the U.S.A." Investigation led her to discover a burgeoning sweatshop industry in New York and Philadelphia, where thousands of Asian immigrants toil for as little as 50 cents an hour. (See Lii, 1995.)

Since the early 1980s, millions of Americans who "always thought we would have a job" have had to accept a place lower down on the ladder or leave the work force altogether. It wasn't supposed to work that way. From the end of World War II until the early 1970s, a growing economic base fueled an expansion of the middle class. Blue collar and white collar workers were neighbors in the burgeoning suburbias across the country (Beatty, 1994:65). Republican President Dwight Eisenhower and his successor, Democrat John F. Kennedy, symbolized the centrist politics of that period. The divisions that rent the national fabric in the 1960s and early 1970s were not over competition between middle and working classes, but over race and foreign policy.

The economic floor began to give way around 1973, and a new term was introduced into the national vocabulary: stagflation. Real median family income, which had risen at an average rate of 2.7

percent since 1947, declined just as steadily into the 1980s. Between 1960 and 1974, the real salaries of experienced workers, regardless of education, rose 20 percent. Between 1974 and 1989, they fell 21.7 percent. From 1980 to 1990, middle income households fell from 73 percent of the total to 63 percent. During the same period, low income households increased by more than a third (Beatty, 1994:66).

The effects were especially devastating among young men, who had assumed they were safe. An increasing proportion of healthy men in the prime of life were unemployed or had left the job market altogether. In the 1970s, four out of five men aged 22 to 58 worked full-time. That had dropped to 70 percent in the 1980s. After inflation, men were earning a fifth less in wages and benefits. Rather than increasing their work to make up the difference, they were working less. What growth there was, occurred in what had traditionally been considered "women's work." During the 1980s, there were 27 more clerical, sales, and service jobs per thousand working-age Americans, while there were 16 fewer jobs per thousand in production, transportation, and common labor (Nasar, 1994). Overall, blue collar employment declined from 40 percent of the work force at the end of World War II, to 25 percent in the mid-1990s. By then, 40 percent of young males were not making enough to support a family of four (Zuckerman, 1994).

But the downward trend was not just hitting line workers. Two million middle management positions were permanently eliminated. As the loss of middle-class employment deepened, recovery from lay-offs became harder. In the early 1980s, 90 percent of those laid off from white collar jobs were reemployed in a similar position for equal or higher pay. In the late 1980s, that figure had slipped to 50 percent. By the early 1990s, it was down to 25 percent and still falling (Nussbaum, 1992:58).

What made the descent from the middle more devastating was the perennial reassurance that the state of the economy was basically sound. In 1989, President Ronald Reagan announced that nearly 19 million nonagricultural jobs had been created during his time in office. In 1995, President Bill Clinton announced that six million jobs had been created during his time in office. The fact was that the biggest job growth was in retail trade and services, two fields toward the lower end of the pay scale. Through the 1970s, approximately 1.5 million new manufacturing jobs were added each decade. In the 1980s, there were 300,000 fewer, and it was predicted there would be another million fewer by the end of the 1990s, despite the fact that this was a period of economic recovery (Barlett & Steele, 1992).

For some, the apparent security and fulfillment of the American dream vanishes. For others, the dream dies aborning. Michael and Julie Harlow of Cary, North Carolina, considered themselves middle class. When interviewed in early 1992, Michael, a 30-year-old veteran of eight years in the U.S. Air Force, was a night clerk in a hotel. Julie, 33, with a degree in business administration, divided her time between managing a gift shop and caring for their two-month-old daughter. Together they were making $20 to 25,000 a year. Said she, "Sometimes I think the American dream is about dead."

During the 1960s, commentators noted a paradox: as government opened up more opportunities for poor and minority Americans, instead of quelling the fires of discontent it seemed merely to fuel them. The explanation for this phenomenon was a "revolution of rising aspirations." The idea was that modest advances in civil and economic rights created hopes that rapidly outran them. As the system was unable to deliver on the promises, real or implied, frustration boiled over among those still mired in age-old patterns of discrimination. It became apparent that legal rights did not automatically translate into economic justice.

The frustration that surfaced in the 1990s was of a different sort. Here were people who assumed they had already made it into the mainstream and now felt the ground giving way under them. The depressed mood has hit not just people in the middle of a career, but college students looking ahead to a bleak future.

Well into the 1980s, representatives of just about every large company in the United States descended on the campus of Pennsylvania State University each spring, looking for talent to recruit. Seniors in engineering, business, and the sciences would go to the University's job center, arrange five or six trips to interviews around the country, and end up with a $45,000 job. But those days are gone forever, according to Penn State's director of career development. By 1995, on-campus interviewing had fallen by almost half over a five-year period. A feeling of "Why bother?" has set in among students, according to the career planning director at one college (Vigoda, 1995). It was a pattern that was visible all around the country. This is a predominantly Caucasian population which grew up in comfortable circumstances and whose parents shared their middle class optimism coming out of the postwar era of expansion. The question for these young people is not rising above their origins, but merely hanging on to what they have been accustomed to.

Downward mobility evokes a reaction which is different from the response to frustrated upward strivings, according to the respected Italian sociologist, Gino Germani (1966:375). Persons who are blocked from achieving upward mobility tend to adopt a progressive ideology, whereas those moving down the social scale are more likely to be reactionary. Studies have indicated, for instance, that manual workers whose fathers and grandfathers were also manual workers are more likely to lean leftward in their politics than persons who have entered the ranks of manual laborers from higher up on the social status scale. There is also some evidence that the downwardly mobile harbor greater ethnic prejudice than those whose status is stable (Lipset & Bendix, 1959:70-71).

Social scientists say downwardly mobile persons coming from the middle class, which tends to be more conservative, retain these attitudes because they feel, despite evidence to the contrary, that the descent is temporary. In other words, they have trouble believing they have permanently left their roots behind (Smelser & Lipset, 1966:49). They are particularly threatened if they perceive other groups as moving up when they are moving down. Germani (1966:374) believed this helps to explain the middle-class support of rightist totalitarianism in Germany during the 1920s and 1930s.

Compounding the feeling of lost ground in the economic realm was a different kind of a threat: the undermining of traditional assumptions about gender, race, and life-style values. It impacted most heavily on Caucasian males, Christian conservatives, and regionally on the southeastern United States. In the beginning, the cause of racial justice was as much a matter of liberal white *noblesse oblige* as it was black demands for justice. Even at this point, school desegregation and voting rights were the occasion for bitter conflict in the South. As African Americans became more militant and independent of their white allies and major cities erupted into violence, some of the earlier white support eroded, and issues such as affirmative action split the old civil rights coalition apart.

In the 1950s and early 1960s, male dominance in the home and the workplace was so much a part of the social fabric that women as well as men accepted it as the natural order of things. As women began to challenge the status quo, a strong backlash developed. By the mid-1990s, *Ms* magazine was reporting that domestic violence was the leading cause of injury among U.S. women, exceeding muggings, rapes by strangers, and auto accidents combined; that at least one in four women victims of domestic violence were pregnant at the time; and more than three million children witnessed acts of domestic violence each year (*Ms*, 1994). The rate of forcible rapes had increased more than 27 percent between 1983 and 1992 (U.S. Bureau of Census, 1994:198).

Traditional religion had provided intellectual underpinnings for the subordinate status of women. Coincidental with the rise of feminism was a revolution in sexual mores, and together these evoked a harsh reaction, particularly among Protestant fundamentalists. The abortion issue united this religious constituency with an unlikely ally: Roman Catholics. A cluster of issues, ranging from abortion to homosexuality to drug abuse on college campuses and opposition to the war in Vietnam, became the rallying point for a new kind of populism on the right. The demise of the labor movement had left a political vacuum in the ranks of working-class Americans, and now what was to become known as the religious right moved into it.

It is the combination of lost economic power and the backlash against a revolution in national mores that has given the politics of frustration its tremendous force. But the angry American middle class of the mid-1990s was a volatile mix. Pollster Stanley Greenberg (1995) has suggested that no political party can count on its support. Overriding everything else is the feeling of resentment and disillusionment, something which Ross Perot parleyed into a 20 percent vote in his 1992 third-party bid for the presidency. It is important not to read data from one slice of time as representing long-term trends. For example, Kevin Phillips (1993) saw in George Bush's poor showing a rejection of supply-side economics. Yet two years later, voters gave a congressional majority to Republicans calling for something very much akin to supply-side economics.

LOOKING FOR VILLAINS

Who or what was responsible for Larry Weikel's being laid off for good after 24 years of working for the Diamond Glass Company of Royersford, Pennsylvania? Was it the heirs to the century-old family-owned business who sold it to new owners in the early 1980s? Was it the new management team that had acquired a second glassmaking plant in West Virginia from a bankrupt firm? Or was it their decision to go public two years later? Or the subsequent purchases of other troubled glass manufacturers? Or the heavy borrowing, to finance the expansion binge? Or the Wall Street investors who made a killing in the millions of dollars in the process? Or the U.S. Congress, which allowed such high-stakes financial manipulations to go unregulated (Barlett & Steele, 1992:13-14)?

Whom should Marie Whitt, displaced after 17 years of loyal service at Leslie Fay's Wilkes-Barre plant, be mad at? The company for shifting her job to Central America? The overseas competition? Or the young girls putting in 54-hour weeks for a pittance?

One of the frustrating things for downwardly mobile American workers in the 1980s and 1990s has been the amorphous nature of the enemy. It is hard for workers to know whom to blame. Mergers, take-overs, buy-outs, corporate downsizing, globalization of production–these arcane transactions involve people far removed from where the pain is, both geographically and structurally. It can be just as baffling for middle managers who thought they were secure.

Workers and supervisors in Plant X hear their company has been merged with Company Y. Not to worry. Operations will continue as before. Your check will look a little different, but your pay and benefits will all remain the same. Then a new management team arrives. At first things seem the same, but then the staff notices a change in attitudes. These new people are strictly business. No more old-boy network where everybody knows everybody else. There are rumors that the plant is going to close, but management assures the employees that it is here to stay.

Then one day comes the word: selective lay-offs in order to remain competitive. Later on the news that the local operations *will* terminate, after all. In two months. Please be sure to empty your desk and remove all personal effects no later than . . . .

Whether the underlying cause is corporate restructuring or reckless borrowing or inability to compete in the global market, the effects are equally devastating for employees. Not only is it hard to figure out who the villains are, but while one's own fortunes are plummeting, the media report on how the economy is forging ahead. One reaction is to blame the self. Another is to lash out at something, anything, that can be identified as a target. On a personal level, the target can be a spouse, a child, an employer, or a coworker. On a political level, the targets become more generalized.

In the 1930s in Germany, the targets were Jews and communists, the two often being lumped into the same category. The American radio priest, Father Coughlin, began by attacking capitalists, then focused specifically on bankers and eventually Jewish bankers. While anti-Semitism is still prevalent in this country, although often of a more subtle variety than what occurred in the 1930s, other groups have become the focus of the anger. Two in particular, as we have seen, are women and racial minorities.

It is not that these target groups have surpassed the majority economically. For example, in 1992, the poverty rate was virtually identical among Caucasian families headed by a high school dropout, Hispanic families headed by a high school graduate with no college education, and African-American families headed by a person with some college (U.S. Bureau of Census, 1994:478). And female-headed households continued to be the most poverty-stricken of all. Women who managed to move ahead career-wise were still expected in most cases to carry the major burden for child rearing and household chores, as well as care of aging relatives. But clearly, gender roles in the home as well as the workplace were going through profound changes in the the 1990s, and these exacerbated the feeling among many men that their previous position of dominance was being undermined.

To a large extent, the politics of frustration becomes a politics of symbols. Latent animosities which lie dormant but close to the surface become flashpoints, seemingly without logic. The changing public attitudes about Aid to Families with Dependent Children (AFDC) illustrate the way in which a nonissue in one period is thrust to center stage in another, in response to pervasive feelings of frustration. Since the early 1950s, AFDC recipients have been the subject of negative stereotypes, and there have been countless attempts to shake up the welfare system. Yet the program has survived in essentially the same form. The public has been critical but relatively tolerant of the system. In 1988, when George Bush ran for reelection against Michael Dukakis, welfare reform was a nonissue, as it had been in most previous presidential elections.

In 1992, AFDC still represented about one percent of federal government outlays; reducing it could have little impact either in the national deficit or the taxpayer's burden. In real dollars, the benefits were going down, and federal and state actions were keeping the numbers of recipients within bounds. Yet suddenly it was a national crisis, threatening the integrity of the national treasury and robbing taxpayers of hard-earned dollars. All major presidential candidates vowed strong action to curb the epidemic. In the 1994 congressional elections and in the subsequent session of Congress, welfare reform took front and center as *the* "hot button" issue. Furthermore, the proposals for reform were far more drastic than previous ones.

The frustrations of the middle class expressed themselves in another way. The 1992 elections were noted for the degree of mean-spiritedness which pervaded them. Candidates' personal lives came under scrutiny as never before. Negative campaigning was the rule because negative campaigning worked. Two succeeding presidents, one a Republican, the other a Democrat, hit record lows in their popularity ratings.

In 1992, the year that the one-term Republican president, George Bush, was defeated, two Pulitzer Prize-winning reporters wrote a bestseller which spoke directly to the widespread sense of frustration and insecurity among middle- and working-class Americans. *America: What Went Wrong?*, originally published as a series of articles in the *Philadelphia Inquirer*, was a hard-hitting and well-researched critique of corporate plunder and political failure. It was followed in 1994 by a similar work by the same two authors: *America: Who Really Pays the Taxes?* The authors' prescriptions for redress ranged from tightening regulations on business to making the tax structure more progressive. They were consistent with a tradition of government activism that had occupied the political mainstream since the Great Depression.

The two books, bestsellers, were widely praised by reviewers. The authors were interviewed on television and radio. But in the 1994 congressional elections, the voters opted for proponents of a "Contract with America" which would strip away government regulations and give added tax breaks to large corporations. Clearly, authors Donald Barlett and James Steele (1992;1994) were not being listened to by the American electorate.

Political attitudes do not just happen. They are shaped by campaign rhetoric. Amorphous feelings of fear and frustration crystallize around specific issues and specific targets. In the 1930s, it was welfare state liberals who dominated the rhetorical battlefield, despite the clamor on the far right and the far left. In the 1990s, it was a combination of conservative intellectuals and evangelical religious groups that defined the terms of the debate.

THE RISE OF THE CONSERVATIVE INTELLECTUALS

Franklin D. Roosevelt and Adolf Hitler came to power within a few weeks of each other in the winter of 1933, when their countries were in economic chaos. Their approaches to governing reflected deep-seated differences in the two societies. Hitler, capitalizing on an historic affinity for paternalistic strongmen and militarism, moved quickly to establish a total dictatorship in which any dissent was met by imprisonment or death. In contrast, Roosevelt, stepping into a monumental crisis in a country used to limited government and unlimited speech, took a pragmatic approach that encouraged innovative thinking. Dissenting ideas were not just tolerated, they were actively solicited. As the federal bureaucracy proliferated, it attracted to Washington an army of intellectuals seeking to reverse the country's declining fortunes. The view of government as an instrument of social and economic reform soon invaded the universities and the mass media. Marxism became fashionable in some intellectual circles. Considering the nativistic, nostalgic philosophy that had dominated the federal government only a decade before, it was a transformation of gigantic proportions.

In the succeeding years, the political dialogue between right and left was spirited, but tended to converge at the center. Conservatives were lampooned as a combination of southern segregationists and Babbit-like business executives. Republican leaders found themselves fighting a defensive war against the skillful and ever-popular Franklin D. Roosevelt. A broad national consensus developed, one which emphasized a continuation of modest increments in the welfare state at home and a strong military presence abroad. In the early 1950s, Senator Joseph McCarthy disrupted the harmony with his anti-communist witchhunt, but he never had much impact on domestic economic policies, and the mainstream media were highly critical of his methods. It was his own excesses, against a moderate Republican president, Dwight Eisenhower, and senior military leaders that finally brought him down.

But as McCarthy's star was plummeting, another was rising from the conservative horizon. William F. Buckley, Jr., had the air of a patrician and a gift with words to match. The son of a wealthy Connecticut family and a graduate of Yale University, he was harder for the press establishment to caricature than the surly interloper from Wisconsin had been. In 1955, Buckley launched the *National Review,* "a conservative weekly journal of opinion." Its tone and format mimicked those of the liberal-leaning *Nation* and *New Republic.* Buckley's signature piece, a "Publisher's Statement," made clear that here was no Babbit nor segregationist bimbo:

> It is [on college campuses] . . . that we see how a number of energetic innovators . . . succeeded over the years in capturing the liberal intellectual imagination. And since ideas rule the world, the ideologues, having won over the intellectual class, simply walked in and started to run things. (Buckley, 1955)

The right finally had a voice with which to challenge the rhetoric of the left. Buckley's style was elegant, graced with references to Galileo, de Tocqueville, and Jefferson; it was the language of the intellectual mainstream, but his message was markedly different. For example, in a book whose dedication page read like a right-wing who's who, he asserted that Senator Joseph McCarthy had been vilified because he dared to attack the liberal establishment; the welfare state was an anomally; and, more generally, by definition that government was best which governed least. Buckley was not above criticizing the Republican leadership for its failure to articulate a clear alternative to the left. It was not just that Dwight Eisenhower confessed difficulty in debating with Soviet Marshal Zhukov on the merits of communism versus capitalism, but that he saw the free market system as inherently harder to defend (1959:183-4).

Buckley and a growing number of conservative disciples continued to hammer home their message in subsequent years. The resurgence of the left on college campuses and in the media during the 1960s overshadowed them for a time, but meanwhile they were effectively propagating the rhetoric which would come to dominate political debates of the 1980s and 1990s.

The conservative rhetoric of the 1990s is being written by a cadre of intellectuals who are young, well-educated, and well-connected. Some are the children of senior members of the conservative movement, such as Irving Kristol and Norman Podhoretz. Some got their start by writing for William F. Buckley's *National Review.* They are at home with books, but as children of the television age they can also spit out sound bites that catch the attention of the public (Atlas, 1995). What united them was, first and foremost, a determination to rid the White House of Bill and Hillary Clinton and to turn Congress into an instrument for rolling back the welfare state. They have little patience with the tendency of politicians to compromise and go for the middle ground, whether Democrats or Republicans, and they are supremely confident.

The conservative intellectuals say the tide of history is running with them, and that it is only a matter of time before national policies will reflect what they see as the people's will. This is not just a rightward swing of the political pendulum, they believe, but a trend that will be around for a long time to come. This is precisely the thinking of another political constituency that historically has been held in contempt by intellectuals: evangelical Protestants. Ralph Reed, Executive Director of the Christian Coalition, says his group is thinking in terms of not the next five years, but the next 20 years. Candidates may come and go; but in the end the movement will prevail (Blumenthal, 1994).

THE RELIGIOUS RIGHT

In 1992, the evangelical Christians became the largest single constituency in the Republican Party. They were frank about their political agenda: to create in the United States a Christian nation, by which they meant one that shared their vision of the good society. In states as disparate as Texas, Virginia, Minnesota, and Oregon, during the 1994 congressional election campaigns, the religious right took control of the state Republican party. Moderate Republican leaders engaged in defensive warfare or made peace with the insurgents.

At a political training conference in Fort Lauderdale, Florida, 2,000 activists stood facing an American flag with a cross superimposed on it and recited a pledge which went like this: "I pledge allegiance to the Christian flag, and to the Saviour, for whose Kingdom it stands, one Saviour, crucified, risen, and coming again, with life and liberty for all who believe" (Blumenthal, 1994).

Evangelical Protestants in this country were not always so politically involved. In fact, over the years they tended to eschew partisan political activity. Preachers in this tradition, though many of them were charismatic public figures, urged their followers to look to the afterlife for salvation. It was not until the late 1970s that their concerns became more avowedly political.

In the early days of radio, evangelical ministers were quick to appreciate the potential of the new medium, but religious broadcasting tended to be a local affair, largely in the Southeast. Preaching, Southern-style, far more intimate and personal than the scholarly sermonizing in mainstream Protestant pulpits in the North, was perfectly suited to radio. Not surprisingly, most of the present-day televangelists are from the South (Schultze, 1991:83-5). With the advent of television, the potential audience expanded. Evangelists, lacking the financial support of large institutionalized churches, were compelled to engage in self-promotion and fundraising via their preaching in a way that was not true of the more established denominations. Selling became second nature to them (Schultze,

1991:153-4). It was a short step from huckstering in the business sense to political huckstering.

In the late 1970s, there was a convergence of events that accelerated the rise of the televangelists. Crumbling racial and gender barriers and an apparent relaxation of traditional sexual taboos, which occurred in the 1960s and early 1970s, were provoking a backlash. The message of the evangelist preachers seemed to respond to the need for social stability. Television became the medium of choice for transmitting the message. It both isolated people from one another and provided an illusion of intimacy. But television took money, a lot more than radio, so the ability to enter people's living rooms depended on organization and well-heeled backers.

In 1974, Arizona congressman John Conlan, and Bill Bright, president and founder of the Campus Crusade for Christ, formed a tax-exempt organization under the name of Intercessors of America. Using telephone "prayer chains" and a mailing to 120,000 members of the clergy, they promoted a political action manual written by Bright. It told readers how to take over local precincts. Intercessors of America set up a "Christian Embassy" on Capitol Hill and began evangelizing members of Congress, the military, the judiciary, and the diplomatic service. With the endorsement of Billy Graham and Norman Vincent Peale, they got 20 businessmen to donate $50,000 apiece. The goal of their saturation campaign was to train five million people from 150,000 churches to carry on the crusade.

When Intercessors of America collapsed, Bill Bright carried on the same campaign under a different title–Here's Life, America. He raised $100 million and set his sights on bringing in $1 billion. Business interests invested heavily in the effort. In one weekend, Texas oilman Nelson Bunker Hunt raised $20 million from business associates and added $10 million of his own. By the mid-1980s, Here's Life, America had garnered $170 million from Pepsico, Mobil Corporation, the Adolph Coors family, and other sources. Many of its big contributors were actively involved in right-wing political causes. It would serve as a model for a later generation of evangelical activists (Liebman, 1983:50-2).

The West Coast-based Christian Voice, founded in 1978, was more explicit in its social and political agenda: anti-gay, anti-pornography, anti-abortion, pro-family, pro-school prayer. It opposed the teaching of evolution in the public schools and warned of the dangers of "secular humanism." It held the government to be immoral in its "betrayal" of ruling regimes in Taiwan and Rhodesia. It accused the National Council of Churches of promoting Marxist policies at home and marxist guerrillas abroad. Its "Congressional Report Card," mailed to 37,000 pastors and 150,000 lay persons rated members of Congress on these and other issues (Huntington & Kaplan, 1980).

The evangelical lobbying group that would bring together these initiatives and turn them into a powerful political movement was the Moral Majority, founded in 1979 by the Reverend Jerry Falwell. It included Moral Majority, Inc., a lobbying operation; the Moral Majority Foundation, to educate ministers and lay persons and conduct voter registration campaigns; the Moral Majority Legal Defense Fund, to counteract the influence of the American Civil Liberties Union; and the Moral Majority Political Action Committee, whose function would parallel other PACs. Its emphasis was on grassroots mobilization. With chapters in all 50 states, it was able to register two to four million new voters (Liebman, 1983:54).

Television and other media of mass communications were an integral part of the Moral Majority's strategic arsenal. The televangelists spread its message nationwide, so it soon reached far beyond its original base in the Bible Belt. Not all preachers of the airwaves joined the new political movement. Oral Roberts, Rex Humbard, and Jimmy Swaggart, household names among Christian fundamentalists, stayed out of the political arena by and large; however partisan their implicit message. But a growing number, led by Jerry Falwell, Pat Robertson, and Jim Bakker, made no bones about their intention to reshape the political landscape (Wuthnow, 1983:173).

The strategy was working. For example, nearly one in four viewers of Pat Robertson's "700 Club" said a "very important reason" for tuning in was to find out whom to vote for (Gantz & Kowalewski, 1979). Regionally, the core constituency was Southern. Demographically, it was not far out of the mainstream. For example, one survey in Metropolitan Dallas, Texas, found that 60 percent of supporters of the Moral Majority were white collar workers, as opposed to 70 percent of nonsupporters. Supporters tended to have less formal education. The major distinction was in religious affiliation: 29 percent of Moral Majority supporters identified themselves as fundamentalists; only 9 percent of nonsupporters did so (Shupe & Stacey, 1983:106).

Televangelists have been effective in cultivating their image as simple, backwoods folks with little knowledge of modern technology. In fact, they are highly sophisticated in using the electronic media. They use state-of-the-art equipment and expert engineering. Evangelist Robert Schuller was using high-definition TV in his Crystal Cathedral long before it had found its way into major league sports stadiums. Pat Robertson and Jim Bakker saw the potential of cable television early in its history. In the 1950s, while many parts of the United States outside major metropolitan areas were still discovering television, Rex Humbard built a church in Akron, Ohio, engineered specifically to use high-tech TV production methods (Schultze, 1991:37-8).

It is not only the engineering that has been sophisticated. Televangelists historically have been excellent entertainers. They are able to understand mass audiences and what they are seeking. They know instinctively how to speak to the hunger of lonely and frustrated people, in an age when the way to reach them is through the electronic media. In short, these objects of ridicule among sophisticated journalists are far ahead in the race to move into the politics of the information age.

An old labor union anthem asks, "Which side are you on?" The obvious answer is, with the workers and against the bosses. In 1994, virtually the same words were used at a political convention in Virginia. Only this time it was under Republican auspices, and the candidate who dominated the proceedings was Oliver North, the arch-conservative who had masterminded the Iran-Contra arms-for-hostages deal. It was a graphic demonstration of the Christian right's mastery of politics as theater.

The 14,000 convention delegates sit jammed into the cavernous convention hall as the theme song from *Rocky III* booms out from loudspeakers. Suddenly the room goes dark and a huge black-and-white picture of Jane Fonda is flashed on a 30-foot-tall video screen. Booing wells up from the audience. Then a huge picture of

> Jesse Jackson. More booing. The *Rocky III* theme gets louder. Picture of CBS anchorman Dan Rather. More booing. The music goes up a few decibels. ABC newsman Sam Donaldson. More booing. Bill Clinton. The booing is practically a shout now. Then in block letters that fill the screen, WHOSE SIDE ARE YOU ON? Quickly followed by a promotional piece for Oliver North. And then, standing alone under the glare of the spotlights is the candidate himself, and the hall breaks into pandemonium. The soldier hero has come to rescue the country from the forces of darkness (Blumenthal, 1994).

North was the leading actor, but Ralph Reed, head of the Christian Coalition, was the producer. The zealous and single-minded promotion of a narrow agenda lends itself to ridicule in the mainstream media when its advocates are clearly in the minority. But when the political tide is running its way, as appeared to be happening with the far right in the mid-1990s, it has great power to define issues and direct the policy debate. The widespread tendency of political interest groups to compromise and seek common ground enhances the bargaining power of a constituency that sees all issues in stark moral terms and would rather lose the battle than the purity of its position.

In early 1994, it appeared that the Christian Coalition, the driving force behind this movement, was broadening its agenda beyond the so-called "social" issues when Ralph Reed, the executive director, announced a million-dollar campaign to promote the GOP "Contract with America," many of whose items concerned economic issues and the downsizing of government (Berke, 1994). But 15 months later, a Christian conservative spokesperson complained, "The Republican leadership wants to back away from the party's moral stance." The major irritant at the time was a welfare reform package, sponsored by the House GOP leadership, which was feared might inadvertently encourage more abortions, an anathema to Christian conservatives. But the seeds of the problem had been planted long before when the crafters of the "Contract with America" had refused to include potentially divisive items against abortion and for school prayer (Thomma, 1995). In time, the coalition of conservative forces would spend their energy. The frustrations among voters to which they were appealing were volatile and could easily turn against them. Old animosities within the movement would come back to haunt them. But as the end of the twentieth century approached, the coalition dominated the political landscape.

LOBBYING IN A TIME OF POLITICAL FRUSTRATION

I have no way of knowing what your political orientation is. You may be an enthusiastic "ditto-head" who hangs on every word from radio and television commentator Rush Limbaugh, a proponent of less government, especially in the human services realm. Or you may favor an expanded welfare state. I shall assume, for purposes of this text, that you are closer to the latter than the former. That is not because it reflects my own political biases (it does) but because, in thinking about how to cope with the politics of frustration, it is useful to begin with the worst case scenario.

We will find that there are many lessons to be learned from the people who moved from the political shadows to the point where they were setting the agenda and winning elections. How did they do it? First of all, they assumed they would ultimately prevail. Second, they assumed they would prevail only through hard and persistent effort. Third, they became experts regarding the issues they cared about. Fourth, they became experts in the political process. Fifth, they mastered the art and science of communication. Sixth, they took advantage of every opportunity that came their way. Let us look at each of these things they did.

Assuming that history is on your side. Which it is. Also on your opponent's side. The fact is, no movement, particularly one that defines things in absolutes, prevails forever in this society. A basic characteristic of Americans is their mistrust of extremes, and in time the pendulum swings to the other side of dead center. That is a cause of hope, not complacency. How long it takes for the swing to occur and how far the swing goes is *not* inevitable. And it needs to be seen in terms of thousands of lives affected, thousands of dreams aborted while awaiting the shift.

It is no accident that the religious right has been a major factor in the conservative swing of the pendulum. I have been struck by the optimism of truly religious folk under the most daunting of circumstances. Whether African Americans struggling against the drug dealers down the block in a Northern city, or rural Southerners scratching an existence out of a hostile environment, or Central Americans hiding from the death squads, they believe God will not let them down. But you don't have to buy the notion of Supreme Being in order to have faith that setbacks are only interruptions on the way to ultimate victory.

It has become fashionable to be pessimistic in the name of "realism." Somehow the person who expects the worst is thought to be more world-wise than the person who is too hopeful. In the very short term, the desperation born of imminent disaster may mobilize one's resources–for example, on a sinking ship or in a burning building. But over the long haul–and we are talking about a very long haul–the belief in eventual success is energizing.

The road to hell is paved with good excuses. To demonstrate the importance of persistence in lobbying, I shall use a very different kind of task: working one-on-one with high school drop-outs in an inner city neighborhood. The ones I know personally start out "knowing" they cannot learn, cannot find a job–in short, can succeed at little but watching TV, shooting baskets, and hanging out on the corner with their friends. People say they have lots of potential, but somehow the potential never gets translated into action. As one man put it, potential is another way of saying unused ability.

I know of people who have succeeded in working with such youths. Some have professional credentials, some do not. The distinguishing feature that marks them all is their total personal investment in their work and the fact that "give up" is not part of their vocabulary. The youths will put them to the test, trying to get them to go away, so they can say to themselves, "See, I knew they didn't care. See, I'm not worth helping." But the mentors keep coming back, keep finding new ways to try to punch through the wall that the youths hide behind. Sometimes it works, sometimes not. But then, the only way to know for sure whether your efforts will succeed or not is to give up. Then you know for sure that you will fail.

Translating all this to the political arena, rarely will you find that success comes easily. Typically, a policy change takes several sessions of Congress or the state legislature to become law. At the end of every two years, bills still pending automatically die and have to be reintroduced in the next session. So if you are advocating a change in policy, especially a major one, count on spending years on it. Even then, you may see a very watered-down version of your plan adopted. Or none. Not that your time has been wasted. In the process of promoting your cause you have educated a lot of people, some of whom you will never meet. And elements of what you want will find their way into the national culture, even without a piece of legislation or regulatory change.

Becoming an expert on the issues. During the many years that they were on the outside looking in, conservatives discovered the advantage of backing the cause that nobody loves. Namely, the need to know the arguments better than anybody else. While the majority were so sure they were right that they didn't bother to find out what the minority were saying, the latter were forced to look for every scrap of evidence to support their case. As a result, they were often able to argue more effectively than the majority, to raise doubts in the public mind about the conventional wisdom, and then to knock it down. It does not mean they were "right" in some cosmic sense. Just that many of them handled themselves more effectively in the give-and-take of battle than their opponents.

Knowing the political process. Many elections are won or lost on the basis of who knows the rules better. When does one have to file as a candidate? How many signatures are needed on the petitions? How many extra signatures should one get in order to make up for the ones that will be nullified as not valid? Many legislative contests are decided in the same way. Experienced lobbyists know which mark-up session to attend, what kind of language to insert in a bill–sometimes what mark of punctuation. The details are boring, which is why it is possible for insiders to leave many constituencies out of the process until it is too late to affect the outcome.

That kind of knowledge is there for anybody to use. Leaders of the religious right and other conservative groups were the ones who did so. They paid close attention to the details of the political process. They published manuals on how to take over precinct jobs that nobody else cared about. They built grassroots power step-by-step. Knowing the importance of money, both how to attract it and how to spend it, they were able to accumulate the resources to expand their influence where it counted. There is nothing to prevent you from doing exactly the same thing. Maybe not raising large amounts of money. But making every bit of resources available count to the maximum.

Adapting to the information age. It may seem paradoxical that people whose policy agenda appears to some to be stuck somewhere between Calvin Coolidge and Herbert Hoover are using the most advanced techniques for getting their message out. Chapter 2 describes a revolution in communications technology and how this is being used in the political arena. Anybody who wants to be a significant player will have to become part of this revolution–either directly, with her or his own expertise and equipment, or piggybacking on somebody else's.

Taking advantage of the openings. The people who led the conservatives out of the shadows and into center stage never conceded an advantage to their opponents if they could help it. Clear on their agenda and zealous in its pursuit, they took advantage of every opening afforded them. Such single-mindedness is well suited to the kind of attack politics we have seen in recent years. I am not suggesting that you have to imitate them in this regard. Standards of fair play may deter you, for instance, from exacting an eye for an eye and a tooth for a tooth from a combattive adversary. But there are still useful lessons to be learned from this.

Consider the mass media. As is discussed in Chapter 11, there is a lot of free mileage via the letters columns of daily newspapers and call-in talk shows on radio and TV. Depending on the particular program, your call may be screened out because of your point of view. You then have to become creative in saying enough but not too much to make it onto the show. Will you win the debate with the person who controls the microphone? Chances are you won't. No matter. You can still draw attention to *your* issue.

Suppose, for example, that instead of one person you are a group of like-minded folk, wishing to present an alternative point of view to the audience of a call-in show. It could be locally or nationally broadcast. The group has decided which issues to focus on and has done its homework. It anticipates the kinds of counter-arguments that might be forthcoming. Not every member of the group gets through, but some do. When the host tries to shift attention to a related issue, the caller says not to change the subject and brings the discussion back to the original focus.

At this point, my intent is not to get into specific tactics but to think more in terms of a mindset–one which believes in the ultimate success of its cause, is prepared to invest time and effort over the long haul, girds itself with the necessary expertise, and is constantly on the alert for ways to promote its agenda. We are not talking about money or built-in influence. All the elements are there within you if you have but the will. The rest of the book tells you how to get the maximum mileage out of your efforts, but cannot create that initial mindset. You are the only one who can do that.

POINTS TO REMEMBER

1. The 1990s have been a period of deep fear and frustration in the electorate, brought on by a sense of downward mobility and rapid social and cultural changes.

2. The fear and frustration have been translated into a mistrust of government and more generally a conservative outlook. Yet it is volatile and can rapidly change.

3. Political attitudes do not just happen. Conservative intellectuals and the religious right have been effective in defining issues.

4. We can learn from the experience of the people who led the return to power of conservatives. They teach us that a belief in ultimate victory, persistence over the long haul, willingness to acquire the necessary expertise, and constant alertness to opportunities for advancing one's agenda can be empowering.

Chapter 2

Lobbying in the Information Age

Bill Clinton thought he had Congressman John Breaux's vote for the 1993 BTU tax bill. Aimed at the giants of the energy industry, it was right in line with the Louisiana Democrat's populist leanings. But when Breaux returned to the district that summer, he found the streets lined with angry, sign-carrying protesters worried about their jobs. He backed off, and eventually so did Clinton.

What Breaux could not know at the time was that the demonstration was part of a well-orchestrated campaign financed by a coalition of energy companies and employing state-of-the-art technology. Initially, the opponents of the tax had sent their lobbyists out to work the Capitol corridors and mounted a massive advertising campaign, but that proved to be counterproductive. It was obviously a self-serving operation by moneyed interests, playing right into Clinton's strategy of casting the opposition as fat cats intent on reaping huge profits at the expense of ordinary Americans. So they adopted what has become a hallmark of lobbying in the information age: grassroots pressure mobilized by carefully targeted appeals, using advanced communications techniques (Dowd, 1993).

Welcome to the world of cyberspace, Internet, Fax, and E-mail. With the aid of computers, it is now possible in a matter of a few hours to identify swing districts, obtain profiles of each voter within them, test out messages for maximum impact, and issue personal appeals for action in order to generate an apparently spontaneous voter reaction. Lobbying in the information age still uses age-old principles of influencing policymakers' decisions, but the new technology has transformed it into a new game. And, despite the optimism of some observers that it is democratizing the process, it has widened the gap between the haves and the have-nots considerably. At least for now. In this chapter, we will consider not only the new challenge facing the low-budget lobbyist, but also what can be done about it.

THE OLD POLITICS MEETS THE NEW

The November 1994 elections were a political watershed for reasons other than the fact that they signaled the end of 40 years of control of Congress by Democrats. This was also the point at which old-style politicians fell in unprecedented numbers to young unknowns using modern technology. Some of the old-timers, such as Senator Edward Kennedy of Massachusetts, managed to survive by adapting to the new style of campaigning. But many could not make the switch.

For Illinois Congressman Dan Rostenkowski, the defeat in the November 1994 election had to be as humiliating as it was unexpected. Rosty, a veteran of 35 years in the House, lost by 10 percentage points to a 31-year-old political unknown with minimal funds. Pundits gave Rostenkowski a six- to seven-point edge right up to the end of the campaign, but the challenger, Republican Michael Flanagan, had better polling data, showing him with a comfortable lead. The National Republican Committee, which had written off the race until the closing weeks, rushed in with a $50,000 television blitz on the final weekend. The ads were the result of careful testing of where Rostenkowski was most vulnerable with voters.

Actually, Flanagan employed some very old-fashioned campaigning techniques, such as walking the district and knocking on doors–necessary in view of his modest resources. But, starting with Rostenkowski's indictment on corruption charges the previous spring, the campaign shattered many a piece of conventional wisdom in American politics. And in Chicago of all places!

Dan Rostenkowski never really left Chicago's 32nd Ward, where he was born. The son of an alderman, he came up through the ranks, serving in both houses of the Illinois legislature before going on to Congress. Even as the chair of the powerful House Ways and Means Committee, he returned to the district every weekend to listen to constituents' complaints and check in with ward leaders and other barometers of district sentiments.

Rosty came out of the old school where loyalty is *the* cardinal virtue. In the classical mold of big city machine politics, he brought home generous chunks of federal largess in exchange for loyalty from the voters. Machine is too cold a word for the web of relationships based on affection as well as mutual need. Still, in this world jobs are passed out on the basis of patronage, dues are extracted and woe be to him who crosses the boss. "Rostenkowski has the memory of an elephant," wrote Dan Hofstadter (1994:52) in a *New York Times Magazine* profile, "He remembers who has helped him and who has hindered him."

He countinued on loyalty and appreciation for all he had done for the district to see him safely through the 1994 election. Indictment on corruption charges in May and his subsequent relinquishment of the Ways and Means chair posed a threat, but still the smart money was on this politician's politician. After all, Chicago had a long if not honorable history of public officials surviving corruption charges. The fact that his alleged missteps appeared to have been as favors for constituents rather than for personal profit made them seem less onerous to many observers. The *Chicago Sun Times* scolded but endorsed the veteran warrior. Even the Republican-leaning *Chicago Tribune* refused to endorse his opponent. When he made it through the primary with little trouble, it appeared that, like countless other political figures of the past, Dan Rostenkowski would still be there at the helm when the dust cleared. But times had changed.

In the end it was not Michael Flanagan who brought Rostenkowski down but the incumbent's own ethical lapses, and a political climate in which such scandals loom larger in voters' eyes than old loyalties. It is a climate which is part and parcel of the information age. Illinois's 8th Congressional District is still predominantly Polish-American, but its sense of a tight-knit community is diminished. St. Stanislaus's parish has shrunk from 2,000 to 200 in a generation. People are more likely to stay behind closed doors and get their picture of the outside world via television and talk radio. The gradual shift from personal interaction to reliance on the media for information has the secondary effect of making people feel less in control of their world, more resentful of those who appear to control the national destiny from inside the Beltway. In such an atmosphere, repeated charges that an officeholder has betrayed taxpayers' trust and misused their money fall on fertile ground.

The politician best known for nurturing this climate and using it to defrock the mighty in Congress is Republican Congressman Newt Gingrich of Georgia. He is given the major credit for having brought down House Speaker Jim Wright, the Texas Democrat, in this manner. In many ways, Gingrich epitomizes the new style of politics. He could not be more different from Dan Rostenkowski. Gingrich was born in Harrisburg, Pennsylvania, the son of a career Army officer. Army "brats" are used to moving around, and their loyalties are not tied to a geographical locale. It was only happenstance that landed Gingrich in Georgia. His first introduction to politics was not through attendance at ward meetings but via history books. After a stint of teaching at West Georgia College, he made two unsuccessful runs for Congress and was elected on the third try in 1978.

According to one observer, "Gingrich has become a prototype for the new entrepreneurial politicians, the independent contractors who use sophisticated campaign techniques to bypass tedious years on school boards and zoning panels" (Sternberg, 1993:26). Reliance on old loyalties back in the district is *not* characteristic of this kind of officeholder. A former congressional aide and adviser is quoted as saying, "Gingrich engages in retail politics with his constituents only to the extent that it's necessary to get re-elected. He's not there to do the ribbon cutting and baby kissing. . . . Instead you've got a history professor who took a keen interest in politics because he thought that was the way for him to have an impact on the course of history."

Dan Rostenkowski was known as a master of compromise, where everybody could come away with something to take back to the constituents. Newt Gingrich has seemed to prefer the rough and tumble of attack politics, in which the objective is not simply to win, but to annihilitate your opponent. This approach fits well with information-age politics because it lends itself to attention-grabbing sound bites, the life-blood of television news coverage.

Traditionally, members of Congress have avoided making too much of their colleagues' pecadillos, for fear of having their own exposed in retaliation. But Gingrich, who has himself been the subject of a number of ethical accusations over the years, has not hesitated to make an issue of the ethical lapses of congressional Democrats, apparently counting on his ability to turn aside the counterattacks.

Gingrich is at home with information-age politics. He has made floor speeches to an empty House chamber–and the cameras of C-SPAN. He has videotaped lectures on history which were then broadcast by satellite over National Empowerment Television, a right-wing cable network that reaches into ten million homes, and taught for credit in 25 universities. He regularly faxes material to talk show hosts and newspapers around the country. He enlisted the help of pollster Frank Luntz in formulating, then pretesting before focus groups, the "Contract with America." A group of Republican proteges have listened to his tapes and studied his lists of key words with which to paint Republicans (positive) and Democrats (negative).

One bit of conventional wisdom which has fallen victim to the new politics is the reputed power of incumbency. Just get past three or four elections, went the story, and you have a hold on a seat virtually for life. Gingrich's own experience at the polls stands as graphic evidence to the contrary. After his election to the House in 1978, he was returned by the voters five times in a row. Then in 1990 and again in 1992, he won by fewer than 1,000 votes. Nor can these close calls be attributed to national sea changes such as the GOP sweep in 1994 and the post-Watergate rejection of Republicans 20 years earlier. In a time when hot buttons can be pressed with precision, the political arena has become a less predictable place.

No set of political tools works forever. All the players eventually come to use the same guidebook. The public, at first infatuated, becomes bored or outright resentful at the feeling of being manipulated. But as of the mid-1990s, information-age politics was having a major impact on the national landscape, primarily in favor of conservatives.

THE USE OF INFORMATION IN LOBBYING

To say that the basic principles of lobbying are what they have always been is like saying the basic principles of flight have been known since heavier-than-air craft took to the skies. The jet engine did not change the action of air currents in creating a vacuum above a molded wing, but it transformed the practice of aviating into something very different from what it had been. Supersonic flight added another dimension and flight beyond the earth's atmosphere yet another. Lobbying in the information age still involves understanding the target of one's efforts, developing a convincing case and presenting it in a persuasive manner. But the technology now available even to small organizations with limited means has changed the ball game forever. Would-be players need to know what is out there, whether or not they are able to use the same tools.

Central to the lobbying task is the gathering and dissemination of information. The speed with which this can go on over wide areas is what has changed. We shall look at each of these functions: acquiring information and transmitting it.

Acquiring Information

Your profile is on a lot of people's databases, some of whom you have never been involved with or even known of their existence. That is because you shop at discount houses, use credit cards, fill out warranty forms for TV sets and other household appliances, take out a mortgage or school or auto loan, write to your congressperson, and/or belong to one or more organizations. You are such a valuable commodity that people pay high prices to obtain information about you. Before the advent of the computer, it would have been too time-consuming and expensive to make it worth gathering all those bits of information. But now it is easy to put together a dossier, each fact being brought together with all other facts to form a composite picture.

Commercial firms want to know you, the better to induce you to buy their products. Lobbying organizations want to know you for much the same reason: to induce you not only to agree with their point of view, but, depending on what your profile looks like, to pick up the phone and urge your representatives in Congress or the state legislature to vote the "right" way. Or an organization may skip over you because your profile says, "Let this sleeping dog lie; we don't want her or him making waves."

This is called targeting: identifying the constituencies that are most disposed to agree with a point of view and act on it where it will do the most good. Targeting has always been around, only now it is so good that it is possible for an organization to profile every voter in every precinct in the country. It means that when a crucial vote is due to come up on the floor of U.S. House of Representatives, targeted constituents in the districts of wavering representatives can be mobilized, creating massive grassroots pressure.

One of the most rapidly changing fields is that of public opinion polling. A few well-publicized fiascos, such as the *Literary Digest's* prediction that Franklin D. Roosevelt would be a one-term president and the premature exultation by the *Chicago Tribune* over Harry Truman's presumed demise in 1948, have given polling a bad name. But the means of tapping constituent opinion has become highly sophisticated in the information age.

Most polling is done by telephone, the only reliable means for rapid feedback at a time when virtually all U.S. homes have phones (the remainder are least likely to contain voters), people in even low-crime suburban communities hesitate to open the door to a stranger, and there is a premium on speed (Selnow, 1994:47). Sampling methods are more sophisticated than ever. Computers can process and spit out in hours data it used to take days to prepare, and the analyses can be more varied, tailored to diverse needs.

Interviewing techniques are also improving. Computers have not replaced humans in this process–the mechanical voice is a turn-off–but the person asking questions has become part of an integrated, machine-dominated system known as Computer Assisted Telephone Interviewing (CATI). Based on a sampling strategy, a pre-selected number is dialed. When the person answers, an opening question is flashed on a screen in front of the interviewer. Depending on the response to that, a follow-up question is flashed, triggering a series of probes, answers, and further probes. Then on to the next opening question. The computer can be set to randomize the order of opening questions, to avoid biasing the responses. If the initial call gets a busy signal, the computer notes the fact and redials at preprogrammed intervals (Frankovic, 1992).

Computers can continuously update the data fed into the system. The underlying function is no different from what one might do with a box of index cards. It is just that many times the information can be processed at much faster speeds.

The system looks for *patterns,* the profiles of people with different views on an issue–for example, those strongly in favor of a measure through those strongly against–and *parcels*, sets of issues about which constituents with a particular profile feel strongly. The patterns around a given issue help the lobbying organization know where to go looking for people to mobilize in relation to a bill. The parcels of issues that tap a given constituency's hot buttons might be used to decide how to get voters in a district to stay home or come out on election day.

In-depth profiling of candidates and public officials calls for a different approach to data gathering. Here, every available scrap of information is gathered and fed into what amounts to an electronic dossier. For example, supporters of a candidate for office might look for negative information about both the person and her or his opponent, to prepare a defensive strategy to meet damaging information or mount an attack on the other contender. Or lobbyists might look for a public official's pet interests and prejudices, in order to know how to approach her or him. The tactic is as old as politics itself, but the technology makes it faster and more comprehensive.

Individualizing the Message

In a way, the art of political influence is coming full circle. Historically, information was carried person-to-person, relying on the kind of trust relationship that it took a Dan Rostenkowski years to develop with his constituents. The message was shaped for the small, intimate group or the individual by a personal aquaintance. Lobbyists worked at gaining the confidence of the officeholder, or sought out opinion leaders in the union local or the neighborhood, to help get the word out.

In recent decades, the focus has been shifting from retail to wholesale communications, with television and other mass media playing an increasing role in shaping constituent opinion. The President uses his news conference to rally public support for his program. A senator or representative appears on "Meet the Press." Newspaper editorial writers are cultivated by advocates or opponents of a policy. Public demonstrations compete for attention on the evening news.

Now the pendulum is shifting back toward a retail approach, thanks to technology that allows precision tailoring of messages and precision targeting of audiences. There was a time when advocates sought the widest possible audience, the ultimate example being a president who comandeered all the major networks for a prime-time address on an urgent issue. It is no longer enough for the president to ask. Networks sometimes pass up such occasions and broadcast taped segments at a later time, in order not to lose advertising revenue. More important, there is less interest in aiming at total national coverage now. The information age has given birth to the concept of "narrowcasting"–targeting a message at selected audiences. Cable television has spawned specialized channels. Audiences can now select information they are most interested in.

Newspapers, the first medium of mass communications in this country, stressed local interests, and thus encouraged geographical diversity. Ethnic and other specialized publications pushed the separation of different segments of the population to another level. Movies and radio changed that. When I was a child in Maine during the 1930s, my friends and I would come back to school on Monday morning talking about what funny things Jack Benny and Charlie McCarthy had said the night before on the radio. I am sure the same kinds of conversations were going on in schoolyards in Muncie, Indiana, and Savannah, Georgia, and San Luis Obispo, California. Walter Winchell was helping to shape our parents' political views and our own. There were barely any African Americans in the town I grew up in, but I "knew" what they were like, because I saw them in the movies.

Television, pressed by enormous production costs to maximize its viewing audiences, was an even greater force for national homogenization. Not that the mass media eliminated local and regional differences, as witnessed by the civil rights struggles in the South. But the models children and adults emulated tended to be national models.

Meanwhile, radio, forced to cultivate new fields, began to specialize. One could choose to be exposed, not just to 24 hours a day of music, but a particular kind of music. Or all-news stations (actually a mixture of news, weather, and traffic conditions, with local police and fire reports given the lion's share of news time). Or talk radio reflecting a particular political bias. Cable television and VCRs have brought a similar range of choices to the small screen.

The political process has adapted rapidly to the new media reality. As a result, targeting of messages to specific audiences has become central to information-age politics. It is less important that the National Empowerment Television (NET) cable network reaches into 10 to 22 million homes than that the occupants are the most likely among viewers to respond to its conservative message. Radio talk show hosts are listened to most often by people who agree with their viewpoints. Politicians are quick to pick up the beat.

A television viewer sees a commercial that rings alarm bells about taxes or abortion or social security. Moved to outrage, he or she picks up the phone and dials the 800 number being flashed on the screen. A voice on the other end of the line offers the following choices: Press 1 to send a telegram to ~~your~~ his or her senator or congressperson. Press 2 to be connected directly with your Washington office. Press 3 to record a voice-mail message. Press 4 if you plan to write a letter. (Presumably there is no fifth option to ignore the appeal.) Offering options gives the viewer the feeling of being in control. The viewer does not need to know the name or number of the bill in question nor even the name of his or her representative; that is all taken care of by computer-assisted targeting. Within minutes of having seen the inflamatory message, and without a lot of time to ask questions or even reflect on the issue, the viewer is coached on the kind of message to send and is soon talking to a congressional aide. This constituent's anger may cool within an hour, but to the congressional staffer it is a genuine expression of grassroots sentiment. The key link in this chain is the "patch-through" telephone hookup.

Fantasy of the twenty-first century? Many organizations, including both the National Restaurant Association and the U.S. Chamber of Commerce have patch-through capability now. The restaurateurs used it to defeat a cut in the tax deduction for business lunches in the early 1990s, turning what looked like defense of a government-subsidized bonanza for rich capitalists into a crusade to save the jobs of low-paid servers (Dowd, 1993). The Chamber has business leaders throughout the United States in its database, organized by state, congressional district, size of company, and area of interest. The businessperson receives a call giving a brief update and ending with an invitation to give his representative a piece of his mind, right then and there. It is an offer that is very hard to turn down, if you are in business and feel threatened by what is happening in Washington. In strictest terms, this tactic leaves the decision to act in the hands of the viewer, who can decide to ignore the initial message on the screen. But once provoked, she or he becomes a cog in a highly integrated machine for delivering pressure when and where it is needed.

But such developments leave maximum control in the hands of the consumer. Armed with a hand-held remote tuner, the viewer is free to flip channels or mute the sound at will. Advertising messages must be immediately engaging to avoid being tuned out. So directing appeals to a mass audience, however narrowly defined, limits the power of the advocate. Now through a variety of technological developments, it is possible to bypass the mass media, or work in tandem with them, to penetrate the individual's personal space.

Individualizing the Delivery

A major means of penetrating people's private domains is one of the oldest forms of communication: letter writing. Only now it is precision-targeted letter writing, cheaper and faster to do in large volume than ever before. The person credited with having invented modern direct-mail lobbying is Richard A. Viguerie, a devotee of conservative causes. He has become a legendary figure in the field of direct-mail lobbying, partly because of his own self-promotion (Viguerie, 1980).

Viguerie credits direct-mail campaigning with having rescued the conservative movement from the backwaters of American politics: "Without direct mail, there would be no . . . New Right" (Viguerie, 1980:120). One of the early people to use this technique was not a conservative, but liberal Democratic presidential hopeful George McGovern. In 1972, McGovern borrowed $200,000 to pay for sending letters to a million liberal members of the party. He anticipated–correctly–that he would receive enough contributions in response to pay off the initial loan. This made possible the launching of his campaign.

Because direct mail can be highly selective, it is especially useful to single-issue groups and third-party candidates, since broad-based appeals in the mass media mean huge outlays with only limited yield. Illinois Republican Phil Crane took the same gamble in his 1978 bid for the presidential nomination. With a personal loan for $15,000, Crane was able to raise $3 million, which brought federal matching funds of $2 million. Equally important, he had a list of 80,000 contributors, prime prospects for another round of fundraising. When John Anderson made a run for the Republican nomination for president in 1980, his campaign organization mailed out seven million letters. This resulted in a list of 157,600 contributors and a fund of $7 million.

In 1975, the National Right to Work Committee (NRWC) was fighting a "common situs" bill, which was being pushed by labor unions. An obscure issue with little public attention, it could easily slide through unnoticed, since union members were the only ones with an apparent stake in it. NRWC mailed out four million letters to a list of its sympathizers accumulated over the years. The result was 720,000 letters and post cards to the White House, urging President Ford to veto the bill (Viguerie, 1980:121).

Each mailing and the subsequent returns help generate further lists of sympathetic constituents. Those who send money are prime targets for next time, gradable by the amount donated. Those who respond but send no money are in a second category. In 1980, Viguerie claimed he had a database of 4.5 million individuals with interest in conservative candidates or causes, and expected to have another four million within three years (Viguerie, 1980:128).

In the early 1990s millions of elderly Americans received an urgent message through the mail. "ALL THE SOCIAL SECURITY TRUST FUND MONEY IS GONE!" screamed the message on the outside of the official-looking envelope. Inside, one found a letter from George Murphy, former screen actor and U.S. senator, and honorary chairman of the United Seniors Association. The letters continued to go out that way after Murphy died in May. The campaign netted millions of dollars in contributions to the United Seniors Association, whose moving spirit was none other than Richard Viguerie. The organization had no paid lobbyist working to save social security. It didn't even have an expert on social security. There was every indication, in fact, that the United Seniors Association was simply a front for generating revenue for Viguerie Associates, at the time much in need of cash.

The operation was within the law, even to the point of being able to claim tax-exempt status, because the IRS considers such letters to be "educational." The money that came in was used to send out more mailings. Some client organizations have gone into debt paying the cost of direct-mail solicitations, but Viguerie Associates first scoops its commission off the top, according to news reports (Eckholm, 1992:Al, B14).

What is new about this is not direct-mail solicitation per se, but the ability to send a large volume of letters to a selected population in a very short space of time. It means that Congressman Jones, sitting on the House Ways and Means Committee, can be deluged with letters from his home district supporting or opposing a complex amendment while it is still being debated in the Committee. But as the Viguerie operation makes clear, it takes money to generate, and so the fundraising function of direct mail can come to control the lobbying function.

In the eyes of some observers, the information age has ushered in a vast democratization of the political process. With C-SPAN, ordinary citizens can watch congressional debates they might not even have heard or read about in the old days. Voters have instant access to their representatives in the state capital and Washington via fax machines and E-mail. And voters are taking advantage of the opportunity. In the first six months of 1992, members of Congress received 11.4 million calls from constituents. During the same period of 1993, the number jumped to 16.7 million, a 46 percent increase. On an average day, 2,500 people call the White House; another 2,000 send computer mail (Dowd, 1993:62).

The new technology has found its way into protest movements in developing countries. Labor unions in the United States have provided their counterparts in other countries with computer hardware. Some African regimes have discovered that unions in their countries have more sophisticated technology than they themselves do. The Internet allows dissident groups to bypass government restrictions. When opposition groups in South Africa were banned, they fed information from personal computers to liberal newspapers. A women's group in Mexico City used the same database consulted by American companies to collect information about United States firms moving in to recruit cheap labor (Holderness, 1993). Fax machines and satellite communications are credited with having helped speed the downfall of communism in Eastern Europe (Freeman, 1993:51).

Yet access to the most sophisticated equipment takes money. Especially as one combines computers and satellites with the more mundane postage stamp and phone bank, which give the whole thing the essential "human touch," disparities in resources will continue to count heavily in the political process, only more so.

INFORMATION-AGE LOBBYING IN OPERATION

Information-age lobbying makes use of the new technology without disposing of more traditional tools. In the early 1990s, the $75 billion drug industry had an image problem. With profit margins routinely three times those of other Fortune 500 companies and three out of four Americans in favor of government controls, the drug firms were vulnerable to government restrictions. President Clinton threatened to crack down, citing a 1,250 percent increase in the cost of immunizing children between 1981 and 1991 (Levine & Silverstein, 1993:713, 730).

Traditionally, the drug companies had relied on generous donations to friendly members of Congress. In the 1992 election campaign, the companies gave $4 million to congressional candidates, up 27 percent from two years before. They launched an $850,000 advertising campaign in 40 national newspapers, using contrived "persons" to tell their stories. There was a $2 million public relations blitz that included media training for drug company executives, and meetings with national and local reporters and administration officials.

Still, any public presentation was quickly seen as special pleading on the part of rich companies. It was necessary to generate a grassroots protest. The means selected was a massive direct-mail campaign. A letter over the signature of the Chief Science Officer of the Eli Lilly Company was sent out to targeted audiences, yielding 50,000 letters and messages to members of Congress. Although the basic response was a form letter, people were encouraged to append their own personal notes. More than 200 CEOs of phamaceutical companies sent hundreds of thousands of letters to workers and shareholders asking them to write to their representatives. The techniques were the same as those used by consumer groups–phone banks and direct mail. In fact, the sources of some of the communications were patient advocates and civil rights groups, third parties with no apparent industry affiliation (Levine & Silverstein, 1993:731).

The new allies included the National Multiple Sclerosis Society, the Cystic Fibrosis Foundation, and the National Coalition of Hispanic Health and Human Services Organizations. What moved these groups to join the fight to protect the earnings of a billion-dollar industry? The fear that reduced profits might cut into new research. The strategy worked and the campaign succeeded in getting the administration to back off.

This case points up the importance of targeting. It was possible to contact, in a short space of time, very large audiences with a high probability of responding. The other aspects of the operation were ones that have been employed over the years: direct mail and enlistment of the support of third parties seen as neutral or potentially antagonistic. In the next case, the urgency of time dictated that information-age technology be employed in the communication itself.

In 1993, the U.S. Senate voted for lobbying reform. In 1994, a coalition of groups was successful in getting a reversal. The Christian Coalition saw lobbying reform as a threat to its ability to influence legislation. When alerted to an impending vote on the issue in the Senate, the Coalition mounted a crash campaign to defeat the bill. Fifty organizations, including both abortion rights and anti-abortion groups, hand gun control advocates, and the National Rifle Association, were brought together to form the Free Speech Coalition (FSC). It was important to the strategy that the movement include people from across the political spectrum. Using computer bulletin boards, telephone trees, faxes, and talk radio, the FSC was able, according to one spokesperson, to mobilize 250,000 persons in a 24-hour period. The message was simple: the lobbying reform was "a gag rule for grassroots advocates" (Seelye, 1994:A22). The campaign was successful in stymying the President's effort to lead a populist attack against the well-financed lobbying groups

A similar strategy was employed by the Christian Coalition to promote the GOP's "Contract with America." Ralph Reed, Coalition director, promised a million-dollar campaign, complete with phone banks, fax networks, satellite TV, computerized bulletin boards, talk radio, and direct mail (Berke, 1994).

Aside from the speed with which groups can respond to breaking developments in Congress, the new technology allows the development of a sense of momentum, so that people are swept up in an apparent tide of public opinion. The defeat of President Clinton's proposed BTU tax on energy was made possible in part by the apparent spontaneity with which key members of Congress were pressured by constituents.

LOW-BUDGET LOBBYING IN THE INFORMATION AGE

You do not have a database of four million names which can be pulled up according to one or another characteristic. Nor four thousand names in your congressional district. Nor a patch-through phone system to plug constituents into their representatives' offices. You are not even on the Internet. Nor do you own a fax machine. Maybe you are still struggling to feel comfortable with computers. Has the world of political influence passed you by? Not in the least. You have a very important role to play, regardless of the state of your technological resources. But you must adapt to the context in which you are functioning.

The first thing to do is to see information-age politics in perspective. One can get the illusion of a smooth-running machine which never errs. But, like Dan Rostenkowski's old machine in the 32nd Ward, this one is run by humans, who are as fallable as ever. The experts in the new technological environment are still capable of bad judgment, or bad luck, or both. The "patch-through" phone call backfired in one case in which a congressional aide overheard an operator coaching a constituent on what to say. Once exposed, the flood of phone calls lost its punch. On one occasion a computer-generated letter from my senator thanked me for my letter urging passage of a bill that I had written in opposition to. I was distressed that my "vote" ended up in the wrong column, but reassured by the fact that someone out there, or some computer, was capable of making mistakes.

Snafus aside, politicians are quick to see through phony "mass" pressure. Much of the new technology relies on speed and numbers. When a public official refuses to be stampeded, checks in with trusted sources, or asks questions to see if a constituent knows what she or he is talking about, the crash campaign can come crashing down. A representative may respond to a mass appeal, not because he assumes it is spontaneous, but because he or she respects the power of the organization which is able to muster it. A representative knows the same power can be turned against him or her in a future election.

There are two ways of coping with a technology gap: piggybacking on somebody else's modem, and stressing those things machines cannot do.

Working in organizations, rather than as the Lone Ranger, is doubly important in the information age. Just about any organization of any size has members who have access to sophisticated hardware and software and know how to get the most out of it. If your group lacks this kind of resource, it would be wise to try to recruit it. Forming coalitions with other groups can put such talent at your disposal. But rather than using the computer experts as a crutch, use them as teachers. Take advantage of opportunities to master the new medium. The prices keep coming down, so machines that were once out of reach can be within your pocketbook. Universities and other institutions are continually upgrading their technology, and so are often willing to sell old equipment at a very reasonable price, or even give it away. The same is true of individuals who want to stay on the cutting edge.

Some tools are more important than others. Given the emphasis on targeting grassroots pressure on short notice, a good database of names, addresses, and phone and fax numbers should have high priority. Whether it is a hundred people or a thousand, you need to be able to sort by zip code in a hurry. The basic core of information can be augmented with other facts that help you target with pinpoint accuracy–for instance, parents of young children, or people who have been most active in the past and thus are more likely to pick up the phone and dial their representative. It can be done by hand.

Index cards can have the different pieces of data located in different corners for a quick sort.

A computer with a modem gives you access to a wide range of information that is continually updated. Some advocacy organizations offer the same thing with telephone messages that are updated periodically. Computers as word processors make editing and updating easy. They catch spelling errors, though they will not stop you from using "veto" when you meant to say "vote." They are particularly good for getting action alerts out to a list of constituents in a hurry.

Telephones are good for instant contact with a representative's office. Fax machines are better because they are not put on hold, or given a taped message and set going on telephone tag. E-mail and other options make phones more versatile, but after a point the cost outruns the usefulness. There is also a kind of information inflation: as there is more and more of it at our fingertips, the value goes down. The human mind just cannot absorb all that content. After all, only so much data can be compressed into a sound bite.

The more our technology expands the range of human potential, the more we yearn for a simpler world and something machines can never replace: our humanness. It is no accident that the information age has been a time of political nostalgia, of trying to turn back the clock to an earlier day. A major appeal of talk radio, a reason why it has exploded into a huge industry, is the illusion of intimacy. In a poignant moment of self-revelation, one radio listener said of Rush Limbaugh, "He's the best friend I have." To an extent, the need for the personal touch can be manipulated, but over time contrived closeness tends to wear thin and be exposed for what it is. The feedback public officials receive via the fax machine and the telephone and the mail box, to say nothing of the public opinion poll, they view with a considerable degree of skepticism. They know how easy it is to whip up a mob, whether in the streets or via E-mail. They know a lot of the techniques because their own campaigns have employed them.

You can present something different: information and a commitment the representative and her or his staff can come to trust. A way of approaching this is to stop and think what machines cannot do, then do that. They cannot hand-write a letter, though I believe there are factors more important than whether a letter is penned or typed. Machines do not take the time out of a busy schedule to visit the representative's office. And especially these days, people are coming to trust machines less and less. That is why lobbyists use human contact people in a machine-driven campaign. But such orchestrated outpourings lack the feeling of genuineness that you convey out of your conviction that brings you back to the representative's office again and again. It shows in everything you do. The receptionist realizes it. The aide realizes it. Which means in time the public official does, too.

There is still a premium on good information on policy, especially if it is in an area with which the representative is unfamiliar. Are you on the "wrong" side of the issue? All the more reason to make sure you keep your representative informed of the facts. You can become a trusted source of knowledge even when you and the representative have long since agreed to disagree. Particularly when you are close to the problem, see how existing policy plays out in the lives of constituents, and report your observations to the representative and her or his aides, you can play a strategic role. Most representatives feel more comfortable with anecdotes than statistics. The canned scenarios that show up on the fax machine and in letter-writing campaigns come to sound that way. You can offer an alternative to the noise that public officials are constantly exposed to.

Politics in the information age puts a premium on speed and numbers–hundreds of thousands of phone calls or computer messages or letters generated within hours of an event. What it sacrifices is depth and persistence. That is where you can come in, the tortoise plodding steadily past the sleeping hare, who is preoccupied with the next media blitz. You may be your representative's favorite constituent, or somebody she or he wants to hide from. But in time, the fact that you are still around after the dust has settled comes to be appreciated.

POINTS TO REMEMBER

1. Advances in the technology of information gathering and distribution have transformed the practice of lobbying. The basic strategies are the same as before, but the speed with which large

amounts of data can be gathered, organized, and disseminated has created a new political environment.

2. While seen by some as the dawn of a more democratic era, the new technology has widened the gap between those with resources and those without.

3. Even organizations with limited funds can acquire the tools to expand their influence, through more precise data on target populations, continual updating of information on policy changes and proposals, and faster and more targeted dissemination. Coalition politics become even more important under these circumstances.

4. Most organizations have people aboard who know the new technology and are willing to share it. You can borrow their expertise, and master it yourself at the same time.

5. You should consider what machines cannot do and emphasize those qualities in your approach. In particular, you should be prepared to build up a sense of trust with your representative and her or his staff over the long haul.

PART II: BASIC STEPS

In this part of the book, we look at the step-by-step process the advocate must go through, regardless of the specific kind of lobbying involved. The process begins with a careful assessment of what you have going for you and the limitations on your ability to influence policy. The more obvious sources of political power–large sums of money, blocs of votes, and connections in high places–are probably not available to you. But that does not mean you are totally lacking in power. In Chapter 3, you will discover hidden strengths. At the same time, it is necessary to be realistic about power in the political arena. You should come out with neither an inflated view of your ability to bring about change, nor an underestimation of it.

Chapters 4, 5, 6, and 7 move you from settling on your action objectives to identifying whom your lobbying should be directed toward and mapping a strategy for persuading your target person(s) to act.

Chapter 3

Assessing Your Strengths and Limitations

It is hard not to be cynical about the possibility of changing social policies. Professional lobbyists are backed by big bank accounts and can muster thousands of letters on any issue. The same powerful interests shape public opinion by dominating the mass media. The bottom line for any elected official–or anybody hired by an elected official–has to be reelection. And with the cost of campaigns skyrocketing, everybody is vulnerable to the influence of moneyed interests.

These facts can be rather discouraging if one thinks only about radical change in the political and economic order. There is no question that money is a powerful force in the making of policy, and those with lots of money have great potential influence. However, many important policy questions do not involve that kind of monumental change. Modest expansions in social welfare benefits, a marginally better balance between individual liberty and protection of the innocent, incremental reductions in pollutants in the environment: these are not revolutionary leaps into utopia, but can empower oppressed people and make the quality of life better for all of us.

It is important to think about fundamental questions of social justice and recognize the relative impotence of even large organizations in addressing them. But that should not be allowed to immobilize one. Even with very limited resources, advocates have been able to make critical differences in public policy. In assessing one's assets, it is necessary first to acknowledge one's limitations.

I will assume you are not an elected official nor a cabinet-level appointee, so you do not have formal status to trade on. Do you have thousands of dollars with which to seed election campaigns, hire lawyers and other experts, and send out massive mailings to computerized lists of voters? If not, money is not one of your major assets. Can you deliver a thousand votes on election day? Hundreds? One hundred? If not, blocs of voters are not one of your major assets.

Now for those assets you do possess, or can acquire regardless of who you are: commitment, time, allies, organization, and information. The first of these, commitment, is the one asset that is entirely in your hands. It is also without doubt the most underrated. There is, finally, an asset that builds on all the others and in some ways is most crucial: confidence in your ability to be an advocate.

COMMITMENT

In the beginning, Lois Gibbs had nothing working in her favor except fierce commitment. Painfully shy, lacking any formal education beyond high school, firmly believing that a woman's first duty was to look after her kids and keep her husband happy, she sneered at women's libbers. Politics was a strange and intimidating world. But that was *her* child the school officials were saying not to worry about, *her* child having the unexplained seizures and asthma attacks. And that made all the difference. Once they went into action, Lois Gibbs and the other citizens with whom she allied herself were able to meet and defeat bureaucratic indifference and every obstacle an unyielding system could put in their path. Their story, the Love Canal story, is an excellent example of what a small band of people with limited resources can do about a problem in which they have a huge personal stake.

Opinions vary as to the kind and amount of help the anti-abortionists have had from powerful interests–the Catholic church hierarchy, wealthy fundamentalists, and an array of right-wing demagogues and lobbyists. But much of the power of the anti-abortion movement comes from the zeal of the activists at the grassroots. Their single-mindedness and the belief that they are fighting what amounts to a holy war against Satan has given them tremendous power.

The pro-choice faction, while in many ways just as committed, has a broader agenda. For a few, freedom to abort a pregnancy has been central to the struggle for women's rights. Freedom to determine what happens to their bodies–especially freedom from control by the male-dominated medical profession–is the ultimate sign of deliverance. Unlike the anti-abortion activists, though, they are unwilling to subordinate all other policy issues to this one.

The way people entered the two movements is instructive. Luker (1984) found that the typical anti-abortion activist became incensed at the idea of "baby murder" and went looking for a movement to join. She had never been involved in politics before and tended to remain focused squarely on the abortion issue. The pro-choice activist, on the other hand, was recruited by those already active, and the message about abortion was linked to a broad spectrum of women's rights issues.

Strong personal commitment to a cause leads one to persist when it would be much easier to quit. The committed person will put in that extra time and effort that others are not ready to invest. It means going to meeting after meeting, being there at the beginning and staying through to the end, staying alert while other minds wander, always with that single agenda overriding all others. It means wading through page after boring page of legislative jargon and statistical tables. It means developing close working relationships with people one has little interest in, even some one personally dislikes.

Typically, it is a dedicated core of active leaders who keeps an advocacy effort going. Sociologist Adeline Levine says of the handful who led the successful two-year effort by Love Canal residents to get action on their demands,

> Most important, the workers gave of themselves. They provided a constant presence; they persisted; they were always there. They did all the tedious, laborious tasks familiar to anyone who has ever worked in a voluntary organization. (Levine, 1982:189)

Many socially committed persons have a special liability: too many agendas. Their names appear on countless lists of supporters on the assumption that if commitment to one cause is good, supporting three causes is three times as good. One trouble with that theory is that one cannot invest the necessary time and effort to become a true expert on everything–the kind that others turn to for information, the kind legislators learn to treat as a trusted resource–on more than one or two issues at a time. Another problem is that policymakers know that the advocate who tries to influence them on a wide range of issues cannot hold them accountable on any one issue. If they see you as being hooked into every urgent cause that comes along, they will calculate–correctly, no doubt–that your readiness to stay the course for any particular cause is limited.

One state chapter of the National Association of Social Workers (NASW) joined a coalition fighting a particularly onerous welfare reform bill being pushed by the governor. The trouble was, they were also desperately seeking passage of a social work licensing bill, and many of the legislators in favor of licensing were equally committed to the governor's welfare reform program. The NASW leadership tried to rally the membership behind both issues, but for the rank and file majority, licensing took precedence over anything else. The result was a divided chapter, with a few pro-welfare "generals" leading the charge with no troops.

The only reason a democratic form of government like ours actually works, actually gets things done, is that the majority of people have low commitment on the majority of issues. Were that not so, the country would be in one gigantic gridlock and never achieve any results. Policymakers avoid offending anybody, so if everybody was intensively involved in everything, the interest groups would cancel each other out, and no public official would dare to do anything for fear of antagonizing somebody. One factor that helped anti-abortionists in the early days of the movement was that the issue held so little interest for other people. In a way they had the field to themselves. In time this changed, of course, as the pro-choice forces became aroused.

That lack of commitment by most people most of the time can be one of *your* biggest assets, because you, being strongly committed on *your* issues, get the attention of the policymakers. And that is more important than whether you agree with their biases or are even considered an expert on the subject.

One piece of conventional wisdom in policy advocacy ought to be disposed of at the outset: the belief that people invest only in what has a personal, material payoff for them–it is a belief that politicians subscribe to. But many persons work long and hard, at great personal sacrifice, for causes they believe in. For evidence of that statement, one need only consider the abortion issue.

The core of activists who have worked zealously over the years to outlaw abortion are not in it for personal gain. By definition they are driven by a concern for those who cannot even show their appreciation, the unborn. I am not referring here to politicians who use the abortion issue to make political gains, but to the people who give so generously of their time and money to pass petitions and travel to the state and national capitals to lobby and picket abortion clinics. One may criticize some of their tactics–just as one can find questionable tactics being used on behalf of most causes–but their sincerity is hard to question.

This is not to say that a self-interest stake in an issue is unimportant. There is no question that mental health professionals lobbying for better services are doing it for more than altruistic reasons. For many, their own jobs, maybe careers, are on the line. Good-hearted people concerned about the plight of this or that consumer population have a way of fading–or more typically being drawn into some other fight for some other worthy consumer population. Any of us has only so much energy to devote to the common good. But if professionals are driven by a concern for both the recipients of their services and their own careers, they are likely to keep working longer and harder. Mental health advocates should certainly not feel defensive about wanting to be able to continue in a career in the service of other human beings.

Acknowledging an element of self-interest in much advocacy work helps one empathize with the target of the advocacy, the public official. Do not judge too harshly the legislator who takes a particular position in order to get votes. That is, after all, how he or she stays in office. Elected officials are all keenly aware that they will do precious little good, as lawmakers at least, if they are voted out of office.

Commitment means little unless it is translated into action. The most obvious expression of one's commitment is the use of one's time.

TIME

Time is in many ways more valuable than money. In fact, a major use of money is to buy somebody's time. That has advantages and disadvantages. The salaried employee is likely to be more dependable than the volunteer, in showing up when expected and adhering to the party line. Money can buy high-priced talent that is often unavailable to efforts dependent on volunteers. However, the salaried employee may or may not share the zeal of the committed volunteer.

When sociologist Kristen Luker (1984) wanted to identify a sample of anti-abortion activists–the most committed–she used as a major criterion the amount of time they devoted to the movement. Her cut-off point was ten hours or more per week. She found that many activists spent as much as 40 hours a week. These were, by and large, homemakers, while the pro-choice activists were tied to work schedules and had to fit their political work in around the job. One tangible advantage for the anti-abortionists was that they worked out of their own homes, thus they were available to get and relay phone messages at all hours. The pro-choice volunteers were more likely to be out when called. Answering machines are useful tools, but lack the personal touch so necessary in lobbying and recruiting members.

The Love Canal Homeowners' Association (LCHA) relied almost entirely on unpaid volunteers, including a handful of lawyers and scientists. Their single-minded dedication made them a match for local and state public officials who had to juggle several issues at once and whose general orientation was to avoid damage to their agencies.

The activist core in the grassroots struggle at Love Canal, not surprisingly, was made up of homemakers, retired persons, and workers on night shift. Lois Gibbs, a leader in this effort, had quit her job a few years earlier to raise a family, so she had flexibility in her schedule which full-time workers lacked.

Large corporations and entrenched political interest groups count on other people's lack of time as well as lack of commitment. By scheduling a public meeting in Albany, the state capital, hundreds of miles from Love Canal, officials hoped to cut sharply into the number of angry residents they would have to face.

The time investment exacts a price. Lois Gibbs describes how her work as an advocate kept preempting her time as a parent:

> It was Michael's birthday, and I didn't have a gift. No cake. Nothing. . . . I did manage a small birthday, however. I went out to Child World and bought a bunch of toys; but I didn't

have time to wrap them. I bought a cake at the bakery and put some candles on it. The party had to be early, because I had an association meeting that night. (Gibbs, 1982:52)

To a great extent, the LCHA volunteers simply absorbed the costs. Physical and emotional health and some marriages suffered. The small core of activist leaders was up against public officials who had vast staff resources at their beck and call, and a corporation that could buy the time of experts on everything from engineering and toxicology to the finer points of the law. This fact seems to have escaped the writer of one magazine article who chided Lois Gibbs for not spending time combing through old school board records. (See Zuesse, 1981:30.) But policy contests rarely take place on a level playing field. Rather than waste time and energy bemoaning that fact, advocates must pick their issues and do the best possible job with the time available. The only test in this business is results, as cruel as that may seem.

Because there are limits on the time any of us can devote to advocacy without running oneself and one's supporters into the ground, advocacy requires the help of a network of allies, all of whom have their own reasons for becoming involved.

ALLIES

The image of the loner is deeply ingrained in the American psyche, whether it is wearing cowboy boots or a cape and a big S on the chest. The 1930s movie, *Mr. Smith Goes to Washington*, told of a young congressman who battled a big tycoon single-handedly, to protect the interests of the little people. The climax was a filibuster in which the young hero, exhausted from the ordeal, fainted amid a shower of supportive telegrams from around the country. The audience knew he had won the day. It was right out of the O.K. Corral–and just as realistic.

Policy advocacy is not a solo operation. Especially because you lack a big bankroll and blocs of votes, you will need to combine forces with people who share your concern. The lineup may change from issue to issue. Whatever the issue, there are sure to be advocacy organizations working on it–if not in your own locality, then in the state capital or Washington. If you have trouble locating them, call an agency that provides a related kind of service. Somebody there will know.

If the abortion issue or welfare reform had suddenly intruded into the agenda of the Love Canal Homeowners' Association, the group would have become badly split. LCHA was made up of Caucasian blue collar workers and their families. They never succeeded in forming a close working alliance with African Americans in the area, who faced exactly the same threat to their health.

It is particularly important to stay focused on one's goals in considering alliances. The groups one has least in common with may be the very ones with access to an unfriendly legislator. As a general rule, then, enemies are a luxury the advocate can ill afford.

Ordinarily, one might not think of welfare rights advocates and chamber of commerce leaders as having a lot in common. But when the Pennsylvania legislature was considering a punitive welfare reform measure, the Philadelphia Chamber of Commerce came out against it. Perhaps individually the Chamber of Commerce leaders agreed with the attitude of the governor, who saw his reform bill as forcing able-bodied welfare recipients to go out and find a job. They also understood, however, that a sharp reduction in the welfare rolls could have a devastating effect on the city's retail trade. They had the potential for swinging critical votes of conservative legislators who tended to tune out any message coming from welfare rights advocates.

There are two important caveats which must be balanced against the general rule of finding bedfellows wherever one can. The first is that it is essential to know as well as possible why the group or individual is supporting this particular cause. Is it with the expectation that the favor will be returned at some future time? It is good to avoid making long-term, binding commitments, especially to parties whose intents are unclear. The second caveat concerns the network of allies. Will the advocate's involvement with one group alienate others, now or in the future? The solution is not necessarily to forgo the alliance in question but at least to try to reassure the others and help them see the necessity for it.

Alliances between different groups that want the same thing for different reasons are common in policy advocacy. A bus caravan goes to the state capital carrying ex-mental patients, family members, and mental health professionals. All three constituencies want additional funding for community-based services. For the ex-patients, the services are not only valuable in their own right but could mean the difference between being able to stay in the community and ending up back in the hospital. Some parents may be along because of the disruption or threat their children pose at home when services are lacking. For the professionals, there is the dual commitment to the welfare of the mentally ill and their own careers.

As long as the coalition stays focused on the business at hand, the alliance will hold and the powerful combination can have an impact. If they get diverted to the subject of involuntary commitment to mental hospitals, the ex-patients (for many of whom hospitalization is an anathema, a painful memory), and the parents (many of whom would feel safer with easier commitment procedures), may find themselves on opposite sides of the fence.

The right-to-life movement needed organizing ability, political sophistication, money, and the kind of computer hardware possessed by ultra-conservative lobbyists. The latter saw an opportunity to mobilize a huge, highly committed constituency to support their conservative agenda. Paige (1983) suggests that the anti-abortionists allowed themselves to be used by the right-wing organizations.

Mutual suspicion about who is using whom has been a chronic problem for those seeking humane welfare policies. Grassroots organizations of welfare recipients worry about the intentions of professors, lawyers, suburban church members, and other "do-gooders" who join their cause. Sometimes, indigenous leaders are suspected of harboring personal ambitions instead of the interests of the rank and file. The test of anyone's intentions is in the outcome. If a local leader aspiring to political office performs effectively for the movement, what does it matter that he or she also has a personal agenda? At the point that the leader ceases to work for the cause or begins doing things that undermine it, then it is time to drop the connection.

Occasionally, there is a more insidious side to such second agendas. Those without the best interests of the group at heart may infiltrate to sabotage the effort. A troubled individual may play a divisive role out of personal need. While it is necessary to be alert to such possibilities, the organizational paranoia thus generated can be far more destructive than any number of multiple agendas. Perhaps the time to be most suspicious of intentions is when an ally claims to have no special interest other than to do others a favor. Altruism in politics does exist, but it is typically mixed with other considerations, especially where organized groups are concerned.

This mutual aid principle presents a special problem to a group that has little to offer its allies. There are no free rides in politics, and this certainly applies to coalition politics. Groups need to find a useful role to play or they are not needed by other constituencies. That also applies to individuals who want to join an advocacy effort. They need to make themselves useful to the group effort or they become something of a liability. Usefulness can mean willingness to put in time on the dirty, boring little jobs as well as the more exciting tasks, being available when and where needed, not just when it is convenient, and informing oneself about the issues. It may also mean willingness to be a team player instead of trying to lead the march. If you are a potential leader, that will become apparent readily enough.

A specific kind of ally worth cultivating is news media staff. One should be aware that an overriding commitment for such professional communicators is getting the story. This typically takes precedence over helping your cause, a fact that has sometimes led to resentment when an activist felt "set up" by a reporter. Chapter 11 discusses using and being used by the mass media.

ORGANIZATION

The 1996 presidential campaign was in its early stages as this book was being written. If one took the news media version as the reality, the election would be won on the basis of the candidates' positions on issues, their personalities, or how they came across on television. Not to deny the importance of any of these factors, but to a great extent elections are won or lost on the basis of effective organization. This is even more true in state and local contests.

The ability to raise large sums of money is one of the more obvious functions of good organization. Anyone who has worked to any great extent in election campaigns knows how much time and energy go into updating voter lists, running phone banks, and keeping track of the candidate's schedule. What is true of election campaigns also applies to public policy campaigns. Keeping track of legislators' positions on a bill, alerting constituencies to where the bill is in the legislative process, getting mailings out on time, making sure to get feedback from individuals who lobby their representatives–mind-numbing work, but crucial to the outcome.

What confounded Luker (1984) about the anti-abortionists was their apparent lack of the machinery ordinarily associated with political effectiveness. They rarely attended meetings, yet were able to coordinate their activities down to the parish level. While the Catholic church hierarchy surely helped in this, the activists themselves were the backbone of the effort. Along the way they learned how to stay in touch with one another. At modest cost they were able to use telephone answering services with call forwarding, so if one advocate was not available, the call would automatically go to another. With the advent of personal computers it was possible to generate thousands of letters with relative ease. Using electronic banking, contributors could have donations automatically deducted from their bank accounts each month–an especially useful device for low budget organizations whose constituency might balk at large annual donations. Such technical aids have been put within the reach of groups of modest means. But even without them, a well-organized constituency can multiply its effectiveness manyfold. It is more than worth the effort.

The Love Canal leaders had to invest a great deal of personal time in keeping their members informed and energized. As it turned out, one of their allies in this endeavor was the state department of health, the agency that in other ways proved to be an obstacle. The department provided the LCHA with an office and telephones. It may have seemed like an inexpensive goodwill gesture, but as anyone who has worked in campaigns knows, it was an invaluable asset to the residents.

The ability to maintain an effective organization, keep good records and a constant flow of essential information to key constituencies is not a universal attribute. In fact, some of the most creative and forceful advocates are terrible organizers. However, good organization is a must in any sustained advocacy effort, particularly where the work of several allied groups must be meshed. So, if you are not a well-organized person, you need to team up with people who are.

INFORMATION

We next consider the asset that translates the others into an effective operation: information. That is what a major part of the book is about–determining what information is needed, where to find it, and how to make the most productive use of it. To a surprising degree, the information you need is easily accessible. Not that special expertise and funds to hire other people's expertise and computers and years of accumulated experience are not extremely valuable. Much critical information, however, is sitting in libraries, free for the asking. You can also capitalize on other people's knowledge, including that possessed by those who do not agree with you.

There are two complementary kinds of information: substantive *policy content* and the arguments with which to support or oppose a particular change, and *strategic content* regarding the process by which the change takes place, and the actors and forces that influence decisions. Policy information can be found in books and other published materials, though not exclusively. Strategic information is more likely to come from contact with the people with hands-on experience, though not exclusively.

Policy Content

I teach a course to social work students in which the final assignment is to go out and *be* a policy advocate. In most cases that means lobbying one or more legislators. When the students discover what they are expected to do, many go into a panic. But, before they venture out into the political arena they spend weeks preparing a "brief," which is anything but brief. It is an exhaustive summary of the arguments on the critical issues, both sides of the issues, with supporting evidence drawn from a variety of sources.

They will never use most of that content in their contact with a legislator, but they are prepared, and know it. If they had any doubts about the value of all that research, they get over them quickly after realizing that in most cases they know far more about the subject than the person they are talking to. And the person knows it, too. So, the students are convincing advocates in the eyes of two parties: the target person and themselves. Especially as they continue to advocate for their chosen cause after the course is over, as I encourage them to do, that depth of knowledge really pays off. They frequently become important sources of information for other advocates as well.

At one point Lois Gibbs tells how she made an important discovery while sitting at her kitchen table charting on a map the locations of people with health problems. This process led to the realization that toxic chemicals were traveling out of the Love Canal cavity along subterranean channels.

What struck me about this was the fact that I once made an important discovery while sitting at my kitchen table. The governor, whose welfare reform proposal would virtually eliminate all able-bodied adults without dependents from general assistance, had made a speech in which he said that jobs were easy to find if one only had a little initiative. Why, the newspapers were full of job ads. It was an argument for tough welfare rules that Ronald Reagan has also made.

So I sat in the kitchen one Sunday morning with the employment section of the *Philadelphia Inquirer* and went through the job ads. Out of the first 1000 ads, I found a total of 27 for which the average general assistance recipient would qualify, according to the state's own statistics. That discovery led to a letter to the editor, which got wide distribution by organizations opposing the governor's plan.

Critical evidence for policy arguments can be that easy to obtain. In both Lois Gibbs's case and mine, the advocate had been living with the issue for months and knew what to look for. But in neither case did it require special expertise, just a little imagination and the time and patience to plow through detailed information. Still, one often does need the help of experts and access to information that is not readily available.

The data requirements vary with the policy question. Discoveries may occur regarding the medical side of abortion. There will certainly be new information on the social and psychological consequences of policies that make it harder or easier to obtain one. But, in large part, the arguments are couched in moral terms and by now are quite familiar.

Many arguments regarding welfare reform are of this sort, although researchers and practitioners are continually turning up new evidence about poverty, the actual impact of welfare on work motivation, methods of job training, and the economic side-effects of public assistance payments.

Technical knowledge in the mental health field is necessary to make a convincing case for the spending of tax money on community-based programs. A standard question in legislative hearings on appropriations for such services is whether the services have been proven to do any good. It is tough to answer because there is little solid evidence of the success of mental health treatment. Often, the biggest challenge for the mental health professional is not the need to be current on the research literature, but rather to translate esoteric principles into common, understandable language.

The issue of toxic waste disposal is another one in which mastery of technical content becomes important. The problem did not exist until a few decades ago–at least not on the scale it does now. Not only is there very little experience with policies in this area, but one quickly gets into very technical content. That may seem to make toxic wastes an issue only for the professionals. But as Lois Gibbs demonstrated, a young homemaker with no advanced education can learn to hold her own in this policy field, as in any other. She does not do it on her own. This is where allies with the right expertise become a critical asset.

Strategic Content

All the facts in the world will do you no good if you do not know when, where, and how to use them. For this there is nothing like a wealth of personal experience on which to draw. This book suggests some principles for identifying key decision makers and who and what influences them. These principles must be adapted to fit the particular case you are working on.

This is where good working relationships with other advocates are beneficial. In particular, the people who do this sort of thing for a living have to be conversant with the formal and informal policy-making system. When I want to lobby a legislator on a bill, I frequently get on the telephone to a trusted friend who works the corridors of the state capitol to find out what kind of reception I can anticipate. My contact is also likely to know the best time and place to act. The way to develop such ties is to be helpful in return when one can. For instance, if you are doing background research on an issue, you may have useful data to share with a lobbyist. There is one cardinal principle in this, which must never be broken: *Be sure you know what you are talking about.* Giving wrong information to a lobbyist or a legislator is one sure way to end the relationship–permanently.

In each of the four case examples in the "Introduction," strategic information was essential to whatever success advocates were able to achieve. Because of the volatile and emotional nature of the abortion controversy, knowing when *not* to make a particular argument–or even not to raise the subject at all–can be crucial. Knowing that a legislator has a family member who has spent time in a mental hospital is the kind of information one normally finds only through experience and informal contacts. Mental health professionals also find they are able to offer helpful advice regarding constituents' requests for help.

Welfare reform rhetoric and welfare reform legislation can be very different. In Pennsylvania, one key Democratic senator was disposed to vote in favor of a bill that was opposed by welfare rights advocates. They could have written off his vote, but instead began to educate him on the negative consequences for his own constituents. In time they turned him around on the issue. To force a favorable vote, legislative leaders attached one amendment to the bill that would provide essential funding for child welfare services, and another that would restrict funds for abortions. Pro-welfare lobbyists had to advise friendly legislators on how they wanted them to vote.

Leaders of the Love Canal residents had to gain their strategic information the hard way: by sometimes bitter experience. They began by assuming official announcements could be taken at face value. In time they learned to be skeptical and to ask for proof. It was demoralizing to be repeatedly reassured, then let down. Among other things it made it more difficult for the leaders to retain the confidence of the rank and file and keep the diverse factions together.

It is hard to be skeptical without sometimes being cynical–never trusting anybody and assuming that no matter what you do it will come to naught because "they" will always betray you in the end. That attitude can be as self-defeating as assuming that everybody is working with equal zeal for the same cause.

CONFIDENCE

There is another asset that comes as a result of all the others: a belief in one's own abilities. In many ways it is a make-or-break factor. A sense of self-assurance is not something achieved entirely from a book or a course of study, though both may help. In a way, the best means of gaining confidence in lobbying is, as with so many things, to do a lot of it. As you discover for yourself that legislators are not ten feet tall, that you do know a great deal about an issue, and–perhaps most important–that you can survive a setback or two, your confidence will grow.

One of the heartening parts of Lois Gibbs's story is what happened to this shy, retiring individual as a person. When she started out, she had a fairly shaky ego. She tells about her first attempt to interest her neighbors in taking action against the lethal dump underneath their homes:

> I went to 99th and Wheatfield and knocked on my first door. There was no answer. I just stood there, not knowing what to do. It was an unusually warm June day and I was perspiring. I thought: *What am I doing here? I must be crazy. People are going to think I am. Go home, you fool!* And that's just what I did. (Gibbs, 1982:13)

Within months this same woman was taking on highly placed officials in the U.S. Environmental Protection Agency and fielding questions on national television.

First-time advocates often assume that the legislator they are going to see will pepper them with difficult questions and generally make a fool of them. They are even a little disappointed when they are greeted by a warm, friendly, though usually noncommittal individual, who must be helped to understand the intricacies of the subject they are so thoroughly steeped in.

A small, soft-spoken woman in one of my classes called the office of her state senator for an appointment. Expecting to get a secretary, she was surprised to find the senator himself on the other end of the line. He was obviously in no mood for small talk. When she stated her business, he suggested in a loud, unfriendly voice there was no point in talking with him. Having come this far, she was not about to be turned away so easily. She waited for the tirade to subside, then asked quietly if she could come to see him. He finally gave her a few minutes the following week.

Back in the safety of the classroom she was still shaking from the ordeal and wondering if she should cancel the appointment. With the encouragement of the rest of the class she agreed to carry through with the task. When she did meet the senator, she was shocked to find him gracious and ready to give her an extended visit. She was not sure she had convinced him of her case, but her confidence in her ability to lobby had grown dramatically.

BEING REALISTIC ABOUT LIMITATIONS

I am somewhat reluctant to talk about limitations because of my conviction that most people's problem is *under*confidence rather than *over*confidence. However, it is necessary to realize that one is up against formidable forces in the policy arena. When billions of dollars are at stake, as they are in the case of welfare policies and toxic waste disposal suits, the interested parties are going to mobilize their resources accordingly.

We can take inspiration from the ability of a relative handful of Love Canal residents with very limited means to force concessions from the State of New York and very possibly from the Occidental Petroleum Company. To a significant extent, Lois Gibbs and her neighbors were lucky. They had an issue that seized the public's imagination and sympathy. Contrast this with the problem of the advocate for the welfare poor–stigmatized, viewed as hopeless, helpless, shiftless, or all three. If anything, public attention to the problem may make positive changes even more difficult.

At this point you may be prompted to ask, if it is so easy to have an impact, why does not more happen? You are right to be skeptical about the advocate's ability to make dramatic changes in a well-entrenched and powerful system. By being realistic about the limits of the feasible you can avoid the disillusionment that may follow exaggerated expectations. Admittedly, we live in a political environment whose reactions to policy innovations range from apathy to outright hostility. But there have been enough instances in which persons without the obvious trappings of power were able to make small changes that resulted in big improvements in people's lives, to warrant investing one's time and effort in policy advocacy.

This book will help you maximize your potential impact. That is different from saying the principles here are guaranteed to turn you into an effective advocate. At best, they can help you capitalize on the assets you already possess and will acquire as you go along. At some point, now or in the future, you will find that something you care very much about can be affected by a change in public policy. At that point you will plunge in with intense commitment, take time away from other things if necessary, look for allies, organize your forces, and arm yourself with the necessary information. The willingness to invest yourself in this way cannot be manufactured, but your ability to translate the will into effective action can be cultivated.

POINTS TO REMEMBER

1. Personal commitment to a cause is one of the most underestimated resources in advocacy. It is also entirely within your control.
2. Time, the availability of it and your use of it, is what translates your commitment into productive action.
3. Lobbying is not a solo activity. You must multiply your own strength by joining with kindred spirits. This may require balancing your agenda against items in somebody else's.
4. Good organization and care in making sure the necessary supports are in place means maximum pay-off for the investment. It enables relatively weak groups to have an impact on policy decisions.
5. A well-organized case, thoroughly grounded in solid information, is a critical element in successful lobbying. Another is knowledge of how and in what kind of environment decisions are made.
6. All of the above elements are what give you confidence, perhaps *the* critical ingredient in lobbying.

Chapter 4

Setting the Action Agenda

Before one can map a course of action for change, it is necessary to answer the question, action for what? That sounds so obvious as not to need to be stated, but too often advocacy groups neglect this important step. They are then vulnerable to divide-and-conquer strategies of a determined opponent. General goal statements, the kind that find their way into fliers and posters, are the easy part. It is much tougher to struggle with specific language so everyone is working in the same direction. The same principle applies to action by an individual advocate. Without a clear set of objectives, he or she is vulnerable to being sidetracked or overwhelmed by the enormity of the task.

To avoid these problems, you should observe the four cardinal rules of agenda-setting: (1) know your agenda beforehand, (2) decide between incremental and fundamental change goals, (3) be clear about your priorities, and (4) develop fallback positions. To see what can happen if you neglect these important rules, let us look at the plight of Betty and Brad Advocate: a tragedy in four acts.

Act I: Betty and Brad corner Senator Artful in a corridor of the Capitol. They tell him they are very upset about the way women keep having babies and their boyfriends take no responsibility because they know their women friends can always get welfare. "You have to do something about this mess," says Brad. He has been seeing on television and reading in the newspapers how families in urban America are being destroyed by welfare. "What are you going to do about this?" they ask. "What do you want me to do?" asks Senator Artful. Betty and Brad look at each other. There is a lot of hemming and hawing, while a glaze comes over the senator's eyes and he thanks them for coming by.

Act II: Brad tells Betty about a new bill in Congress, HR 13, that would provide funds to move mothers on welfare into mandatory job training. "We need to write to our congressman and get his support for HR 13," he says. Betty is appalled. "That's like putting a Band-Aid on a running sore," she says. "Job training without creating more jobs in the inner city is useless. We need a gigantic urban development program, one that will give hope to the people at the bottom. As long as that problem is neglected, a zillion job training programs are a waste of time." Brad disagrees, saying Betty's approach would take such a massive amount of money it would sink the economy. They finally decide the problem is so huge that there is little anybody can do about it.

Act III: A number of groups are now urging people to support HR 13 as a step in the right direction. Betty says they should support it. Brad says he is not so sure because he has seen one prediction that the program would cost billions in the coming years. "That is going to make the federal deficit worse," says Brad. "But if we can do something about the welfare problem, it is worth it," Betty replies. They get into an argument and end up not speaking to each other.

Act IV: To pick up the votes of several conservative senators, HR 13 has been changed from a comprehensive job training program to five demonstration projects running over the next two years. Brad says the original bill has been gutted and it would be worse to pass HR 13 in its amended form than to take no action. "This will allow them to claim they've done something and kill any chance of a real attack on the welfare problem." "Are you kidding?" asks Betty. "If we give up now it will send the wrong signal. They'll figure we don't care about the problem, and if we don't, they won't." By the time Betty and Brad decide whether to support the watered-down HR 13, it has been voted down by the House.

It does not have to be tragic, but this is one kind of scenario that never ends. Unlike Shakespeare, the drama of public policy has no final curtain, it just goes on and on. That is part of the frustration: one is never finished with the work of fighting for better policies.

Betty and Brad Advocate have failed to observe the four cardinal rules of agenda setting:

1. Know your agenda.
2. Decide between incremental and fundamental change goals.
3. Be clear about your priorities.
4. Develop fallback positions.

RULE 1: KNOW YOUR AGENDA

Knowing what one wants sounds simple, but it is a step that is all too frequently ignored in advocacy. In the first scenario, Betty and Brad never got beyond being angry over the welfare problem. They could tell the senator at length about the terrible conditions in America's inner cities. They were also keeping up on coverage of the issue in the mass media. Unfortunately, the media frequently tell us what is wrong without saying much about what would improve things. The Advocates have to get beyond that point and define what they would like to see happen. Fumbling in the senator's office is not the only problem that can occur. Suppose somebody else comes along with a family therapy program they claim will salvage inner city families. Will Betty or Brad latch onto that "solution"? By knowing where *you* want to go, you are least likely to be talked into backing somebody else's agenda, one that may have little to do with seriously attacking the problem you started with.

One advantage of the anti-abortion activists is that they are crystal clear about their agenda: stop abortion under any circumstances. Other interest groups, including many pro-choice activists, are much less certain about what would be a desirable policy. They have no trouble saying what they are against: the adamant position of the anti-abortionists, their rigidity being part of the problem. But, abortion on demand at any point during pregnancy? There are feminists who hold out for that, but many pro-choice activists have trouble with that position. Abortion on demand up to the point at which the fetus could survive outside the womb is a goal that can attract wider support.

Particularly as one enlists others to fight for reproductive rights, it is essential to establish a common ground. The group must arrive at a position that all can live with comfortably. Otherwise, various members can send different messages, sowing the seeds of dissension and confusion in the minds of others.

Spending proposals are always hard to sell. When the product is community mental health services, the problems are compounded. Lawmakers who will allocate billions for exotic military hardware without blinking an eye, suddenly become very protective of the taxpayer's money when it comes to human services. Not only do mental health programs smack of a tax-and-spend welfare state mentality, but psychiatry is still a mysterious realm to the public. It is one thing to feed the starving, house the homeless, and treat cancer patients but quite another to pay people high salaries to talk to other people about their problems, organize therapy groups, and create halfway houses.

So, not only must one be clear about what is being sought, it is also necessary to be able to explain this to others in plain English. The legislator asks, "What exactly do you propose to do with this money if we appropriate it? Why does it take that much? Do you have any evidence that these programs actually work?" These are legitimate questions which deserve good answers. Later we will look at how to answer them. The process starts with one's own clarity about what is being sought.

In a society used to thinking of poor people, especially public assistance recipients, as lazy ne'er-do-wells, simplistic answers such as cutting people off the welfare rolls or assigning them to menial jobs to work off their grants are especially appealing. Issues of race and class are usually involved. Champions of welfare rights tend to be thrown on the defensive, so that they devote more energy to answering the critics than thinking through what sorts of policies they favor.

"You don't approve of workfare? Just what do you propose to get people off welfare–or do you favor making welfare a permanent way of life?" Later we will consider ways of dealing with such questions. At this point we are looking at another issue: the need for the pro-welfare forces to think the problem through and come up with a clear agenda. Do they support the main thrust of a proposed work and training program but with safeguards against exploitation? Do they favor a totally voluntary approach to participation by clients? Do they feel priority should be given to day care, transportation, and other support services? Do they favor an increase in AFDC grants? Do they favor it even if it leads to automatic cuts in other means-tested programs such as housing and food stamps?

The residents of Love Canal were angry and frightened–so angry and frightened that in the beginning they had trouble articulating specific goals. On the one hand, it was tempting to want revenge on the villain of the piece, the Hooker Chemical Company. On the other hand, offers of a quick settlement on terms that were to the residents' disadvantage were also hard to resist. One of the main challenges for the leaders of the Love Canal Homeowners' Association (LCHA) was to figure out what they wanted. But without a clear conception of their goal they would have been an easy mark for other interests wanting to use the residents' plight for their own purposes.

By focusing on demands to be relocated and get adequate compensation for their homes, the LCHA leaders could keep the members energized and united over the long haul. The specific objective was less important than the fact that they knew what they were after and were able to communicate this to others.

RULE 2: DECIDE BETWEEN INCREMENTAL AND FUNDAMENTAL CHANGE GOALS

One may believe in the need for radical change in the long run, yet in the interim work for improvements within the existing structure. In order to lobby effectively, one should be clear about which of these is being sought *now* since some incremental and fundamental changes may work against each other. Making modest improvements in the status quo may simply create the illusion that real change has taken place. Conversely, by holding out for total victory, an opportunity to make tangible gains may be lost. On the surface this may seem like the previous issue. But whereas the previous problem was a matter of unclarity, this issue involves a clear difference between alternative directions in which to move.

Betty and Brad Advocate are on the horns of a familiar dilemma. They know that their ultimate aim is saving the family in inner city America, but are unsure as to how to approach the problem. Do they focus on job training programs, a stop-gap approach to Betty's way of thinking, or do they work for a massive economic development program? Either approach could be considered "right," in the sense that it has the potential for reducing the poverty of *some* families. The two strategies are not inherently incompatible; Betty and Brad could work on both levels simultaneously. They are aware that Congress is unlikely to invest large amounts of resources in both, so in effect it is an either-or situation. Unfortunately, the Advocates end up not making a choice–which is, in reality, a choice not to act.

* * *

In the mid-1960s the pro-choice forces in California became split over the issue of abortion as a right versus liberalized abortion policies under the control of the medical profession. The proponents of repeal of the state's abortion law, the more "radical" faction, saw the issue in terms of the second-class status of women:

> When we talk about women's rights, we can get all the rights in the world–the right to vote, the right to go to school–and none of them means a doggone thing if we don't own the flesh we stand in. . . . (Luker, 1984:97)

Those who favored reform of the law included members of the male-dominated medical and legal professions who sought to ease what they considered to be archaic restrictions. The abortion reform act, passed in 1967, left intact the principle that abortion should be allowed only under circumstances considered harmful to the women. Discretion was left in the hands of the doctor. While this did not deal directly with the issue of women's status as rights-bearing citizens, what followed was, in effect, abortion on demand. Of the women who sought abortions, over 99 percent got them. The number of legal abortions in California escalated rapidly, and, says Luker, medical control of abortion became a legal fiction (1984:94).

Was the repeal faction wrong? One might argue that way, if abortion is considered in isolation. But the repealers were part of a much larger movement and undoubtedly their strong stand helped mobilize forces that might otherwise have lain dormant. During the abortion fight in California of the mid-1960s, they and the reformers needed to be clear about what they were after. Opposed to them was a powerful political force, the anti-abortionists, who had no such dilemmas.

Welfare–public assistance to the needy–has been looked upon as (1) the enemy of capitalism, (2) a tool of capitalist oppression, or (3) a humane attempt to mitigate the worst effects of capitalism, flawed not in concept but in implementation. Its abolition, or at least drastic paring down, has been proposed by conservatives. (See Murray, 1984; Nozik, 1974; Friedman, 1962.) On the left, Piven and Cloward proposed a strategy of overloading the welfare system with the thousands of poor persons who were eligible for benefits but did not apply for them. They saw this as a way to force a basic redesign of welfare (Piven & Cloward, 1971:321n). Through it all, the system has shown remarkable resilience, bending to accommodate political, economical, technological, and social changes, but never breaking down.

Up to this point, incremental change and fundamental change have been referred to as if they represented clear positions across the social change spectrum. However, they are relative terms. In one sense, turning family assistance, now a series of state programs, into a uniform national system with grants based strictly on need would be a radical change. But as a means-tested system in which recipients have to demonstrate need, it fits a conservative view of what to do about poverty.

In the late 1980s, welfare reformers were confronted with several major proposals for changing the system. All emphasized ways of moving the able-bodied poor, particularly mothers of young children on Aid to Families with Dependent Children (AFDC), into the labor force, thus buying the underlying assumptions that had guided the system for decades. If one wished to impact the congressional deliberations on welfare reform, it was necessary to adopt a reformist posture. Proposals for more fundamental change were simply tuned out by the policymakers.

The tragedy at Love Canal helped speed the passage in 1980 of the Superfund legislation to clean up toxic waste sites around the country. (See Zuesse, 1981; U.S. Senate, 1979.) The act did not provide for compensating victims of pollution, such as members of the Love Canal Homeowners' Association. The Superfund was an example of incremental change, in the sense that it focused on cleaning up existing lethal dumps and offering industry incentives to stop polluting. It left untouched a market system under which government regulates privately run corporations, offers them incentives, and helps clean up their messes, but does not take outright control of the production process. The latter steps would indeed represent fundamental change.

* * *

Who is to say which is better, incremental or fundamental change? There are arguments for each. As an advocate you need to know what kind of strategy you are following, because tactics that promote incremental change could be seen as undermining the potential for fundamental change.

RULE 3: BE CLEAR ABOUT YOUR PRIORITIES

Brad Advocate cares a lot about the inner city family. He also cares about other issues, including the size of the federal deficit. Brad and Betty are treating the problem as an either/or proposition. In so doing they have created a *false dichotomy.* Some economists say we cannot expand social programs because to do so would simply add to the federal budget deficit. There are ways, however, of reducing the federal deficit other than cutting back on social programs. We can reduce other expenditures, such as the amount we spend on weapons systems. Taxes can be raised, which many politicians agree to privately but not publicly. Still, some economists say the federal deficit is a phony issue. (See Eisner, 1986.) The real dilemma for Betty and Brad is that they have several priorities and cannot agree on which comes first.

There are several ways in which confusion about priorities can get in the way of effective advocacy. Here we look at four common situations which I shall call "You Can't Have It Both Ways," "Getting Justice or Getting Results," "Trade-offs," and "Whose Agenda Are We Working On?"

You Can't Have It Both Ways

Unlike the false dichotomy that Brad and Betty have erected in their path, there are times when one *must* choose between alternative goals. One cannot support greater freedom of choice for pregnant women wanting an abortion *and* restrictions designed to protect the fetus. For the anti-abortion activists this presents no problem. "Protect the fetus at all costs," they say. Some persons who identify with the feminist position on most issues have moral qualms about abortion. As long as they are not able to resolve this dilemma, they will be immobilized.

Some issues may pose either/or questions in practical terms, even though, strictly speaking, there are alternatives. A large percentage of chronically mentally ill persons live in nursing and boarding homes under horrible conditions. Most states have done an inadequate job of regulating these privately run operations. One argument raised against cracking down on the boarding home industry is that this would reduce the supply of an urgently needed resource. Not surprisingly, the operators are often the ones who pose this problem. There is a reality to the question, at least in the short run. Unless the state legislature is willing to spend large sums to develop alternative housing for the mentally ill, the supply may indeed go down as a result of strict enforcement of stringent rules. The lobbyist must think this issue through if he or she is not to be left fumbling when a state legislator asks, "What would *you* do if you were in my shoes?"

Getting Justice or Getting Results

Justice is never retroactive, and the way to avoid injustice is to prevent it in the first place. Redressing wrongs through the court, aside from the expensive, prolonged, and inefficient process involved, rarely ends up truly balancing the scales. Party A can sue Party B for a fatal accident that killed Party A's wife, but that will never restore her to life. The starting point in public policy is *now*, after damage may have been done. The task of the advocate is to move on and reduce the likelihood of future damage.

The Love Canal residents' sense of outrage at the Hooker Chemical Company was understandable. Lawsuits against Hooker had a dual purpose: getting reimbursed for the costs–economic, physical, and mental–of the toxic waste dumping, and getting back at the company for what it had done. Having to pay punitive damages may act as a deterrent to future dumping, in which case something practical will have been achieved. But that can never really undo the damage.

Vengeance is a powerful motivator. The death penalty is presented as a deterrent to future crime, but it clearly has another function: satisfying the lust for revenge. Nations rally their populations to battle by appealing to that same emotion.

The leaders of the Love Canal Homeowners' Association could have been drawn into an abortive contest with the Hooker Company, trying to match their limited resources against those of a sprawling multinational corporation. They wisely kept their sights on something more practical: being compensated for the damage they had suffered and getting help toward making a new start in a new location. As they became big news in the national media, Lois Gibbs and her neighbors had an opportunity to make Hooker look bad in the public eye. It is doubtful that the company or its parent corporation, Occidental Petroleum, would have suffered greatly from this kind of campaign. Since Hooker sold its products to other industries, not to the public, it would have been hard to hurt the company through public pressure. In time, the resident leaders would have had trouble keeping their followers involved if the only satisfaction they could offer was an outlet for anger.

The wish for revenge sometimes leads activists to make threats of reprisal at the polls against an unsympathetic lawmaker. Opponents of a punitive welfare reform bill vowed retaliation against a state senator who talked initially as if he would vote against the legislation, then appeared to betray the cause at the last minute. In so doing, they ran the risk of demonstrating their own weakness and his power by failing in their attempt to dump him in the next election. The threat of political reprisal is indeed a powerful weapon *if* one can deliver on the promise. Such threats should always be based on careful assessment of one's political resources and the legislator's, not on an angry reaction.

Trade-Offs

As they work their way through the legislative process, bills often pick up "sweeteners"–amendments designed to attract this or that pocket of votes. One state welfare reform proposal included a 5 percent across-the-board increase in public assistance grants and a limit of three months' aid per year for certain categories of needy. Pro-welfare advocates had to decide whether they were willing to accept the tightened eligibility as a necessary price of more adequate aid, or to lose the aid by getting legislators to vote down the entire bill. Later, this same proposal was packaged together with state support of child welfare services (urgently sought by certain pro-welfare groups) and an anti-abortion rider (which would appeal to Catholics who had opposed the original bill).

A 1988 welfare reform bill in Congress included sections (1) making an optional provision for assistance to two-parent families mandatory throughout the country, (2) allowing states to force mothers with children as young as one year old to go into work and training programs, (3) requiring states to provide day care and other support services to work and training participants, (4) automatically ordering employers to withhold support payments from their employees' paychecks, regardless of whether or not the worker was willing to make payments, and (5) requiring that minors live with a parent or guardian to be eligible for assistance. The bill was clearly a mixed bag with some things the welfare advocates wanted and some things they opposed. It was necessary to decide what one was willing to trade off in one area in order to make gains elsewhere.

A Pennsylvania mental health reform bill would have made it easier to hospitalize the mentally ill against their will and provided expanded community based services. Mental health consumers' organizations badly wanted the latter but were unwilling to accept the new rules making institutionalization easier. After trying unsuccessfully to get the chief sponsor of the bill to separate the two components, they decided to oppose the total package.

There is no simple rule for deciding what to trade off for something else. One must look carefully at a piece of legislation, decide what is the most important priority, and decide what else is an acceptable cost for obtaining the desired policy.

Whose Agenda Are We Working On?

Coalitions multiply an individual's power many times over. To gain the benefits of coalition politics, it is necessary to serve other people's purposes as well as one's own. The original objectives must not be lost in this process. The New York State right-to-life movement joined forces with other groups whose main goal was opposition to school busing for racial integration (Shapiro, 1972). Each faction needed the support of the other. As long as each was clear as to how the alliance would further its own goals, the relationship could work effectively.

When ultra-conservatives adopted the right-to-life movement, according to Paige (1983:152), it was with the idea of exploiting this rich source of voting strength for its own conservative agenda. Both factions shared a conservative world view, so were natural allies. For the right-to-lifers, with a single, specific goal, there was one major criterion in assessing the relationship: how did it affect progress toward the elimination of abortion? This involved more than simply the need not to be diverted to other right-wing concerns, to the neglect of the abortion issue. The right-to lifers also had to be mindful about the impact of their romance with the political right on other potential allies in the abortion fight. The Catholic bishops, a broad social reform agenda including foreign policy and liberal social programs, became concerned about the ties to the far right.

Fear of being manipulated by others may threaten or prevent alliances. The Love Canal Homeowners' Association had trouble achieving a close working relationship with renters who felt they were being used to protect their neighbors' investment in their homes. Similarly, mental health consumers may fear that they are being used by professionals to protect the latter's jobs. Likewise, the welfare poor may come to view social work activists as being interested only in protecting their own jobs, researchers as wanting to exploit them as subjects, and liberal politicians as merely wanting votes. Any such secondary aims should be presented up front. The fact that people have more than one kind of motivation does not mean they cannot be effective in pushing for a common goal.

The plight of the Love Canal residents was an appealing story, a natural for the national news media and a variety of advocacy groups, each with its own special set of concerns. There is a seductive quality to becoming an overnight celebrity. Lois Gibbs, who made good copy, not only had to keep her sights on her goal, but also deal with the inevitable backbiting from others who saw the whole thing as an ego trip. Ralph Nader and Jane Fonda helped draw public attention to the Love Canal tragedy, but their primary purpose was putting the spotlight on a national scandal, not salvaging the lives of Gibbs and her neighbors. The Love Canal residents could have made the national issue of toxic waste their main agenda, saying in effect that what endangers people in Louisiana, Michigan, and California endangers everyone and unless we deal with the national or even international problem of environmental pollution, we will never be safe. But once they had decided to focus on their own needs as a local community, that was where they had to devote their energies. They then had to gain whatever leverage they could from people like Nader and Fonda without losing sight of their own purpose.

One should always be ready to support the interests of allies, when they are consistent with one's own values and priorities—but then it is doubly important to understand what is in it for everybody. An ally who appears to have no purpose other than being helpful should get a second look.

RULE 4: DEVELOP FALLBACK POSITIONS

The first three rules concern one's initial position: what one would work toward under ideal conditions. But conditions are never ideal. No policy proposal ever comes out of the decision process the way it went in. One must be prepared to compromise. At what point is the original proposal so watered down as to be meaningless—or even worse than meaningless if the illusion of progress has been created, thereby lulling everybody back to sleep?

Our luckless lobbyists, Brad and Betty Advocate, cannot decide whether to keep on promoting HR 13, now pared down to a few demonstration projects, or reject it as actually undermining efforts toward a real attack on the problem of poor families. Without any fallback positions, they stew over the issue until it is too late. It is not possible to anticipate exactly how an original proposal will be altered during deliberation, but it is possible to decide what kinds of changes would still retain enough of the original intent to make it worth fighting for.

The groups seeking to liberalize California's abortion law faced this dilemma in 1967 when Governor Ronald Reagan threatened to veto their bill. The existing law stipulated that abortion could be allowed only when the woman's life was in danger. The reformers wanted to broaden this to include the condition of the fetus as grounds for an abortion. The reform campaign had been spurred on in part by a celebrated thalidomide case, in which a pregnant woman had unknowingly used a drug known to cause severe fetal deformities. Concern about the effects of rubella on the fetus had also gained wide attention. Reagan said he would veto the reform bill unless references to "fetal indications" were removed. The notion that one would destroy a fetus, not to save the mother but merely to produce a whole child, was the most offensive provision in the eyes of anti-abortionists (Luker, 1984:88-89).

After determining that Reagan meant what he said and there were not enough votes to override his veto, the pro-reform forces agreed to the modification. At this point the main movers were not militant feminists but doctors, lawyers, and even California's Young Republicans, so there was little danger that the compromise would cause a revolt in the ranks of the reformers. As it turned out, the concession had little impact on the main thrust of the new law. In effect, California had adopted something very close to abortion-on-demand.

Following the 1973 Supreme Court decision, the right-to-life movement campaigned for a Constitutional amendment declaring that life begins at conception, thus fetuses at whatever stage of development have a right to life, liberty, etc. Amending the Constitution is a long, laborious, and expensive proposition. When it became clear that this strategy would cost more than it would gain, the right-to-lifers switched to adding anti-abortion amendments to other legislation. They were able to limit Medicaid payments for abortions. In many states the anti-abortion lobby sought obstructive measures, such as the requirement that the father participate in the abortion decision and that parental consent be obtained. None of these detracted from the main thrust, since all would make it harder to obtain an abortion. These were also ways of keeping the movement alive and providing political experience for anti-abortion activists looking toward the day when more stringent rules against abortion could be enacted. On the other hand, by implicitly conceding that abortion was legitimate under certain circumstances, some of their bedrock supporters could have been alienated.

Legislation rarely specifies how its intent is to be carried out. That is left to regulations to be written by the department charged with implementing the law. The people who promoted the Community Mental Health Centers Act of 1963 wanted the federal government to subsidize professional salaries in the centers. The American Medical Association fought this provision, fearful of socialized medicine, and that particular provision came out of the final bill (Brown, 1985:41).

The advocates envisioned a bold departure from traditional practice in the centers, but as a concession to the psychiatric profession, the final version required that each center be headed by a psychiatrist. As spelled out by President Kennedy, the intent was that a broad array of community mental health services would supplant state hospitals. States would divert the funds freed up by the closing of hospitals to community-based services. The language on this point was intentionally vague, averting resistance from the states (Chu & Trotter, 1974).

Were the proponents of change right in accepting these concessions, or should they have refused to go along, possibly leading to the defeat of the measure? Some observers feel too much was lost, implying that a firm stand for principle would have been wiser, even at the risk of having to start all over. (See Brown, 1985.) As it turned out, Lyndon Johnson was able to add a provision for federal funding of professional salaries, so the particular concessions made little difference. But by placing psychiatrists firmly in control of center operations and leaving the state role vague, the Community Mental Health Centers Act resulted in a system markedly different from that which the reformers had originally envisioned.

In the fight over President Nixon's Family Assistance Plan (FAP) in the early 1970s, welfare rights advocates came out against the bill because of the low level at which assistance grants were to be pegged. This would have been below existing levels in several northern states with high housing costs. However, passage of the bill, even with the very low assistance payments, would have accomplished much that the welfare rights forces were after by establishing a national plan with national standards and aid based on need, not on arbitrary categories. The law's effects in the Deep South could have been revolutionary in reducing the power of Caucasians over African Americans living in poverty.

After the defeat of the first FAP, the administration came back with FAP II. When this bill faced almost certain defeat it was stripped of most of the provisions for reforming aid to young families in an effort to save other parts of the measure. Included in the law as enacted was a single national scheme, Supplemental Security Income (SSI), for all public assistance categories (with states having the option of supplementing the base amount) *except* Aid to Families with Dependent Children (AFDC). The latter remained a state-by-state program with different eligibility requirements and widely disparate levels of assistance. The revised bill also set up a series of demonstration projects to test the concept of a negative income tax (guaranteed minimum income) system. Not that welfare rights supporters could have stopped enactment of this watered-down measure, but should they have supported the changed bill, as a step forward? Conceivably, it may have been a step backward from the perspective of the welfare rights movement. By creating a national system for other assistance categories, including the blind, the disabled, and the elderly—populations more likely to gain public sympathy—the act further isolated the highly stigmatized AFDC population. This is the program whose clients and their supporters made up the core of the welfare rights movement.

As for the negative income tax experiments, these yielded ambiguous results which have been used to support arguments on all sides of the welfare question. Welfare rights proponents stood little to gain, maybe something to lose, from supporting the final revision of FAP II.

The residents of Love Canal faced a different dilemma in the offers by Occidental Petroleum to settle lawsuits out of court. By agreeing to this, the residents could save legal fees and be assured of getting partial redress without waiting for many years. They would give up the possibility of being awarded higher amounts of money. From a societal standpoint, out-of-court settlements do not set legal precedents, thus cannot serve as a legal standard in future lawsuits against dumpers. Out-of-court settlements are also less likely to deter would-be dumpers.

These examples suggest a set of general principles for determining when a particular fallback position is warranted. Although each case will be different and it is not possible to predict the specific modifications that will be introduced in the midst of the policymaking process, the following questions may help in thinking the matter through.

Is the essence of the original proposal retained, or does the new version undermine the original intent? It can be argued that welfare rights supporters would have been further ahead fighting hard to enact FAP I, despite its stingy provisions and requirements, because of the structural changes that would have been enacted. Conversely, some observers argue that NIMH and other community mental health advocates gave too much in seeking enactment of the Community Mental Health Centers Act of 1963. By acceding to Reagan's veto threat, California abortion reformers managed to enact a bill which might have had tougher sledding a few years later; the modification did little to affect the widened access to abortion contained in the legislation.

Does the new version set a precedent for future action toward the ultimate goal, or weaken the impetus for action by creating an illusion of change? Getting the federal government into the community mental health field paved the way for future expansion, despite the lack of federal support for professional staffing in the original bill. Conversely, a liberalized national welfare scheme for the blind, disabled, and elderly may have been a setback for AFDC recipients. The series of negative income tax experiments may have sounded to some welfare rights advocates like an exciting opportunity to promote such a plan, but did little to advance their cause in the end.

Will acceptance of "half a loaf" help to sustain momentum and morale in a movement or alienate potential supporters by appearing to be a sell-out? The Love Canal Community leaders were constantly under pressure from a variety of sources. Some neighbors wanted to get the matter settled and resented the idea of holding out for bigger gains. Others felt their needs were being neglected; for example, renters who were afraid the homeowners would only look out for their own interests. In accepting or rejecting offers from public officials and the Hooker Company, the advocates had to weigh the impact on these factions. Right-to-lifers saw the series of partial steps toward restriction of abortion in the 1970s and 1980s as a means of keeping the rank and file energized and the opposition on the defensive.

POINTS TO REMEMBER

1. Be clear about what you want. Go beyond saying what you do not want, to deciding what you would like in its place.

2. Decide whether you are working for incremental change, which would leave in place the existing basic structure, or feel drastic change of a fundamental sort is necessary. By opting for incremental steps you are not writing off fundamental change as an ultimate goal, but your energies will be devoted to working within the existing framework, at least for the time being.

3. Stay focused on your priorities. What are you willing to trade off on behalf of your goal? Avoid setting up an either/or choice when you do not have to, but keep your eyes on your own priorities in the process of working on other people's goals. Do not let yourself be distracted by the wish for revenge or personal distaste for a potential ally.

4. Think through the implications of making concessions: will accepting half a loaf now help move your agenda ahead later, or make it harder to achieve in the end?

Chapter 5

Understanding Policymakers

Action agendas must be translated into decisions, so who can make the right decision and who can persuade the decision makers are critical questions. These decision makers are the target individuals or groups, or more simply, targets. As the following true story reveals, the actual channels of influence are often not the obvious ones.

> Senator Daniel Inouye of Hawaii was under intense pressure as he prepared to attend a meeting of the Senate Appropriations Committee one July morning in 1976. So, he did what is standard practice under the circumstances: he turned to his legislative aide and asked her about the vote on the Condor missile program. It was a good plan and should be supported, she told him. Accordingly, he voted for approval of the controversial project, in which the Navy had already invested more than $300 million over a 13-year period.
>
> What Senator Inouye did not know was that the aide's recommendation was the result of months of intensive lobbying by a representative of Rockwell International, the nation's tenth largest defense contractor, in collaboration with Naval officers (*The New York Times*, 1976). Rockwell knew there was little point in working on the senator directly as the liberal Democrat's state had virtually no defense industries. Instead, their representative focused his attention on the staff person who was relied on by the senator for defense information. There was no

exchange of money, no promise of favors for the aide. The lobbyist simply made it a point to impress her with the merits of the project and provide her with language to insert in the final version of the appropriations bill. At strategic times, Navy personnel were enlisted to add their support. The Navy also had a stake in the matter.

The point of this story is not that lawmakers always rely on their aides for advice–in fact, the role of the congressional staff person varies greatly. Rather, it is that advocates need to know whom to court when they are trying to influence decisions. Amateur advocates are sometimes disappointed that they "only" got to talk with an aide to their representative. The pros, like the Rockwell representative, know better. To whom should you direct your arguments? The answer is one you will frequently find in this book: it all depends.

PICKING THE RIGHT TARGETS

A first approximation in selecting targets is to think about who can have the greatest impact on policy decisions. Equally important for you as an advocate is your own access to policymakers. Fortunately, as the Inouye story shows so clearly, your potential influence does not depend solely on direct contact with policymakers.

Elected v. Appointed Officials

We are most aware of the legislative phase of policymaking because it is most exposed to public scrutiny and lends high drama to the process. The president or the governor sends a message to the legislative branch outlining a new proposal, and a bill embracing the plan is submitted for consideration. The news media immediately seek legislative leaders of the two parties to get their reactions. Committee deliberations on the measure may be public, with various interests using the occasion to get their views across to the voters. Even when a bill has little general interest, it may be of intense concern to various factions. By their votes in committee and on the floor, representatives and senators establish their voting records, which may promote their political fortunes or come back to haunt them later.

The bill is passed–always in modified form–the chief executive has his picture taken signing the measure into law, flanked by smiling legislative leaders, and the policymaking process is over. Or is it? Legislation is necessarily written in broad, general, and sometimes ambiguous language. The *real* policy, the sets of rules that will determine who gets what and under what conditions, is now hammered out by people no one elected and most never heard of. The writing of regulations is little understood by the public. But the officials responsible for doing the writing have the final say about what goes into the regulations. If this suggests to you that these appointed officials are important policymakers, it is an accurate perception.

If you are going to be an effective advocate, then you must understand what makes elected representatives and appointed officials tick. Both are potential targets of your lobbying activity.

Elected Officials

In general, you have the greatest access to policymakers who officially represent you. Not only is it the essence of democracy that they listen to what you have to say, but you are, directly or indirectly, the one they depend on for keeping their jobs. That is clearest with your state representative, who has two functions: to enact policies that benefit the majority of constituents, and to assist with personal needs of individual constituents. Thus, responsiveness is built into the relationship, at least in theory. As you become known to this and other policymakers as well informed and strongly committed, your access will grow.

It is good to learn the names, addresses, and telephone numbers–both in the local district and in the state or national capital–of each person who represents you: two U.S. senators and a U.S. representative, a state senator and representative, and local council members in whose district you reside. (Some local government lawmakers are elected at-large, and so represent all the citizens.) Find out what committees or subcommittees your representatives chair or serve on. Do not be surprised if you find you are a constituent of some very powerful people. The president, your state's governor, and the local chief executive should be on your list. In addition, it would be good to list high administrative officers, especially those dealing with issues of special concern to you.

I might be inclined to make less of a point of this if it had not been for an almost-tragedy in my own experience. I was visiting state legislative offices about an issue very soon after I had moved from another state. I had seen frequent mention in the news media about a state senator in my county and jumped to the conclusion that I was in his district. I was lucky enough to find out the identity of my own senator from a friendly representative a short time before I was scheduled to visit the wrong senator's office. I would have felt ridiculous lobbying the wrong person–more importantly, I would have undermined my credibility as an advocate.

The nice thing about direct contact with your representative is that the more of it you have, the more significant you become to that person. It does not take too long for you to become known, usually on a first-name basis, not only to the representative, but also to his or her staff. And never underestimate the importance of being on good terms with receptionists and other clerical staff.

It is not necessary to agree with the representative's political views, but you must treat everybody with respect–the way you would want to be treated by a constituent if you were in the other person's shoes. Regardless of your position on issues, at the very least you have to be part of the representative's reelection calculus. A well-informed visitor or letter-writer, especially one who shows a persistent interest in a problem, is known to be the kind of person who will remember on election day. In Chapter 8 we will look at dircct lobbying in more detail.

Working Through an Intermediary

As Senator Inouye's experience so clearly shows, there are times when a staff member is a better audience for your information than the legislator, for whom you are less likely to be an information source than a vote in the next election. For this reason, I find it useful to talk about two kinds of targets: *ultimate* targets, whose decisions you are trying to influence, and *intermediate* targets, who transmit the message to the real quarry.

When reaching a decision maker through an intermediary, it is necessary to keep in mind that you are actually dealing with two audiences: the contact person, and the ultimate target you may never speak to. What will make an impact on the aide and what will influence the policymaker are not the same. As you have contact with a representative and his or her staff over time, you will get to know what kinds of arguments are most effective with both.

Some legislative aides are very well informed about policy content. However, you may be talking with a person whose greatest expertise is in dealing with constituents' complaints or keeping local interest groups happy. The latter is most likely to be the case with state legislators' staffs and home district staffs of U.S. senators and representatives. It is not always easy to gauge how much a staff person or a representative actually knows, because some feel impelled to present themselves as knowing everything–an impossibility, given the vast scope of legislative business.

Occasionally an aide will question an advocate's stand, not because of personal doubts, but to force into the open the best arguments on the issue. Under such circumstances, it is important to keep in mind that your task is not to win a debate but to get across your message. Showing that you are well informed and thoroughly committed to your position is what will most impress the targets. Showing them that you are smarter than they will impress them, to be sure, but not in the way you want to.

One group of advocates for community mental health services were disappointed to learn that they would not be talking to their state senator but his aide instead. The aide questioned them closely on their proposal for funding and also their views on the senator's own plan for involuntary hospitalization. It became clear to them that this aide was heavily involved in the issue and would report back to the senator in detail on what they said. By sending his aide instead of meeting with the group himself, the senator was able to avoid committing himself to a hard position or making promises he could not later keep.

Appointed Officials as Targets

"Bureaucrat" was a dirty word until the sociologists explained that a very large percentage of the work force, private as well as public, consisted of bureaucrats, i.e., specialized employees of large organizations. The people I shall refer to in this section are more accurately civil servants. Not only do they turn legislated programs into rules for setting up and funding programs, but many legislative initiatives are first "thought up" by departmental employees who see first-hand what is wrong with existing policy.

Civil servants include everybody from senior administrators to mail carriers and schoolteachers. The civil servants we shall be concerned with here are the people in the upper echelons who have responsibility for translating legislation into regulations. This is a group responsibility and, depending on the political sensitivity of the subject matter, the drafting involves substantial consultation with others within the department. The person may also discuss the work with professional colleagues and legislative committee staff. Once the regulations have been written, they are published in an official document and comments are invited from the public. In actuality, most of the public is unaware of all this; it is legislators, lobbyists, and interested organizations who know what is going on. The department may or may not rewrite the regulations on the basis of suggestions it receives. It can ignore them if it sees fit. After several weeks the final form of the regulations becomes official policy—that is, they now have the force of law. The courts can overturn them, but the only way the legislature can change them is by replacing or amending the law they are intended to carry out, or by eliminating from the budget the funds required to implement them.

Notice that unlike the elected representative, the appointed official is relatively free to ignore outside pressure. Because of technical expertise and available resources, this official may know more about the content of the policy than the people doing the lobbying. This is less likely to be true of legislators, whose special expertise is in getting elected. That is not the advocate's only problem. It is also sometimes a challenge to find out which appointed official to lobby. The process of writing regulations goes on in small offices well insulated from public view.

Assuming you want to have an impact on this process, how do you proceed? You begin by turning to the people who *do* know their way through the bureaucracy. Professional lobbyists, including those who work for public interest organizations, make it their business to know this sort of thing, as do legislative staff aides, especially those employed by committee chairs and ranking minority party members of committees. This is one more reason to work closely with allies, as was discussed in Chapter 3.

The next task is to get access to the regulation writers. Some make themselves available, particularly if you are from the same professional community. Remember they are under intense time pressure and may not welcome visits from outside nonexperts while they are in the throes of writing. Needless to say, one must be thoroughly familiar with policy content, very focused and concise, and absolutely truthful. It may be wisest to attempt this kind of lobbying in the company of somebody who knows the ropes. Later we shall look at the world through the eyes of appointed officialdom in order to know the best strategy to employ.

Interest Groups as Targets

Instead of a legislator or bureaucrat, your target may be an interest group representative. Your first task is to decide whether you are trying to convince the group that this is a cause they should work on, stir them to action, arm them with information, or work with them on how to lobby. Anti-abortion advocates have little trouble in getting people involved in their cause. Their job is more one of providing basic information about pregnancy and teaching constituents the most effective way to lobby.

Social workers seeking to enlist their professional association in a fight over welfare reform had to get across to these colleagues–whose own practice was mainly in other fields–why the bill in question was relevant to them. This was also the challenge facing the leaders of the Love Canal Homeowners' Association, some of whose constituents had jobs in chemical companies and therefore ambivalence about making too much of a stir regarding toxic waste disposal.

Targeting Multiple Audiences

Often, the problem is that one is dealing with different targets simultaneously, for example in a legislative hearing. On several occasions I have given testimony on welfare reform in public hearings before state legislative committees. Typically, I am dealing with three different targets: the committee members, who are of course different targets with different agendas; others in attendance, who tend to be the most partisan on the issue; and the news media. All three are intermediate as well as ultimate targets. The committee members are decision makers in their own right, but they also communicate with their colleagues. Allies in the audience are people to whom I want to provide information and help mobilize, but I also want them to carry the message to their wider constituencies. By providing information to the news media I help shape their perception of the issues, and possibly their editorial position. Ultimately they are important insofar as they reach the public. Depending on which of these I have seen as my primary focus, I have shaped my testimony accordingly.

Sometimes I am aware that the committee hearings are a way to publicize an issue rather than inform the legislators. On one such occasion, I was testifying to a friendly committee regarding proposals to liberalize a harsh welfare policy. The state administration opposed the changes on the grounds that the state's economy was in trouble. I deliberately inserted into my testimony an analogy to a sinking ship which tries to deal with the problem by throwing half the crew overboard. The argument had nothing to do with welfare reform and state finances and did nothing to inform the committee members, all of whom were familiar with the subject. The reference to the sinking ship, however, was picked up by at least one major radio news program that evening.

When Lois Gibbs, of the Love Canal Homeowners' Association (LCHA) made public statements, she had to keep in mind that several audiences were being addressed simultaneously. Unless she gave the news media a fresh angle or new information, they would not use her material. Unable to pay for advertising and lacking the natural platform that public office provides, LCHA was dependent on the news media to rally support, create a positive image in the public's mind, and most of all keep Love Canal from being forgotten as a critical issue. So Gibbs not only had to say something attention-grabbing, but also had to do it so as to win public sympathy and not alienate the majority. Meanwhile, she had to respond to the frustrations of other residents and mollify factions eager for a more violent confrontation with the authorities.

The LCHA's campaign basically left alone what to many will appear to be the *real* villain of Love Canal: the Hooker Company. In fact, Hooker was the focus of a number of articles in the mass media that linked Love Canal with other toxic dumps the company had created in different parts of the country. (See, for example, Nader & Brownstein, 1980; Tallmer, 1981.) For its part, Hooker made it a point to avoid being a target. At first it kept a very low profile. Then, when new media attention and a series of large lawsuits made it impossible to remain out of the limelight, the company tried to control media coverage of its role. To a great extent, it was able to let local and state public officials take the brunt of the residents' wrath.

Were the residents being naive in not going after Hooker? No, LCHA was simply focusing on its agenda: obtaining redress from governments with the power and clear obligation to help their citizens. The government agencies in turn went after Hooker and its parent corporation, Occidental Petroleum, in the courts. The State of New York and the U.S. Justice Department were in better positions to take on a $9 billion multinational corporation than was a local association of working class families struggling to survive a massive economic, physical, and psychological threat. Hooker was in a good position to fend off a public assault. Aside from its huge resources, it was too far up the production chain to be easily embarrassed. In general, companies that sell their products directly to the public are the most vulnerable to media exposure. Chemical companies that sell to other companies are much less so.

In terms of precedents for the future, the strategy was important in putting all governments on notice that they must assume the role of protector. There was undoubtedly another good reason for LCHA to focus on public officials rather than Hooker. The company was a major employer in Niagara Falls, and many potential supporters of LCHA would not have supported a direct attack on Hooker. In addition, everyone was aware that this corporation was in effect the surrogate for other employers in the area, and an attack on it could be interpreted as an attack on the chemical industry as a whole. In this way one important target group, employees of chemical companies who also had a stake in a safe environment, was kept from defecting.

All this may or may not have gone through the minds of the LCHA leadership. It is nonetheless instructive in suggesting that identification of targets is a crucial step in planning one's lobbying strategy–not that one never focuses on the corporate sector. The real point is the criterion for the choice: what will help accomplish one's objectives.

WHAT MAKES POLICYMAKERS TICK?

What determines a policymaker's behavior is basically the same as what leads any of us to act in a certain way. This rather complex subject can be reduced to three basic factors: (1) the capability of acting (i.e., the competence and opportunity), (2) the incentive or motivation to act, and (3) the justification for acting. (See Compton & Galaway, 1989:144-147.) For the advocate, it is the second and third of these which are the most important. Motivation is the more obvious factor. If one can tap into the existing motivations of a policymaker, that would seem to evoke the desired response. But it is not that simple. As is discussed later, the policymaker must also justify the action. The advocate may be able to modify the policymaker's behavior by challenging the justification.

What Motivates Elected Officials?

If you think elected officials are preoccupied with being reelected, you are absolutely right. Put yourself in the legislator's place. If you, as this legislator, have chosen politics as a career (one in which you hope to serve your fellow human beings in addition to gaining whatever material and ego rewards may accrue to you), you are not about to throw it all away for somebody else's worthy cause. Even if this is only a transitory stage, a means to other opportunities, nobody likes to be fired. The problem is that every two or four years, somebody, maybe many persons, want your job. They are not nice in the way they go about seeking it, either. If you, the legislator, lose your job, everybody will not only know about it, but most are likely to attribute your ouster to your failure to perform effectively and deliver on promises you made when you took the position. So you have a lot of pride wrapped up in keeping your job, as well as a livelihood now, and economic security in the future. And if you do get "fired" from your legislative seat, your ability to use this position to improve the world will come to an abrupt halt.

Another thing to keep in mind about policymakers in government is the sheer range and volume of material they must handle. A legislator must address hundreds of issues during a typical session. It would be thousands of items if committees did not screen out many bills. Think of the junk mail *you* get in the course of a week. You are on the mailing lists of many worthy and not-so-worthy causes, in addition to commercial enterprises that take advantage of the low cost of bulk mailings. If you study each letter and the accompanying brochure carefully and try to weigh the merits of every one, you are a rare exception. Most of us take a quick look at the outside of the envelope, make a snap decision whether to open it, make another snap decision when we read the opening sentence, etc.

Now multiply that experience severalfold. In addition to appealing letters, legislators are constantly bombarded by telephone calls and visits to their offices by people wanting something. Unlike Jack and Jill Citizen, they must act interested and at least minimally informed on everything from unemployment compensation rules to land use policy. Because many persons with a personal stake in an issue try to cast it in terms of the public interest, lawmakers soon become skeptical about any person presenting himself or herself as concerned mainly about the public good.

How do legislators manage this awesome task? One way is to develop a kind of shorthand. To start with, there is a basic view of government and his or her role in it. This is typically the basis on which the person ran for office. Having been successful, the legislator is likely to assume that what he or she stood for in the election is what the constituents want.

That general philosophy of government is the first screen with which the legislator tests a proposal. (See Hurwitz, 1986.) Many issues are not that simple. Opinion may be divided in the district, or the party leadership may push for one position and strong interest groups in the district for another. The president, governor, or the party whip in the legislature may be on the line asking for your help–a flattering but also potentially threatening appeal. Lobbyists representing powerful interests let lawmakers know, sometimes not so subtly, that they can be helpful in the next election. Mail and telephone calls are flooding in. Or, conversely, the issue is ambiguous and the representative has no clear notion of which way to jump.

Under these circumstances, a common practice for lawmakers is to turn to one or more colleagues who share the same general philosophy and, because they sit on the relevant committees or are known to be well-informed, can be trusted. If the "cue-giver" is for the measure, it makes sense to be for it as well (Bibby, 1983:22). But, just as lobbyists can undermine their credibility with misleading or unfounded assertions, the cue-givers within must earn their colleagues' trust. They, in turn, may rely on other sources. A legislator may have several cue-givers of this kind, each looked to for guidance on a different policy area (Clausen, 1973:33).

Not surprisingly, political scientists have a lot of interest in what influences legislators' decisions. According to studies by Ray (1982), legislative colleagues and organized interest groups had the most influence, appeals from the executive branch and one's own research on the issues had the least, and in between were the party leadership, legislative committee reports, and communication from individual constituents.

Songer's (1985) interviews with state legislators from Kansas and Oklahoma gave this ordering: first, after the person's own value screen, was constituents; second, interest groups; third, fellow legislators; and last, party leaders.

How do legislators assess the will of their constituents? There is a tendency to generalize about the voters in one's district as being liberal or conservative, and to act in terms of that general view. Especially on controversial issues, the legislator will make it a point to explain his or her vote. Just as there are cue-giving colleagues within the legislative body, there are key individuals in the district who will be consulted on problematic issues. Legislators have a dual function: deliberating on policy and providing services for constituents. Some see a responsive service operation as allowing them to be more liberal or conservative than the district voters.

You may be distressed to learn how little emphasis is given to personal reading in these studies. But remember the deluge of material the legislator faces. Kingdon (1973:224-227) has found that lawmakers rarely make an extended search for information. They will do more reading and talking to others when the issue is controversial or has high visibility in the news media. Their preference is for short summaries that evaluate as well as describe the policy and take political factors into consideration.

The greatest amount of background reading is normally done in one's role as a committee member, where one is supposed to be something of an expert and very likely a cue-giver for fellow legislators. According to Whiteman (1985), the search for material by committee members is determined by how they define the problem. (The critical role of problem definition is discussed later in this chapter.) Members use such information in three ways: to gain substantive knowledge of the problem or policy in question, to extend and refine an existing position on the issues, and to justify one's position.

These are generalizations about elected officials. In Chapter 8 you will meet three actual state legislators and find out how they arrive at conclusions on issues.

What Motivates Appointed Officials?

Except for outright political appointees whose fortunes rise and fall with those of their elected bosses, civil servants establish job rights as soon as they get past a short probationary period. Then the only way to get rid of one of them is to get rid of his or her position. This job security may mean that this kind of work attracts people who by nature are not risk takers. But regardless of who it is, the civil servant is keenly aware that his or her career prospects hinge directly on the continued flow of funds. Not surprisingly, then, avoiding reduction of one's budget is a high priority. According to one study, it is the first priority (Arnold, 1979:21).

That is not meant as a cynical comment. Just as legislators know they will cease to serve the public as elected officials if they are defeated at the polls, dedicated civil servants (of which there are many) will think twice before jeopardizing their opportunities to serve the public in the role for which they have been trained. The popular image is of people constantly seeking to increase their budgets at taxpayers' expense, but studies indicate this is clearly secondary to avoidance of budget cuts (Arnold, 1979:21).

Aside from continued funding, the civil servant is dependent on positive evaluations by superiors and, even more important, effective working relationships with departmental colleagues. For this reason, there is a natural tendency to protect the people with whom one works, and, more generally, the department itself. A by-product of all this is resistance to outside interference, particularly by those who do not understand the agency's mission and technology (Gruber, 1987; see also Aberbach, Putnam, & Rockman, 1981).

Given all this, it is easy to stereotype civil servants as merely obsessed with hanging onto the job and unwilling to let any fresh air into the office. However, reality is different. Gruber (1987) has identified three kinds of bureaucrats–experts, workers, and administrators:

- *Experts* are mainly interested in the challenge of the task, which fits in with their professional training. They share a commitment to excellence and public service with their professional colleagues, and they respect advice from people who are seen to have the same attributes. Competence ranks particularly high with them.
- *Workers* come closest to fitting the popular stereotype of bureaucrats. They are mainly concerned with mastery of the workplace and, more than other kinds of public employees, are preoccupied with job security. They respect senior officials to whom they are officially accountable.
- *Administrators* are mainly concerned with getting a job done effectively. They are more flexible and more ambitious, career-wise, than the other two. They are also more likely to respect the opinions of outsiders, whether elected officials or the public.

It is useful for the would-be advocate to take the above factors into consideration when planning to lobby appointed officials. It is less than useful to make too many assumptions about the particular official you are going to see. Each civil servant is a distinct individual, with gifts, feelings, and biases of his or her own, as is true of the rest of us. But the generalizations help in alerting one to the kinds of questions to ask, before meeting the person. Experienced advocates who have dealt with the particular department are a good source of such background information.

The Need to Justify

There are two things nobody wants to be: evil and stupid. People will go to tremendous lengths to convince themselves that they are neither. But in this competitive and moralizing world, we are continually exposed to signs that, yes, we are deficient in our competence, our goodness, or both. So each of us is engaged in a never-ending process of reassuring ourselves, and others, that we are really all right. To be inconsistent is to violate this image: either we do not know what we are about or are not abiding by our own rules of conduct. (See Aronson, 1980; Festinger, 1957:1,2; Lecky, 1961.)

One way to feel smart, moral, and consistent is to block out any signs to the contrary. One can do that by simply ignoring the signs or distorting the information, to bring it in line with good self-concept (Lecky, 1961). The problem is compounded when one is also trying to convince other people and has taken a public position. This is precisely what elected officials are faced with all the time.

In one experiment, householders agreed to reduce the use of their air conditioners to save energy. Those who did so only as a private vow were most likely to forget their promise, while those who declared their intent publicly tended to act accordingly (Pallack & Cummings, 1976). In the same way, legislators who publicly declare they will not compromise on an issue are less likely to do so than those who do not make such a declaration (Hurwitz, 1986; see also Deutsch & Gerard, 1955; Tedeschi, Schlenker, & Bonoma, 1971).

State Representative John Smith has to vote on a bill that would require pregnant teenagers to obtain parental consent in order to have an abortion. His attitudes on abortion and pregnant teenagers and parental consent have evolved over a lifetime of hearing what his own parents thought about such issues, reading newspapers, magazines, textbooks, and watching television, being married to a Roman Catholic, exchanging views with schoolmates and colleagues, etc. His sentiments are a tangle, some of which he is not consciously aware of. Most of the time he does not think about these questions and would prefer not to have to, especially since his district has a substantial number of Roman Catholics who are in favor of the bill, and many members of a well-organized feminist group that is just as strongly opposed.

Representative Smith is going to have to decide something: to vote in favor, to vote against, to abstain, or to be out of town when the vote is taken. There are potential costs, no matter what he does. But there is a prior task. First he has to decide what he thinks about parental consent, and he has not done that yet.

Eventually, John comes to the conclusion that he personally is opposed to requiring parental consent. It may come about after his wife says something to him at breakfast, or he sees a particularly arresting story in the morning paper, or he has an argument with his independently minded teenage daughter. This is the trigger, the small incident that shoves him over the brink of indecision. We know that it is not the real cause of his position–that has come from the accumulation of his lifetime experiences.

Once John has taken the plunge, however, he begins to develop the explanation for his stance–initially to himself, then to his wife and other people around him. The explanation will have to "make sense" and be consistent with his values and his self-image. The more he repeats it and elaborates on it in subsequent conversations with himself and others, the more firmly committed to the position he will become. His self-persuasion, in other words, will take on a momentum all its own.

Being flexible by nature and buffeted by shifting political winds, Representative Smith may change his mind before the vote is taken. But if he does, he will have to rearrange his explanation. He cannot simply talk one way and abruptly go off in a different direction. Aside from his credibility with other people, his own sense of personal consistency and integrity would be shaken.

Note the sequence of events. First came an evolving process of attitude development resulting in an amorphous set of biases which were not at the center of his attention. Then something brought this question to the fore, so he had to think something about it. *Then* came the process of deciding why he felt that way. That is basically how all policy decisions come about, a fact which flies in the face of common sense notions about policy decisions. I am talking about the point at which most policy issues surface in public debate. This says nothing about the kind of in-depth analysis that may go into formulating policies in the first place. A professional policy analyst arrives at answers as a result of painstaking analysis. Typically, elected officials do not do that. You should not conclude from this that analysis is only window dressing, designed to mask the true nature of policy. The analysis is vital, and good policy requires it. That is because societies and interest groups must justify what they do–to themselves as well as others–and analyses that challenging initial assumptions can force people to revise their views.

Whether your name is Martin Luther King, Jr. or Adolf Hitler, you have to convince yourself that what you are doing is right and makes sense. It is true whether you are deciding to invade another country or vote for a tax bill, pursue a career or buy a new raincoat. When the question is a public policy issue, something else is added: the need to convince others as well. Let us begin with a nonpolicy problem for Representative Smith: the point at which he shares his decision with his wife.

Her religious beliefs make abortion under any circumstances abhorrent to her. She sees the requirement that pregnant teenagers obtain parental consent as at least a limited deterrent to what to her is an immoral act. Her reason for supporting the proposal will also be a justification for a web of attitudes that lie deep in her psyche, as is true of her husband. During their years together, John and Mary Smith have not spent much time talking about abortion. Though he has not shared her strong feelings, he has accepted them. Now the public life of State Representative John Smith has intruded itself on the private life of John and Mary Smith. Again, a potentially divisive issue which they could once ignore has become the focus of attention.

John must justify his opposition to parental consent in terms that are meaningful and acceptable to Mary. He will not, for instance, defend his choice on the grounds that abortion is good or that the mother's freedom of choice overshadows the extinction of an unborn child. Were he to do so, it would threaten their relationship and the foundations of their life as a family. Instead, he will seek a rationale that she can accept, for instance the possibility that some teenagers may resort to back alley abortions rather than face their parents.

Very much the same thing will happen when Representative John Smith is interviewed by reporters or reveals his position on the parental consent issue in his letter to the voters in his district. He will find grounds for his choice which will be acceptable to the majority. He must find some way of speaking to the concerns of his Roman Catholic constituents and the feminist activists at the same time. This is not an easy task, but typical of what makes life in the policymaking arena interesting. In this case, he is not only trying to keep a marriage intact, but also trying to stay in office.

Justification of policy choices has a function far more important than the career longevity of individual public servants. By grounding choices in arguments acceptable to effective majorities of the governed, regimes establish legitimacy and assure social stability. We espouse democratic decision making because of deeply held values about the rights of the governed, and that is a value that few in this society would question. This democratic participation also helps to assure willing compliance of the population to government decisions.

When it was revealed that the U.S. government had been selling arms to Iran while preaching boycott, officials sought to rationalize what they had done by saying they were trying to work with moderate elements within Iran. Later, they counted on public boredom with the issue to allow them to focus on other things. When Representative Smith's opponent chides him in a debate on his "flip-flops" on key issues during his career, Smith must either give a plausible reason for them or focus attention elsewhere, for example on his challenger's questionable financial dealings.

For appointed officials, justification is as important as it is for legislators, but the dynamics are somewhat different. First, regulations are supposed to reflect legislative intent–what the lawmakers had in mind when they passed the bill. Understand, of course, that the final version of the law is in all likelihood a conceptual nightmare, consisting of bits here and pieces there designed to corral a few more votes. So the people writing the regulations use a good deal of creativity in deciding what was intended. Many times there is also a lot of innovation, inclusion of things the legislators did not intend. This is a major reason for advocates to focus attention on this phase of the policymaking process.

The civil servants who write regulations are most likely to be professionally trained, either in law, economics, or a field related to the content of the policy itself. They will seek to justify their conclusions in terms consistent with the values and assumptions of their professional fields.

To whom must the decisions be justified? The most important audiences are senior officials in the department and legislative leaders. The writers must also deal with external interest groups that have a stake in the product. While adjustments can be made during the period of public review, before the regulations become final, it is less embarrassing to anticipate criticism than to have to accommodate it afterward.

Overarching all other considerations is the belief among appointed officials that they are problem solvers, not politicians (Gruber, 1987:102-103). However much they may bend to political pressure, their system of justification requires that they deny it. Civil servants will acknowledge privately that, of course, they live in a real world and must learn to accommodate to it, but the public image is apolitical. Challenge that perception frontally and you run the risk of shutting off access to this aspect of policymaking. And remember, the bureaucracy is much freer than elected officials to shut off access.

CRITICAL FACTOR: HOW THE POLICYMAKER DEFINES THE PROBLEM

In the months leading up to the 1988 Democratic and Republican national conventions, the popular view of Michael Dukakis was more positive than that of George Bush. Bush, as vice president, was expected to support whatever President Reagan put forth, regardless of his personal feelings. This exacerbated the public impression of a man who had no mind of his own. Together with certain mannerisms, it made Bush, the image, a wimp. Meanwhile, Dukakis profited from the picture of a child of immigrant parents who had worked their way up in the world. He was also viewed as a super-competent administrator, partly as a consequence of economic good times in Massachusetts, and partly as a result of media hyperbole. And, in a time of concern about the sleaze factor, Dukakis was a symbol of moral rectitude.

One thing that worked for Bush and against Dukakis was expectations built up in the media. If Dukakis, miracle worker, stumbled, the gaffe was magnified many times over. If Bush came off as even a real human being with at least a little backbone, his image soared. Knowing all this, Bush's advisers went to work to create the "new Bush." They uncovered little-known facts which defied the wimp image, buried anything that smacked of weakness, and went on the attack. Dukakis, meanwhile, turned out to be less than superhuman and, accordingly, his public stock fell.

What the Bush campaign was able to do was redefine the situation–definition is that powerful a tool in elective politics. Definition is at least as important in policy making. Let us see what the Bush people did:

1. They *focused attention* on Bush's strengths and Dukakis's weaknesses. In particular they focused attention away from potentially embarrassing issues.
2. They were able to change the *presumptions* (expectations) the public had regarding each candidate. Even the expectation that Bush would be weak worked for him, as he said and did things that defied that image.
3. They tapped into deepseated public *values* regarding patriotism, crime, and race.

I am not being critical of them for doing so. The Dukakis camp was trying to do exactly the same thing. These were the pivotal factors in getting the public to redefine the candidates: focus, presumptions, and values.

Think back to what was said about the basic need to see oneself and be seen by others as competent and moral. I must have a basis for assessing where I stand in regard to these qualities. This requires external standards by which to judge myself: my perception of the real world (a competent person acts in a way consistent with reality), and my value assumptions (a moral person acts in ways consistent with his or her values). This process of defining ourselves and the external world is so much a part of us that we are not even aware of it most of the time.

Two critical components of definition, then, are our presumptions about the real world and our value assumptions. You are probably more familiar with the second of these terms than the first. One place you may have heard about presumption is in relation to courts. John Doe is *presumed* innocent unless proven guilty beyond a reasonable doubt. He is certainly not *assumed* to be innocent, in fact the public may be convinced he committed the crime even before he is brought to trial. The court, however, must start from the opposite end of things. If John Doe were presumed guilty, he would never be able to convince anybody that he was innocent. So a presumption can be thought of as an initial operating assumption, or expectation, which can be overturned by evidence to the contrary. In public policy, we always start from the presumption that changes are not needed. This is not because everything is great the way it is, but because otherwise we would have to prove beyond a reasonable doubt that every wild scheme that came along was wrong, or else we would have to accept it as valid.

The third critical component of definition is the focus of attention. Remember that one way of dealing with discrepancies between where one is and where one would like to be is to shift the focus to something else. Understanding the process of defining gives one a powerful tool for understanding policymakers, thus a powerful tool for influencing them. We should consider each of the three components–focus, presumptions, and values–in more detail.

Focus

Your perceptions of the world are necessarily highly selective. When you enter a room, your attention is focused on specific aspects of the environment and of your own reaction to it, while most of what is there is filtered out. As a student attending a course for the first time, you are likely to focus intently on the professor: who is this person who will be teaching you, what will this person look for in your classroom performance and written assignments, what are his or her biases, is he or she going to be boring? You may also check out your fellow students: are they smarter than you? Depending on your age and current relationship, you may also see if there are any attractive people you would like to get to know better. As the syllabus is passed out, you quickly scan it to see what books you have to buy and in particular, what is required for written reports and exams.

Psychologists refer to *selectivity*, the universal phenomenon by which certain aspects of the environment are continually filtered out and others filtered in. By selective exposure, the person is insulated entirely from some content. Selective attention further filters the content. By selectively perceiving, we narrow the filter even more. And after exposure we recall selectively. (See McCroskey, 1968:42-44.)

These processes, necessary if you are to make any sense of your environment, are not random. They grow out of your attitudes and mind set, which accumulate throughout your life, and, accordingly, your expectations for the future. If you have had a struggle in previous courses in this field, you become preoccupied with how others will judge you. If you have a physical disability, you may be on the lookout for signs of rejection or curiosity from the professor and other students. When you go around and introduce yourself, you may be so preoccupied with the impression you will make that you do not hear what other students say.

In the policy arena, the focus of attention is a critical factor in determining the agenda. It can make a crucial difference in the outcome of policy deliberations even before the deliberations take place. Political scientists Peter Bachrach and Morton Baratz (1970) have suggested the term "nonissue" to refer to a question that never makes it onto the agenda. Parties with control over agenda-setting may deliberately keep certain people and their concerns from getting a hearing, thereby shaping the decisions that can be considered.

Several years ago, the governor of New Jersey proposed a workfare program under which recipients of aid would have to work off their grants in unpaid public service jobs. Here are excerpts from two news items about this policy:

> Governor Brendan Byrne said yesterday he would sign "as quickly as possible" legislation. . .that requires "able-bodied" welfare recipients to work for their relief check. . . .
>
> In his budget message last February, Byrne asked the Legislature to act on the bill, maintaining that no one who is capable of working should be allowed to "sit on his duff and draw a welfare check." (Lamendola, 1977)

> TRENTON (AP)–New Jersey's plan to put employable welfare recipients to work will cost the state more than it would to leave them on the dole. . .state officials said Thursday.

> Human Services Commissioner Ann Klein told the startled members of the Joint Appropriations Committee that the program Gov. Brendan Byrne announced in his annual message would operate under unforeseen restrictions. . . . (*Secaucus Home News*, 1977)

The supporters of the workfare bill focused on the issue of keeping able-bodied recipients from getting something for nothing. The human services commissioner focused on the net cost to the state of running the program. The difference in focus was not accidental. Legislators and the governor were keenly aware of the attitudes of voters toward "shiftless" welfare recipients. The commissioner knew that if her department ran in the red because of actual operation of the program, she would have to answer to those same voters later on.

Presumptions

A presumption is what you already "know" before the evidence has been presented. It is the expectations with which you approach a situation. As a student on the first day of class, you "know" that you will do poorly in this course because you have consistently had trouble in similar courses. It may turn out that your presumption was wrong. (It would be presumptuous of your not to consider this possibility.)

Initial presumptions can be overturned by sufficient evidence to the contrary, as we saw in the case of Bush and Dukakis. However, some people stick to their original presumptions even in the face of overwhelming evidence. Opponents of financial aid to the poor may simply ignore evidence of need. Some people persist in prejudiced attitudes toward racial minorities despite repeated exposure to accurate information about them.

Strictly speaking, the presumption in the public policy arena is that things should stay as they are. The burden of proof is on anybody proposing a change in policy. However, in reality the presumption one must deal with is whatever an effective majority believes. As an advocate, you must size up the presumptions of the target, whether they are in favor of or against change.

Suppose you are invited to take part in a debate on a new bill designed to outlaw all abortions. If the audience is mixed or predominantly pro-choice, you can claim that, since the new bill is a departure from the status quo, the burden is on your opponent to demonstrate the need for a change. Unless an effective case is made, you do not have to open your mouth. If the audience is full of right-to-lifers, you had better be prepared to take on the burden of proof.

Values

Our values are so deeply imbedded in us that we are often not aware of them, and can articulate them only with great difficulty. Any frontal assault on a person's values tends to be seen as tantamount to a direct attack on the person. Moreover, there is an implicit assumption that a person's values are his or her own business ("You have a right to feel the way you want to as long as you do not tread on my right to my own feelings.") Therefore, direct challenge to a target's value orientation should always be avoided.

Assuming that people's values are basic to the choices they make, how can we ever hope to change things unless we do take on a target's negative attitudes? First, it is possible to modify values by presenting new evidence. Second, values are rarely totally integrated. A person may hold contradictory orientations toward an object, and it is possible to support the more desirable side of the dilemma.

Often, however, the advocate seeks areas where his or her values are compatible with the target's, and builds on that consensus. For example, a pro-choice advocate may be able to find common ground with a right-to-life activist on the value of life as it pertains to young children. Without either party giving up its views on the rights of the pregnant woman and the fetus, they may be able to collaborate on legislation to provide better nutrition for low-income families.

Care should be taken not to allow value differences to be translated into a personal attack on the individual holding the value. The advocate should try to empathize with the target and convey respect for the sincerity of the target's beliefs. In Chapter 7 we will look at how to go about making effective arguments for a policy position. It all starts with an assessment of how the target currently defines the situation: What is the focus of attention? What are the presumptions about reality? What is the value orientation?

The right-to-life movement has a highly integrated definition of the abortion question. Its members' focus is on the fetus and the moral as opposed to the social consequences of different actions.

Their presumption, that life begins at conception, is consistent with this focus and the value of preserving this person-to-be at all costs. Because the definition of the situation is so well integrated, it is hard to argue with this position once a person has bought any part of it. Only as the focus of attention shifts elsewhere can the right-to-lifer be unglued from intense commitment to anti-abortion policies.

As a country, we have always had mixed feelings about poor people. When the poor seem to be getting something for nothing, the feelings are negative. Especially if they are males, able-bodied adults should work for a living instead of taking hand-outs from the government. Teenagers who become pregnant, apparently because they do not behave themselves or take precautions, are a source of much criticism in the mass media these days. Those who give birth and then turn to welfare to support them and their offspring are a particular target of public indignation.

But our attitudes toward poor people and pregnant teenagers are mixed. If we see a television documentary on the homeless, especially if there seem to be mitigating circumstances, we may sympathize with their plight. Workers who become jobless because the local steel mill closed down may be more sympathetic toward other unemployed persons than they were when the plant was still operating.

New information can shake up our view of the real world of poverty and welfare. Similarly, we are in a constant dilemma about what is right: vulnerable people should not be neglected, but nobody should get something for nothing. Because of the basic instability of the public definition of welfare, as contrasted with the stable views of the anti-abortion activists, the same arguments keep coming up in slightly different clothing, and new information and changing political winds bring policy shifts.

Paradoxically, administrations and congresses whose espoused beliefs about welfare have mirrored their constituents' negative feelings about "the freeloaders" have allocated billions of dollars for programs that on the surface seem to run in the opposite direction. One factor that has allowed this to happen has been the way issues were defined.

In Chapter 7 we shall see how arguments can be used to alter the policymaker's definition of the situation. That is the key to influencing policy decisions.

POINTS TO REMEMBER

1. Who is the target, that is, the person or group who can make the critical decisions you are after? Know as much as you can about the target, the power to affect policy, and the likelihood that the power will be used the way you would like.

2. Keep in mind that when working through an intermediary, you have two targets: the person you are dealing with and the ultimate target of your message.

3. A high priority concern for elected officials is getting re-elected, and that helps to determine how an advocate should approach them.

4. Appointed officials' careers are closely related to continued funding for their agencies, so avoidance of budget cuts looms large in their thinking. They see themselves as problem solvers, not politicians. Other things being equal, it is harder to get to see an appointed official than someone who needs votes to stay in office.

5. When you are targeting an interest group, be clear as to whether you are out to persuade, educate, train for action, or a combination of all of these.

6. When your message is going to several audiences simultaneously, decide which has priority.

7. Be aware of the deluge of information and pressures with which the target is coping. Think of how you can get the attention of the target, a prerequisite to getting any action.

8. Who are the most important influences on the target's thinking on policy issues? To whom does he or she look for guidance on ambiguous or controversial issues?

9. How does the target define the situation? How do you want him or her to define it? Should you concentrate mainly on the focus of attention, the presumptions about reality, or the value orientation? (More on this question in Chapter 7.)

Chapter 6

Gathering Evidence

In Chapter 3, I stressed the importance of information as an asset to bring to the lobbying task. One kind of information (strategic) had to do with knowing where, when, and by whom the critical decisions were made. The other type of information concerned the content of policy itself, the kinds of data that would support your arguments. It is the latter kind of information that this chapter is about.

It would be good to read this chapter along with the next, which deals with the way of putting the case together, or to read that chapter and then go back and reread this one. The formulation of your case will determine what kinds of data you need. Without the structure of the argument, you could go on amassing facts forever without knowing how to use them.

We will start with the different kinds of evidence and their potential strengths and weaknesses. Following that, some pointers on assessing how good the evidence is will be discussed. Finally, we will look at different sources of evidence and how to use them effectively.

KINDS OF EVIDENCE

Cases in Point

The most powerful images are those of real people and places. Chances are that long after you have forgotten some of the major principles in this book, you will still remember how Senator Inouye's legislative aide gave him advice based on information fed to her by a defense contractor. We are by nature curious about people and our minds find it easiest to place events in actual locations, graphically described. Good storytellers will place their listeners right in the story, so they can "see" what happened, not just hear about it.

Sit in a legislative hearing on homelessness. Watch the body language of the representatives as they listen to a learned recitation of facts about the problem. The numbers are truly staggering, even numbing, as can be seen by the glazed expressions on the legislators' faces. Now see what happens when 70-year-old Jenny Sidewalk tells what happened to her last week. The committee members sit up and pay attention. One individual versus banks of statistics? Obviously a single case tells us nothing about the extent of the problem; find a home for Jenny and her immediate problem is solved. But the purpose of her testimony is policy change, not personal rescue. That single case will stay with the legislators when they have to vote on a bill to finance shelters.

This is not to say that statistics have no place, but without a concrete example or two to bring them to life they tend to be forgotten quickly. The most effective testimony will include both, so we can see the extent of the problem overall *and* how it affects real people.

Jenny has two things going for her: the arresting reality of the concrete example and the fact that she is speaking from her own experience. People whose work brings them in close contact with the victims on a daily basis can be nearly as persuasive. They are actually in a better position to show that this is not one older woman's ideosyncratic problem, but something happening to many persons with whom the advocate works.

Another way of using concrete examples to get a point across to an audience is to get each person to imagine himself or herself in the situation. *You* are huddling on that street corner as the temperature plunges. *You* turn down the opportunity to come into the city shelter because it is actually safer out in the open. *You* refuse to live with *your* son and daughter-in-law because they abuse *you*. Notice that in order to get across my point about concrete examples, I used a concrete example. I put *you* in the hearing room and told *you* about Jenny Sidewalk rather than talk in generalities.

If I were arranging firsthand testimony in a hearing on a homeless shelter bill, I would want to include more examples than Jenny.

Maybe a young mother (families are the fastest growing group of homeless), and a young man just out of a mental hospital. It would be important to have my concrete examples represent the range of situations the bill is supposed to address. Two cases are more than twice as good as one. Three are more than three times as good. Beyond a certain point of course, I run the danger of overkill.

In giving examples, I want to avoid giving my target any excuses for justifying inaction. Several years ago, a group of welfare mothers visited the Ohio State Capitol to plead for an increase in benefits. At that time assistance grants were running at less than 70 percent of the state's own standard of need, so an improvement was clearly needed. The lawmakers appeared to be impressed until one of the mothers lit up a cigarette. That was all some conservative legislators needed. "They get enough to spend on cigarettes instead of food for their kids," one snorted. That image fit in with existing stereotypes about welfare clients drinking up the taxpayers' money while their children went hungry.

Because of their appealing quality and the fact that they involve small numbers of situations, concrete examples are open to misuse. When an opponent trots out a "typical" case, be ready to ask how typical it is. Can he or she back it up with any figures? Even more to the point, is this an actual situation or a hypothetical one; if the former, how does the person know that?

Ronald Reagan used to tell a story about a woman who drove up to the supermarket in her white Cadillac to use her food stamps. Implication: She didn't need them, since she was obviously a lot better off than the hard-working taxpayers who were treating her to this buying binge. Welfare advocates used to comment that this woman sure got around. They had heard about the same woman in Boston, Phoenix, Chicago, St. Louis, and Denver. Implication: The woman was a figment of somebody's imagination. Reagan was able to cite an actual instance of a person who managed to get thousands of dollars illegally through welfare fraud. Critics responded by showing the small percentage of cases of fraud in the welfare rolls, but the image of the fraudulent individual was likely to stick in people's minds better than the statistics. Rather than persist in arguing about the accuracy of the case example, which merely rivets it more firmly into people's minds, it is probably wiser to make a brief rebuttal and shift the focus to the plight of the people who are suffering because of punitive and restrictive policies.

Official Policy Actions

Official documents giving legislative decisions, court rulings, and administrative regulations speak with special authority, since once the decision is made it sets a new precedent. Policymakers tend to follow precedent unless there is a powerful argument to the contrary. Is the current community mental health center's program fulfilling congressional intent? Is a law requiring welfare recipients to allow caseworkers into their homes as a condition of receiving assistance constitutional? Is a chemical company liable for damages caused by its previous deposit of toxic waste if the local school district agreed to assume responsibility for all damages when it took possession of the waste site? "Let the record speak for itself," as they say.

The degree of authority varies. Legislative intent itself carries a great deal of weight, but somebody's interpretation of that intent can be challenged. The intent is stated in general and sometimes vague terms, so the adherence to it is at best ambiguous. The second example, the requirement that welfare recipients open their doors to caseworkers, was the subject of a Supreme Court decision in 1971; a majority opinion written by Justice Blackmun ruled that welfare recipients could be required to admit caseworkers to their homes (*Wyman v. James*, 1971). This could be overturned in the future, but for the time being it is a rule that must be obeyed. Once a ruling has been made it tends to be respected by subsequent courts.

In the case of toxic waste damage liability, the United States District Court for the Western District of New York declared that the Hooker Chemical Company was not absolved of liability for damages caused by toxic chemicals in the Love Canal, even though the Niagara Falls Board of Education signed an agreement at the time it purchased the site from Hooker (*United States et al. v. Hooker*, 1988). Since the company and its parent corporation had billions of dollars at stake in potential judgments against them elsewhere, they were sure to appeal this ruling. The U.S. Supreme Court could overturn the judgment.

In general, administrative rulings are most subject to later reversal, judicial decisions least. Legislative actions are somewhere in between. Decisions by lower courts can be reversed by a higher court. In short, official actions are authoritative but not gospel, and some are more "official" than others.

The *Congressional Record* is supposedly a faithful account of everything that happens in sessions of Congress, and include nothing that does not happen there. But, not only do members include such extraneous material as editorials from hometown newspapers, they can also "clean up" the record after the fact. Some people cite statements in the *Congressional Record,* implying that they therefore must be true. I recall seeing one forgettable book in which the author cited the *Record* to back up several outlandish claims, but did not bother to identify the specific location of the material. Of course it was impossible to check any of his citations for accuracy.

Relying on secondary sources for information about official actions is risky. When possible, check the original source. In one debate on facilitating school desegregation, a student made an impassioned appeal for mandatory busing, citing what he said was the law of the land as interpreted by the Supreme Court. His eloquence was moving, and one wondered what the opponent could say in rebuttal. The opponent pointed out that if one read the Court's decision in full, it was possible to come to a very different conclusion. By showing that she had done her homework, she successfully undercut the student's argument. In the review of the debate afterward, the first student acknowledged that he had not read the original decision but had relied on a popular book on the subject.

Because official acts are subject to legal challenge, they are written in exact but difficult language. To avoid misinterpreting the record, check it out in a number of secondary sources. If *The New York Times,* the *National Journal,* and *Congressional Quarterly Almanac* (standard sources available in most college and university libraries and many large city public libraries) all agree in their interpretation, it is reasonable to go with their reading of policy. However, there are times when consensus among these "giants" is wrong. Lacking such means of corroboration, you might ask a lawyer about court decisions and a knowledgeable (and friendly) lobbyist or public official regarding legislative action and intent.

Precedents are especially persuasive with legislators. These are successful implementation of the same kind of program elsewhere. As is pointed out later, the comparability of the two programs and the respective jurisdictions is a critical test for the relevance of precedents. A program that worked in New York might or might not be appropriate for North Dakota.

Statistical Data

Some people love numbers. They enjoy plowing through census tables and columns of budget figures. I am not one of them. Like a lot of advocates, I have an aversion to wading through endless pages of numerical data. I would rather have a juicy case history or sharply worded polemic any time. But I am aware that in order to know what I am talking about and get a respectful hearing, I must do my homework. So you should develop a healthy respect for statistical data.

Respect, but not infatuation. Cool-headed skepticism works best. We are warned repeatedly that it is possible to lie with statistics and that one can use numbers to prove anything. Still, there is something very convincing about numerical data. There is a natural tendency to trust anything with numbers attached to it. But while figures don't lie, people do, and it is easy enough to distort facts with statistics. More often than outright distortion of the facts, we are likely to get a selected set of figures designed to cast things in a particularly good or bad light.

A policy analyst opposed to raising the minimum wage was making a point about part-time versus full-time employment:

> . . . most of the recent job growth has occurred in the full-time permanent job category. Between December 1983 and December 1987, part-time employment rose by only 1 million, or 5.3 percent, while full-time employment shot up by 9.9 million, or 11.8 percent. (Meyer, 1988)

Of course "*only* 1 million" and "*shot* up" are ways of helping the reader define things the way the writer wants her to. Moreover, the selection of 1983 is not accidental. Another analyst commented,

> It is misleading to use 1983 as a benchmark to examine job creation. In 1982 we had just come out of a deep recession. There is a lag between the end of a recession and the creation of new jobs. Because of that recession, 1983 still had the highest rate of unemployment since World War II.
>
> But if we use 1979 as the benchmark, then the picture changes somewhat. For the period 1979 to the present we see that part-time employment grew at a faster rate than full-time employment. (*The New York Times*, 1988)

Bob Votegetter, a candidate for governor in the State of Confusion, announces at a news conference that since the incumbent, Gary Gladhand, has been in office, the number of auto thefts in the state has risen 25 percent. "That is a lie," says Gary, "Anybody knows that when Bob's party was last in power the rate of auto thefts was actually higher than it is today."

It will take some research to see who, if anybody, is lying. It turns out that neither man is. When Bob talks about an increase in the *number* of auto thefts, he neglects to add that when Gary came into office there were fewer vehicles on the road because of a severe fuel shortage. The number of thefts could increase merely because there are more cars to steal. Gary talks *rates* because that helps his case. What he fails to mention is that the age group that is most likely to commit auto thefts–adolescents and young adults– has been steadily declining in the state over the years. So there are fewer potential auto thieves than there once were. Also, Bob has talked about the year Gary came into office. Gary speaks of the last time Bob's party held the governorship. Those are two different times, because Gary succeeded a member of his own party.

Of course, one could ask other questions, such as what auto thefts have to do with being a good governor. It might be possible to show that the governor presided over an improving economy, which reduced (or increased) the likelihood of auto thefts, or urged the legislature to raise or lower the amount of money for law enforcement. But it sounds as if Bob is stuck for good issues to run on and is trying to focus voters' attention on secondary concerns.

We have uncovered a few caveats in relation to statistical information:

1. Always be clear about what is being measured, particularly the difference between frequency (total number) and rate (the ratio between actual cases and possible cases).
2. Note the time period being selected and ask why that particular time.
3. What is the geographical area being discussed? For example, the rate of auto thefts in Large City, the state capital, may be going up, while the rate for the state as a whole is going down.

Then there are the statistical comparisons. "Did you know," says Bob, "that there were more auto thefts in the State of Confusion last year than in the whole country of Bangladesh?" No doubt. Also more automobiles. So it goes. Whenever somebody starts quoting statistics, be on guard. Back during the Korean War, I was told that more people died in auto accidents on America's highways in the previous year than all the U.S. Navy personnel killed in the war that same year. I forget now whether the conclusion was that we should worry less about battle casualties or more about highway fatalities. But without knowing the potential numbers of each, one would have a hard time knowing what to make of those figures.

Statistics can be intimidating, but as Lois Gibbs demonstrated, advanced degrees in the subject are not necessary to make effective use of numerical data. She had a high school education and a strong motivation to get answers to questions. She knew little about either statistics or toxic chemicals, so she set out to learn about both. Rather than try to master these arcane subjects on her own, she turned to people who were experts and whom she could trust. The credentials of her allies helped, especially when the chemical company and the state bureaucrats tried to discredit their work as "just housewives' research."

When she started, Lois Gibbs had the same problem with experts that she had with politicians: she was both too trusting and too timid to take them on. That changed in time, as she learned how to question their wisdom. After all, it is a basic rule of science that one's assertions are always open to challenge. This brings us to the final kind of evidence: testimony.

Testimony–Expert and Otherwise

I am talking here not just about witnesses in court, but any kind of assertion of fact or opinion, written or spoken. When a person takes a position, a point of view on a controversial subject, one's guard should be up. But when material is presented as factual it is easy to relax one's vigilance. Knowing that, most people pushing a point of view clothe their claims in a mantle of objectivity.

There are two basic questions to ask about any testimony: how much does the person know, and what are his or her biases? These are the questions of source credibility.

How Much Does the Person Know?

Firsthand experience is a very impressive kind of credential. The residents of Love Canal who could not pronounce half of the names of the toxic chemicals under their backyards, to say nothing of understanding their derivation, knew what it was like to have their children come home with the bottoms of their feet scorched. They could speak convincingly of the psychological toll the incident was exacting. That impressed the news media a lot more than the technical bulletins from the State Department of Health. Ex-mental patients and psychiatrists each speak with their own authority about what it feels like to be penned up in a mental hospital.

This is not meant to minimize the expertise of persons trained in a relevant field. The closer to hands-on work the person is, the more convincing the testimony. On the other hand, researchers can provide a kind of information the practitioner may be unaware of.

The first point to understand about experts is that they are just people who have devoted more time to learning about a special area of knowledge than other people. Reasonably, they therefore know more. However, they should be heard with the same skepticism with which one approaches any source. Useful questions to ask about all experts are: (1) What exactly are their areas of expertise, and how are they viewed by their colleagues? (2) Do their professional communities agree with what they are saying, or are there views of theirs a matter of controversy within their fields? (See Gilbert, 1979:76-84.) Before taking on an expert, you might do well to get a "second opinion" on the subject to be discussed.

Written opinion has a credibility in the eyes of the public that spoken opinion lacks. The trust may be misplaced, however. As is discussed later, being published is less important than the kind of publication it appears in. One advantage of the print media over television and radio is that there is a record which can be referred to.

What Are the Source's Biases?

It is rare to find a completely unbiased source of information. Researchers are expected to meet a high standard of objectivity, but even here bias creeps in. This is particularly true in relation to social policy, which by nature is of intense interest to many people and less precise than other kinds of scholarly work. For example, two studies of the economic progress of African Americans, one by a U.S. government commission and the other a highly respected private consulting firm, were found to reflect a conservative bias against government equal opportunity and welfare programs. It turned out that the same individual oversaw both studies. This was not publicly acknowledged in the study reports (Richan, 1987).

News reports are notorious for being influenced by everything from intentional selection and choice of color words, to stereotyping and plain ignorance. This is not necessarily the result of a conspiracy at the top, although that has been known to happen. Reporters, editors, headline writers, and lay-out specialists continually have to make quick judgments, against press deadlines and with limited information. It matters a lot, in terms of public perception, whether an item is in the top righthand corner of page one or at the bottom of page 16, whether its headline covers one column or three, and how the reporter begins the story.

Although radio and television are more restricted than newspapers in explicitly editorializing, their news reporting is more open to bias than the print media because of time pressure and the fact that some on-the-spot accounts are ad-libbed. Use of the mass media in advocacy is discussed in Chapter 11.

The Reluctant Witness

One way to deal with the problem of bias is to use a source that seems to be speaking against its own interests or prejudices. In court, the "reluctant witness" is forced to testify when he or she would prefer not to. The presumption is that if this witness gives damaging testimony it should be believed, because it is against his or her own interests to do so. Lefty is a long-time friend and confidant of Spike. Lefty testifies that Spike was in the vicinity of the liquor store on the night of the robbery. If anything, it is reasoned, he would want to shield his friend, so he must be telling the truth.

A member of Bob Votegetter's own party acknowledges that Bob has a less than pristine record as district attorney. This is far more damaging than for one of Gary Gladhand's henchmen to say the same thing. A retired general speaks at a peace rally with an image of authenticity that an avowed pacifist lacks. Statements by Roman Catholics for a liberalized abortion policy or by feminists against abortion would have the same kind of impact.

Reluctant witnesses must be approached with the same skepticism as one uses in other cases. Especially if such testimony is being circulated by those with an axe to grind, try to determine why the witness is doing the unexpected. We now look more specifically at ways of testing the validity of evidence.

THE QUALITY OF EVIDENCE: WHOM AND WHAT CAN YOU TRUST?

Reducing the Risk of Error: General Rules

1. When possible, use more than one source of information. If the sources are in disagreement, try to get a third opinion and figure out who is more likely to be correct.
2. Test source credibility: Is the source knowledgeable? Is the source free from bias?
3. Is the information original or second-hand? If the latter, get as close to the original source as possible.
4. How current is the information? If related to an earlier time period, is the time relevant to the issue? Be especially alert to time discrepancies in second-hand information. When was the original article written? When were the data gathered? There can be lapses of as much as ten years between an original research project and the point at which findings are printed in a book article.

5. When a comparison is made, is the comparison relevant? If you are looking at crime statistics in California, is a comparison with Utah appropriate? These are literal comparisons between parallel situations; the presumption is that what happens in one state has at least some relevance for another. A figurative analogy–say, using a face-off at the O.K. Corral to make a point about a legislative issue–is purely symbolic, and strictly speaking is not evidence of anything.

When the supporters of the Equal Rights Amendment were trying to get the last few states to ratify it, they sought an extension of the seven-year time period for ratification. One opponent likened the maneuver to the losing side's asking for an extra quarter in a football game in order to have a chance to improve its score. The argument had a certain appeal (fair play and a popular all-American sport), but football games have nothing to do with Constitutional amendments. National defense policy is sometimes translated into terms of police officers walking around with or without guns. Same problem.

The Relative Credibility of Different Sources

Here are a number of sources, roughly in order of presumed credibility:

1. Your own experience or direct observation of somebody else's. For the reasons discussed earlier, knowing a situation first-hand gives you a special kind of authority.

2. Official documents. As was said, you need to weigh the credibility of the specific document and its source. But overall, this is a particularly good source.

3. Articles in juried academic and professional journals, based on empirical research. Juried publications are those in which other professionals–a jury of the author's peers–have reviewed the article and recommended publication or non-publication. The credibility test has thus been administered by people with expertise equal to or greater than that of the writer of the article. These publications require footnotes or other means of identifying source material. The article should include a section on methodology and tables to allow the reader to determine whether the findings support the conclusions. If you have trouble understanding some of the technical jargon and statistical notations, consult a person in the relevant field.

4. Theoretical and other non-empirical papers in juried academic or professional journals. These are of essentially the same caliber as reports of empirical research, but are less rigorous and likely to be based on conclusions drawn from other people's research.

5. Scholarly books. These presumably abide by the same scientific standards as the above categories of scientific work, but the standards vary more. All a scholar need do is convince a publisher there is money to be made (or a pay-off in terms of image). There are also some not-so-scholarly books whose reach exceeds their grasp. You have to be careful in assessing source credibility. One way to do that is to look up reviews of such books in juried journals. Because reviewers can be even more biased and unscientific than authors, it is well to check more than one review.

6. Newspapers, popular magazines, and popular books. Standards vary greatly. Some books are carefully researched, others are not. Some newspapers are more careful than others to avoid bias in their news columns. Magazine articles are written over a longer period than newspaper items, allowing them to go into greater depth. Some newspaper series, on the other hand, are exhaustively researched. Unlike scholarly books and journals, these publications for general readership rarely require documentation so you do not know what a writer is basing his or her ideas on unless such information is incorporated into the body of the article. Newspapers are famous for quoting unidentified sources.

In newspapers, straight news and news features are most likely to strive for objectivity, or at least make a pretense of same. Columns and op-ed items usually have a very marked bias, but may be written as if neutral. Editors often look for controversy in these pages, so diverse views are encouraged. Editorials, avowedly biased, are sometimes good sources of information possibly missed in the news columns. Least to be trusted, of course, are letters to the editor, although sometimes authoritative writers use this method to get their message out. Use these as leads for further investigation, unless what you are looking for is an example of a viewpoint rather than valid information about the subject.

7. Television and radio. The biggest problem with these sources is that there is no permanent record, unless the program is taped or is a documentary or discussion program and transcripts are available. You forget much of what you see and even more of what you hear, so the dangers of distorting what you have been exposed to are great. Still, the broadcast media are valuable sources of information, especially when they do in-depth analyses.

A second problem with these sources is the pressure to be brief and go for attention-grabbing material in preference to thoughtful analysis. This is a highly competitive business where the consumer can turn off a message simply by pushing a button. A third problem is that television and radio depend on the print media for *their* information. Not to say they never do serious journalism, but the evening news is selected at least partly for the spectacular photography it allows; the person reading the news is chosen primarily for physical appearance and on-camera charisma.

8. Public meetings. These can be extremely valuable–and variable as to accuracy of what you are exposed to. Most such meetings include a question-and-answer period which helps to keep them honest, but platform speakers learn to anticipate and have ready answers to the three or four standard questions about the topic. Here again, you have to watch the accuracy of your own interpretation of what you hear; your attention may wander during the presentation. Take notes; your selective recall will trip you up otherwise.

Much depends on the particular public meeting. Is this a learned discourse at a professional conference or a stump speech by Bob Votegetter? Again, the question-and-answer process is a great safeguard. If you are prevented from asking a question in the meeting, either because of lack of time or shyness, you can usually corner the speaker afterward, or give him or her a call the next day.

CONDUCTING THE SEARCH

The Preliminary Phase

The gathering of evidence actually starts in the advocate's preliminary immersion in the subject matter to be argued, well before the issues have been defined. Even to know what one thinks about a problem, it must be explored. That process may have been occurring over the years without much thought being given to it.

Suppose that for several years now, you have been developing a point of view about reproductive rights but have not given a great deal of thought to the abortion question. Then one day a state legislator proposes several restrictions. Now you are ready to go into action in opposition to the bill. Your own experience and that of people you know alert you to what are likely to be some of the salient issues in this fight.

Or suppose you work in a mental health clinic. You think of yourself as a therapist, not a social policy advocate. Now the funds for this and other agencies like it are in jeopardy and you are asked to work on a committee to try to restore mental health funding to the state budget. You may know little about state finance, but you are very clear about the devastating effects a reduction would have on the ex-hospital patients you work with. From colleagues in and out of the agency and through your professional training, you know the problems that a sharp cutback in state support would mean.

There are other ways to immerse yourself in the subject matter. One way is to talk with persons who have in-depth information or experience regarding the problem. In every state there are advocacy organizations whose functions include trying to influence policies in mental health and related fields. They get a large amount of material from national lobbying groups and professional associations. Depending on the problem, newspapers will have additional useful information. Once you have an interest in a topic you will discover a great deal of information you had been ignoring up to that point.

As you consult people, you have to be applying the source credibility test discussed earlier. Do your sources have an axe to grind? How current is their information? Do they know it first-hand? If not, how trustworthy are *their* sources? You need not be shy about asking people how they came by their information.

Building a Data File

As you become immersed in the subject matter, begin to put together a file of information and sources. Contacts made at this stage of data gathering may come in handy later when you are developing arguments. Now is the time to create a system for cataloguing and filing your evidence for easy retrieval when you need it. That way you will not be sitting in the middle of a mountain of extraneous notes, unable to find essential data. If you have a personal computer, it will make filing easier. But the logic of cataloguing is the same, with or without special equipment. The essential thing is to mark each piece of data with (1) a code based on categories you are likely to use in your argument and (2) citation of the source. The following system works well whether you store data by hand or by machine.

The code. Begin with broad, general categories. As you gather more data, you can expand these into subcategories. The subcategories can be further broken down into sub-subcategories as you proceed.

The citations. Rather than repeat all the bibliographical information on each entry, simply put down author and date and keep a separate alphabetized set of bibliography cards. Be sure to include all pertinent information in your bibliographical file. If citing a book: list author, title, city and source of publication, date, and number of the edition if it is not the first. If an article in a journal: Author, title of the article, name of publication, volume number, pages, and year; if each issue of the publication starts with page one, you will also need to indicate the issue by number, season, or month. Newspaper article: author if given, title, date, page, and newspaper (put the city of publication in parentheses unless it is part of the newspaper's name). Public speeches and television and radio material: name of person cited, date, and where heard. Citing an interview: name of interviewee, date, and location of interview. Some kinds of documentation are hard to decipher–for example, federal court decisions. When in doubt, consult an expert in the field.

Format. I have found the layout shown in Figure 1 to be a convenient way to arrange the information on cards. You will devise what works best for you in terms of getting all the information you need and having it accessible when you want to consult your file.

The more detailed the coding system, within reason, the easier it will be to find a needed piece of evidence. As an added aid, you can store the cards or sheets categorized in separate envelopes or file folders. The more organizing you can do in advance and the more religiously you conform to your system, the fewer headaches you

FIGURE 1

Format for Data Card

Code	Author, year
(1st entry:) Page # Content	
(2nd entry:) Page # Content	
etc.	

Example of Data Card on Methadone Maintenance

F/Pol/Preced (Political feasibility; precedents)	Bellis, 1981
39 – Programs exist in Canada, Mexico, Puerto Rico, U.K., West Germany, Sweden, Thailand, Hong Kong, "most nations of the world." In U.K., largely replaced heroin maintenance. 42 – Initial reports from Dole/Nyswander project at Beth Israel Medical Center, NYC, showed over 90% of addicts continued in them.	

will have later when putting together a presentation. Incidentally, this system also works well in the preparation of term papers, grant proposals, and other non-policy arguments. Instead of cards you may prefer to use 8 1/2 × 11-inch sheets, organizing them in a series of file folders corresponding to the major code categories.

The Main Search

Your initial immersion in the subject matter has a function beyond that of identifying the issues. It also provides leads for the main search. You can save yourself a lot of time in libraries if you get some guidance from people who have already been searching. By now you have an initial set of categories, one which you may modify along the way as you get new data and new insights.

Using Libraries

If you and libraries are old acquaintances, you may want to skip this section. But for persons who are not that familiar with libraries, the prospect of finding one's way through the intricacies of these institutions can be a bit intimidating. My intent here is to hit the high spots, not provide a detailed guide to library resources.

In case you are unfamiliar with the main components of nearby libraries, it is time you got acquainted. Visit the ones you anticipate using and familiarize yourself with these features: librarians, card catalog, computer-assisted locator if there is one, reference room, current and bound periodicals, government documents section, census data if that is housed separately, and micromaterials. They are all important resources in your search–especially librarians.

I shall assume you have long since gotten rid of the stereotype of Marion the Librarian who hushes people up, chit-chats with elderly folks, and puts books back on the shelves. Library science is a profession with state-of-the-art knowledge of data storage and retrieval and expertise in major fields of knowledge.

When approaching a library staff member for help, be as clear and specific as possible about what you are after. If you do not understand something, ask for clarification. There is a cardinal principle for getting along with librarians–it is the same one to employ with computer wizards: act dumb. Ask those questions you are embarrassed to ask. Remember, when you do not understand what anybody is saying–be it librarian, professor, news commentator, or other–there is at least a 50-50 chance the problem lies with him or her, not you. Most large libraries have diagrams to show the location of different material. Some have guided tours at regular intervals. Take advantage of both.

The *card catalog* has every holding of the library, filed according to author, title, and subject. Some libraries combine the different files into one. If you are not sure what subject heading to look under, see if there is a directory of headings close by. Books are located by using the catalog number in the upper left-hand corner of the card. The card also contains publication information and a summary of the main contents of the book. In a library with open stacks you can pull out the book yourself.

The *on-line catalog* is a computerized locator system. It serves essentially the same function as the card catalog. It may tell whether a book is out on loan or lost. You should not use it as a substitute for the card catalog. Use both. If computer terminals terrify you (which they may if you are over 40), ask for help.

The *reference room* contains many interesting things such as encyclopedias and foreign language dictionaries. More to the point, it is where you are most likely to find indexes and abstracts of periodical articles. Indexes of government publications may be housed here or in the government documents section of the library. (See below.) It may take a while to figure out the indexing systems in these publications. They may change from year to year in the same index. (See specific reference tools below.)

Current periodicals most likely will be in one location, arranged alphabetically by title. Some libraries keep bound periodicals the same way, while others have them located by subject matter. Ask which system your library uses.

The *government documents section* contains official records of federal and state and possibly local government laws, reports, and proceedings. Journals dealing specifically with government affairs are often filed here. Court decisions may be stored here unless there is a separate law library. *Census reports* may be here or in a separate location with other demographic information.

In order to protect the *micromaterials*–microfilm and microfiche–they are usually kept in a separate room where temperature and humidity can be regulated. If you have not used a microfilm or microfiche reader, ask for help. It is not as difficult as it may seem at first. Some libraries have machines that allow you to duplicate pages from the microfilm.

Most college and university libraries and many large city libraries are tied into large computer networks which allow *computer-assisted searches* for material on any topic you are likely to be studying. Assuming you are making a focused search for answers to specific questions, think twice before investing money in one of these. They can be costly, depending on how extensive the search. The reams of paper you get back with citations, some of which are pertinent to your search and others which are not, may be useful later for padding your dishes when you move to a new apartment. If the service is free, by all means take advantage of it. In this way you will turn up resources you would otherwise miss. It is important to be as precise as possible in defining your terms, the more narrowly the better. But many times you will find that you can do nearly as well by conducting your own search with the printed resources described above. Even if you use the computer search, you should also do a document search anyway. You will know whether the nature of the topic demands the more exhaustive exploration and if the time available allows it.

SOME USEFUL SOURCES

GENERAL INDEXES AND ABSTRACTS: *Social Sciences Index* lists articles appearing in scholarly and professional journals. Author, title, and publication information are listed by subject. *Public Affairs Information Service (PAIS)* is similar though less comprehensive. *Readers Guide to Periodical Literature* lists articles from magazines and other serials for general readership, using the same format. *The New York Times Index* includes all articles appearing in the *Times,* indexed by subject. The newspaper itself is kept on microfilm. The *Times* considers itself a newspaper of record and includes all major national and international news, including reports from all parts of the United States. *The Washington Post* and *Wall*

Street Journal have more limited indexes. *Monthly Catalog of Government Publications* has entries for all official publications of the federal government and is indexed by subject. You may need help deciphering the catalog numbers. *Congressional Information Service* is a similar resource for congressional reports and proceedings. *American Statistical Index* lists government statistical reports. *Statistical Abstract of the United States* is a compendium of population, economic, political, and social data.

SPECIAL ABSTRACTS: *Social Work Research and Abstracts* includes abstracts of journal articles concerning the human services and the social work profession. *Journal of Human Service Abstracts* is similar. Other field-related abstracting services include *Psychological Abstracts, Sociological Abstracts,* and *Index of Economic Articles*. Your library may have other specialized indexes and abstracts.

BASIC RESOURCES FOR UNDERSTANDING PUBLIC POLICY: *Congressional Quarterly Almanac* provides an excellent and detailed account of congressional and administrative actions, congressional voting records, etc. *National Journal* is less comprehensive but goes into greater depth in covering major policy issues.

Using Law Libraries

If you are searching for state or federal court decisions or codes of state and federal laws, a university law school library is your best source. These libraries use their own system of cataloguing. You may also need assistance in understanding some of the legal material in these publications. Here are a few major resources:

COURT DECISIONS: *U.S. Supreme Court Reports, Federal Court Reports* (lower federal courts), and *West's National Reporter System* (state courts).

CODIFIED LAWS AND REGULATIONS: *U.S. Code Annotated, Code of Federal Regulations,* and codified statutes for the respective states (law school libraries will probably have a complete collection).

LAW JOURNAL INDEXES: *Index to Legal Periodicals* and *Index to Periodical Articles Related to the Law.*

Fugitive Materials

These are unpublished study reports and other documents that are circulated within organizations or to special lists of subscribers.

Libraries do not carry them as a rule. You are most likely to run across them as you talk to people with special interest in the subject, such as agency personnel.

Many advocates have learned from bitter experience *never* to request such documents by mail. It is not just that the mails are slow. A request from a stranger (yourself) for a document that somebody has to chase down is likely to sit in an in-basket for days, maybe weeks, before it is answered. If you telephone (make sure they know you are calling long distance), it can get into the mail the same day. If it does not arrive within the next week you can call back and jar them into action. Perhaps the safest course is to call and then follow up immediately with a confirming letter.

POINTS TO REMEMBER

1. Concrete examples are a persuasive kind of evidence. They should be representative. If an opponent uses negative examples, answer briefly and shift to your own agenda rather than fighting a defensive battle.
2. Official policy actions vary in their authority. Judicial decisions are least likely to be overturned, though lower court rulings can be overturned on appeal to a high court. Avoid relying on secondary sources for data on official actions. When in doubt about the meaning of the language, consult someone who is familiar with it.
3. Precedents—successful implementation of programs elsewhere, are powerful evidence, but a crucial factor is the comparability of the cases.
4. Statistical information is useful as evidence but is also open to distortion. Be clear about what is being measured and be on the alert for selection of data that favor a particular viewpoint.
5. In evaluating evidence:

   a. Check one source against others.
   b. Test source credibility in terms of knowledge and possible bias.
   c. Trust firsthand over secondhand sources.
   d. Consider how current the original data are. Especially important when evaluating secondary information.

e. Are comparisons relevant, that is, between comparable cases?
f. Figurative analogies are purely symbolic and are evidence of nothing.

6. A rough ordering of credibility of different sources is as follows:

a. Your own experience or direct observations.
b. Official documents.
c. Empirical research reported in juried publications.
d. Theory pieces in juried publications.
e. Scholarly books.
f. Newspapers, popular magazines, and popular books.
g. Television and radio broadcasts.
h. Speeches at public meetings.

(Keep in mind that the ordering is rough. Some public presentations are more credible than some published articles.)

7. Your initial immersion in the data starts before you develop your case. Organize your filing system right at the beginning.

8. People familiar with the problem or policy can save you time in focusing your search in the relevant places.

9. Libraries are a key resource. Familiarize yourself with one or more near you. The most important resource in a library is the staff. Be as clear and focused as possible in asking for help.

Chapter 7

Preparing the Case

The basic task of the advocate now becomes clear: to create the conditions under which the target will modify his or her definition of the situation. Notice I did not say change the target's definition. The target is an active partner in the process. In effect, the advocate assists the target in finding the justification for the change. That is also what happens when an advocate shares information with which a policymaker can defend a decision to colleagues or constituents. The process by which all this takes place is argument.

Are arguments just window dressing? It is tempting to believe that, but powerful interests would not spend huge sums to hire skilled arguers if it did not matter. In the political world, one is always trying to maximize support from a range of political constituencies. To justify expending their political capital in this way, they must be convinced.

We think of arguments only as disputes. However, some arguments involve no dispute, and some disputes–for example screaming matches between young children–are not arguments. An argument, as the term is used here, is a claim, with justification, that something is so, or else that some action should take place. Some writers say that, strictly speaking, *any* claim is an argument, since it is capable of justification. (See Rieke & Sillars, 1975:48-49.) I find it more useful to limit the term to statements that include justification, through reasoning and/or evidence. "Drink Blotto!," according to this definition, is not an argument unless some kind of support is added.

The approach to argument used in this book is *audience-centered;* that is, the sole test of an argument is whether it persuades a particular audience. (See Perelman & Olbrechts-Tyteca, 1969.)

That is clearly what happens in policymaking. A decision maker or decision-making body must be persuaded in order for the argument to be successful. This is a far cry from classical argumentation in which claims had to meet universal standards of proof.

What has just been said may seem to confirm your worst fears about the world of policymaking: no universal principles of justice or rightness, just interested parties trying to con the rest of us. There are some fundamental values on which this approach is based though. One is free and unfettered expression. The danger of suppression of ideas is far greater than whatever mischief might be caused by the worst demagogue. Just as argument needs an open political system, such a system cannot survive for long without argument.

Every system of communication has its means of protecting its own integrity. The scholar exposes ideas to the community of scholars according to accepted rules of discourse; the clinician is trained in self-insight and professionally disciplined; the attorney abides by legal rules; and every set of interests, including the community itself, has its advocate, in theory at least. For the policy advocate, the integrity is built into the open exchange of views. The advocate for social policies aimed at advancing the common good has a special responsibility to give voice to those views in an arena of contending interests.

MODIFYING THE AUDIENCE'S DEFINITION OF THE SITUATION

Chapter 5 told about three elements of definition: the focus of attention, presumptions about the real world, and values. These are the foundations on which an argument is based. The advocate asks these questions:

1. What is the target's present focus of attention and what do I want it to be?
2. What are the target's presumptions about reality and how might I modify these?
3. What are the target's value preferences regarding this question and how can I connect my argument with these?

Note that these are different questions. The first asks where one wants to focus the target's attention, because that is the easiest aspect of definition to change. The second asks how one might change the existing presumptions: that is usually harder to do. The third asks how one can mesh the argument with the target's existing value-set. That is because, of the three, values are the hardest to alter. If one frontally attacks the target's values, in a real way that is an attack on the target.

Let us see how different writers seek to focus their audiences' attention on the subject of public welfare policy and the related problem of poverty. In this case, the target seems to be "everybody." But even here, the writers have specific kinds of readers in mind, just as this book does. This is how Charles Murray, a well-known writer on welfare reform, begins his book, *Losing Ground:*

> Our topic is the poor and the discriminated-against as they have been affected by "social policy." We may narrow the focus: I shall be discussing the *working-aged* poor and discriminated-against, not the elderly, and *federal* social policy, not variations among states and localities. (Murray, 1984:13)

We may ask why Murray stakes out his territory in this way. Why not the elderly? And why not examine state and local variations? He wants to focus our attention on an age group which it is presumed should be working because a major part of his argument will focus on why they are not working. "Working," incidentally, is an interesting term. To Murray it means being gainfully employed outside the home. A woman who has been separated from her husband and is raising several young children by herself and spends long hours doing that is presumed *not* to be working.

By excluding state and local variations from the discussion, Murray keeps off the agenda the fact that welfare recipients in some states receive grants that are a fraction of the allowances in other states. These are also states that underspend on education and other public programs. Actually, a discussion of federal policy *should* deal with interstate variations, because the federal public assistance laws are set up to allow for those differences. Many social policy analysts believe the rates should be standardized across the country.

An additional point to notice about Murray's beginning is his reference to the "discriminated-against." He is defining not only the topic but himself as well. "I am not against the welfare poor, in fact I sympathize with their plight," he seems to be saying.

Here is how another book on welfare reform begins:

> Over the last decade, the welfare state has become the target of a concerted ideological attack. From the expanding network of conservative think tanks and foundations on up to the president himself, the same themes are reiterated: that social welfare measures are a drag on the economy, an incentive to immorality, and a cruel hoax on the needy themselves. (Block et al., 1987:ix)

A leading figure in this "concerted ideological attack" is none other than Charles Murray. Just as Murray seeks to focus our attention and mold our view of the problem well in advance of any substantive arguments, the authors of the latter volume want to prepare us to be receptive to their evidence before it is delivered. Note also that, whereas Murray wants to narrow the audience's focus by excluding certain aspects of welfare from consideration, Block and his colleagues seek to broaden it. "Don't look at welfare reform in isolation," they are saying, "or you will miss its true significance."

The titles of the two books above are designed to lay the groundwork for their respective messages. *Losing Ground* conveys a sense of hopelessness about federal welfare programs, as well as identification with the plight of their supposed beneficiaries. The title of the second book is *The Mean Season,* a phrase that carries with it the Scrooge-like qualities attributed to the conservative critics of the welfare state. In effect, say the authors of this book, the foes of welfare have already scored an important victory by defining the issues for the public.

> It is their charges that have set the research agenda and dominated ensuing public debate. Researchers who defend the welfare state are reduced to claiming that the charges are not true, that the receipt of welfare benefits does not produce most of the deleterious consequences attributed to it. . . . That the main

> body of empirical evidence provides scant support for the critics is important, to be sure. But it is much more important that the charges have come to frame public discussion. . . . (Block et al., 1987:72)

Environmental protection is a subject of great controversy in this country. Part of the intensity of the debate comes from the monumental, and in some cases, irreversible effects of one policy or another. It is also the majority who are the direct objects of policy actions, not a stigmatized "they." Proponents of strong governmental action emphasize the long-term effects of environmental pollution, the hazard to the health of people from all walks of life, the world our grandchildren will inherit, and the problem of corporate greed. Opponents stress the need for jobs, the elitist nature of the proponents who are said to care more about some species of hop toad than honest working men and women, and the need to defend local control against interference by the federal government.

Presidential news conferences offer an interesting lesson in how to mold the definition of the situation to suit one's agenda. Time was when the public learned of the contents of these meetings between the president and reporters by reading about them in the next morning's paper. The president had to rely on the news media to handle his comments as he wanted them to get to the people. The reporters were thus an intermediate target.

All that changed with the arrival of the televised news conference. The reporters then became bit players in a staged presentation. While they were free to ask any questions they wished, presidents were able to shape the dialogue to a great extent by presenting an introductory statement and particularly by picking the questioners and, after giving an answer which might or might not bear on the question, going on to the next reporter. Reporters have regained a bit of the initiative by asking follow-up questions or simply posing a two-part query. But an insidious aspect of the whole performance is the fact that the reporters, like the president, can now come into American homes in living color. By avoiding a reputation as a hostile questioner, a newsperson is likely to be picked more often.

Presidents exert a great deal of control over news conferences and can have the primary role in defining the situation. A striking example of this fact is seen in the following excerpt from a 1972 news conference of President Richard Nixon. The Watergate break-in had been discovered and there were widespread reports of corruption at high levels, but the administration's image had not reached its lowest point. Nixon, knowing what he did, wanted to keep the focus off of these problems.

> Q. Mr. President, what are you planning to do to defend yourself against the charges of corruption in your administration?
>
> A. Well, I have noted such charges; as a matter of fact, I have noted that this Administration has been charged with being the most corrupt in history, and I have been charged with being the most deceitful President in history.
>
> The President of the United States has been compared in his policies with Adolf Hitler. The policies of the U.S. Government to prevent a Communist takeover by force in South Vietnam have been called the worst crime since the Nazi extermination of the Jews in Germany. And the President who went to China and to Moscow, and who has brought 500,000 home from Vietnam, has been called the number one warmaker in the world.
>
> Needless to say, some of my more partisan advisers feel that I should respond in kind. I shall not do so–not now, not throughout this campaign. I am not going to dignify such comments.
>
> In view of the fact that one of the very few Members of Congress [Representative Jerome R. Waldie of California] who is publicly and actively supporting the opposition ticket in this campaign has very vigorously, yesterday, criticized this kind of tactics, it seems to me it makes it not necessary for me to respond.
>
> I think the responsible members of the Democratic Party will be turned off by this kind of campaigning, and I would suggest that responsible members of the press, following the single standard to which they are deeply devoted, will also be turned off by it.
>
> Q. Mr. President, do you feel, as Vice President Agnew said the other day, that Senator McGovern [Nixon's Democratic

opponent] is waging a smear campaign against you? Would you characterize it as that?

A. I am not going to characterize the Senator's campaign. As a matter of fact, I don't question his motives. . . . Incidentally, I have no complaint when he raises doubts about mine. That is his choice. (Nixon, 1974:952-954)

And on to the next question, which was on the subject of the possibilities of a peace settlement in Vietnam before the elections. You may have a little difficulty recalling what the original question was about. Apparently the reporters did.

STRATEGIES OF ARGUMENT WITH FOUR KINDS OF AUDIENCES

The Active Ally

It may seem at first that argument has no place here. Certainly the target shares the advocate's focus, presumptions, and values. But a problem with active allies is the risk that they will become less active or shift their interest to another problem. So the advocate must keep attention on the mutual concern and emphasize its importance relative to other issues.

Any group of activists loses momentum from time to time. An issue drops out of the headlines, maybe moves from the legislative arena to the courts. In court, obscure, protracted arguments and long stretches when nothing seems to be happening are guaranteed to sap the energy of even the hardiest among us. One of the most draining experiences is to feel that one is fighting a losing battle—all this time and effort going for naught. Opponents sometimes deliberately create that impression. So information about small successes, support from new quarters and the like, can have an important role in rousing the troops to renewed enthusiasm. Allies are also in constant need of updated information to support their position and answer questions from others.

The leaders of the Love Canal Homeowners' Association (LCHA) had to work constantly to keep their members actively involved. As long as the national news media were interested, the leadership of LCHA had a built-in way of keeping up morale. Seeing oneself on the evening news or in the pages of a news magazine was stimulus enough to keep many residents going.

Inevitably, the news media lost interest. Reports of early research that supported LCHA's position were criticized for methodological flaws, seeming to undermine the residents' case. Some people, including the mayor of Niagara Falls, accused the Association of hurting the tourist trade. Conflicting research findings sowed confusion within the group. The Hooker Company eventually abandoned its low profile and placed ads in the newspapers. Seeing the well-heeled opposition presenting its case in this way could be demoralizing to the residents with their meager resources. Then there were the reactions of neighbors who did not feel threatened by the chemical waste as much as they felt their jobs threatened by too much criticism of their employers.

One way of countering flagging morale among the convinced was to continually find new angles with which to interest the news media. When there were no new angles, the public was reminded that the problem was still there.

When their drive to enact a Constitutional amendment failed, anti-abortion activists changed their agenda to seeking to limit federal aid for abortions. One purpose was to keep the movement alive in the face of apparent defeat. Such fallback strategies carry with them a degree of risk as committed followers may interpret the scaled-back tactics as betrayal of the original mission.

The Committed Opponent

The first thing to understand is that your active opponent is rarely the audience you are interested in reaching, unless you are engaged in direct negotiations, as in collective bargaining. Most of the time your real target will be allies or potential allies. So when you are locked in a debate with an antagonist, remember that this is not the party you are trying to persuade. Your task is to compete for the support of those outside of the battle. Strategies for dealing with two such non-participants, the uninvolved and the ambivalent, are presented below. The policy debate before a live audience is discussed in Chapter 9.

When you want to have impact on the opponent, your task is the converse of that in the case of the active ally. Instead of energizing the opposition, the advocate seeks to neutralize it. In most instances, the best way *not* to achieve that end is to engage in acrimonious debate. A frontal attack on the opponent's position is likely to force the person to defend his position all the more vigorously and stimulate even more active involvement in the cause you are against.

Occasionally, an advocate wants to find ways of collaborating with an opponent. For example, the parties to the conflict are wasting time and resources in an impasse, or the fight is creating a dangerous schism. It may be that both antagonists have a common foe and should combine forces against it. Suppose that Caucasian and African-American parents in a low-income neighborhood are locked in a struggle over school policies. In time, they discover that their real problems emanate from a school board that is failing to provide enough resources overall, so the two parties are reduced to fighting over crumbs.

This suggests an argumentative strategy of shifting the focus of attention away from the original fight. The groups can collaborate only when they are able to empathize with each other and view the former opponent as an earnest and dedicated advocate of a point of view. The less defensive the person feels, the easier it will be to work together toward shared goals.

The Uninvolved

In some ways the outright opponent is easier to deal with than the person or group who is not interested in the question. But by using the right argumentative strategy, it is possible to involve people who initially have no interest. The goal here is to get some commitment, however limited, on which to build a larger commitment. Shills on the boardwalk at Atlantic City used to employ the "buy-in" principle. Get the customers to put up a dollar in hopes of winning a big prize. Once in the game they are likely to stay because they do not want to lose that first dollar. Countries sometimes follow the same principle, turning a small investment of military resources into a bigger and bigger war.

Focus is used initially to get the attention of the uninvolved. The public and policymakers are constantly bombarded with various appeals. So, advocates must come up with new and interesting ways to catch people's eyes. The trouble is that everybody soon learns the latest trick and starts using it. Direct mail works until everybody is using direct mail appeals. Then first class mail gets opened while letters sent at the bulk rate are thrown in the waste basket. Famous names add interest until they simply become a signal that there is a request for funds inside. The word "Free" on the outside of the envelope induces people to take the next step of looking inside. Time was when individually addressed envelopes, as opposed to address labels, rated special attention–until computers made it easy to do mass mailings that looked individualized. The same is true of the insertion of the addressee's name in the letter itself.

There are hundreds of gimmicks for getting attention. You are familiar with many of them because you are frequently the recipient. Our focus here is on the intrinsic interest of the content rather than devices for delivering it. By understanding the value orientation of the target it is possible to tap strong sentiments, tying them to the advocate's agenda.

In the early days of the Love Canal controversy, Lois Gibbs struggled to alert her neighbors to the peril in their backyards. People a few blocks from the dump convinced themselves that they were out of danger and that the toxic chemicals were somebody else's problem.

Joe Public loves kids. He is shocked at the idea that very young children have to live in homeless shelters and go to bed hungry at night. But Joe lives in a comfortable suburb where as far as he knows, such problems do not exist. He rides the commuter train through a poverty-stricken area on his way downtown every weekday morning. He has long since blanked out the scene moving past the train window. Of course, chances are he never did associate the abandoned refrigerators and peeling paint with blighted young lives. The kids playing in the vacant lots seem happy enough.

A television documentary on the plight of poor children may get a temporary reaction from Joe Public, but that soon fades into the background; there are more pressing problems such as payments on the new car and what to do about Jane's mother now that she is living alone. It will take more exposure to the reality of poverty, possibly a first-hand look at the problem, to jar Joe out of his apathy. This is only a first step in moving him to actively support legislation to alleviate the problem. He may simply become angry at the parents who allow their children to suffer in ways that Joe is sure he never would. This is at least a starting point on the way to getting his support for positive programs. Better that he be involved and misguided–temporarily, at least–than that he continue ignoring the problem.

We also have to deal with Joe's presumptions. Two kinds are evident: the belief that things are generally all right, so there is no need to be involved in changing them; and the belief that the problem is the behavior of the parents–maybe that more aid from the government would only make things worse by making the adults more dependent.

As we provide information to correct these misconceptions we need to do it in a way that does not tell Joe he is stupid or unfeeling. He is neither. As we tap into his basic humanity and credit him for it, he is free to respond. Once we have begun to involve Joe, it is important to keep on going. Otherwise, he may simply be reminded of his antagonism toward the poor. Better that he be left asleep than that he be roused and then ignored.

Advocates of more enlightened mental health policies have sometimes tried to scare the public into supporting their cause. At points, graphic depictions of life in the snake pit can grab one's attention, but they can also lead people to tune out, particularly if the problem seems insoluble. One sure way to induce apathy is to create a feeling of helplessness. So, in addition to focusing attention on the problems of the mentally ill and dispelling the illusion that everything is all right, advocates for the funding of community mental health programs must show what can be done if adequate support is forthcoming.

The Ambivalent

Ambivalence is not always easy to evaluate because it can look like apathy or opposition. One way a person resolves inner conflict is to deny that a problem exists. Joe Public has never thought a lot about poverty. Jane, his wife, has thought almost too much about it–in circles. As a young college graduate, she was strongly committed to ridding the world of the ravages of poverty. She took a job in a public assistance office. Suddenly, she discovered that poor people were not all paragons of virtue. In fact, the stresses of their existence led many of them into very unadmirable behavior. Unable to adopt the cynical attitudes of some of her co-workers, she "resolved" her dilemma by running away from it. Under that apparent apathy lies an uneasy conscience.

Fred Mobile knows what it is to be poor because he was once there himself. He managed to escape the alcoholic father, the defeated mother, and the siblings who have begun to repeat these patterns. Now having made it to a job in Joe Public's engineering firm and a comfortable apartment in the suburbs, Fred is clear on what to do about poor people: let them pull themselves up by their own bootstraps, just as he did.

This nice, neat analysis breaks down periodically, for example when Fred's sister is deserted by her husband and left to bring up three children on her own. Having dropped out of high school when she became pregnant the first time, she has few skills with which to get a stable job. Fred is willing to help his sister, but the conflicting feelings simply harden his attitude toward poor people and programs designed to assist them.

The first task of the advocate is to understand as well as possible what sorts of feelings lie under the surface. Joe Public, his wife Jane, and his assistant Fred each present a different picture requiring a different argumentative strategy.

Simply focusing Jane's and Fred's attention on the problem of childhood poverty will do little to move them to support positive programs. Nor is it very productive to try to win debates with them when they raise objections to helping "those people." In both cases, their ambivalence and underlying guilt will drive them to fight all the harder to resist your message.

Instead of trying to beat them into submission, you should act as if there is no debate. Focus their attention on your side of their dilemma, for instance by citing concrete situations that have come to your attention involving the plight of poor children.

The same goes for dealing with presumptions. Avoid trying to win a debate. When they present their arguments to justify their position, accept these as sincere and let them know you are aware that it is possible to have mixed feelings about poverty. You may even acknowledge that what they are saying may be true. At no point should you say you share their view that there is no problem or it is all the parents' fault. You can simply agree to disagree. But then keep bringing the focus back to the conditions you have seen or know of from others who have. The more concrete the better. Case histories are far more compelling than abstractions. Statistics have their place in advocacy, as discussed in Chapter 6, but they are unlikely to move a person struggling with conflicting feelings.

As you introduce information, you are helping Jane and Fred find justification for resolving their dilemma in the right direction. In the last analysis, the only person who will convince Jane Public is Jane Public. Ditto Fred Mobile. You are merely assisting them in that process.

How do we help Jane and Fred get beyond their dilemma? The advocate gets them, in effect, to put themselves on record. As with the apathetic target whose small commitments are used to build larger ones, each time Jane or Fred publicly takes a stand it becomes harder to renege. Fred and Jane cannot afford to repudiate their own position. The more public it is, the harder it is to switch sides. If they acknowledge to you in private that they agree with your stance, that is better than no agreement. But, if they do so in the presence of others, the commitment is stronger. If they are led to sign a petition, lobby their representatives, or make a statement at a public meeting, it is even better.

It should be clear from what has been said that it is not always possible to tell what kind of audience you are dealing with. An active ally in your campaign for mental health funding may show up on the other side when the issue is welfare reform. This suggests some presumptions for you. Presume that the target is sincere, shares your concern for people, and is open to change. As with all presumptions, this one may have to be revised in the face of evidence to the contrary. This positive approach is the place to start. If you presume the best, you have not lost anything except possibly some time wasted on a lost cause. If you start by presuming the worst, you are likely to miss opportunities to gain allies and may provoke unnecessary antagonism.

THE POLICY BRIEF

A policy brief is a detailed set of arguments on both sides of a question, with supporting evidence. It is organized around a set of issues designed to cover all bases regarding a policy proposal. By preparing two cases, your own and your adversaries', you are in a position both to present forceful arguments and answer questions that might be thrown at you. It is not fail-safe, nothing is in lobbying, but it greatly increases your effectiveness and your confidence. Think of the brief as a resource paper rather than a document to circulate to policymakers. Occasionally, however, you may want to share your brief with a friendly legislator, as a resource to him. "Brief" is something of a misnomer; a few run 30 or 40 pages. How long should a brief be? Long enough to answer all the major issues and rebut some or all of the answers.

ISSUES

Issues are critical "questions at issue," which is another way of saying potential points of contention in an argument. Think of the issues as the bones that make up the skeleton of the argument. Like a skeleton, they fit together to become one piece. And like a skeleton, if they were missing the argument would collapse. The person proposing a new policy must have good answers to all the issues, while an opponent can overturn the entire case by rebutting the proponent's argument on one major issue. That may seem like an unfair advantage for the opponent, but the logic of it will be clear as we look at how an argument works. In any actual case, the issues may vary, but there are standard questions that must always be answered by the proponent.

Arguments Based on Definition

This is the simplest kind of argument. It states that something is so. John Doe, it is charged, is guilty of murder. There are two basic issues: (1) What is the definition of murder? (2) Has John Doe done something that fits this definition? If the accuser cannot define murder satisfactorily, the case against John collapses. If the accuser gives a satisfactory definition but cannot apply it to what John has done, the case also collapses. The legal system has a well-defined meaning of murder, so court cases are more likely to focus on the second issue–does this apply to John Doe?

Some arguments by definition are more complicated. For example: Community mental health services are a good investment. The first issue–what is meant by a good investment–will be a major point of contention, as will the second–whether one can apply that designation to community mental health services.

Cause-Effect Arguments

Showing that something causes something else is more involved. To start with, the line between cause and effect in social matters is complex, not the unidirectional and unidimensional link that is often portrayed. There can be multiple causes and effects of a phenomenon. Sometimes cause and effect work in a cycle, so effect is also cause. So the question is not whether A is *the* cause of B but whether it is a significant factor contributing to B. The implication of that is if one reduces A, then B will also be reduced to a significant degree.

What are the basic issues in a cause-effect argument? (1) Are the alleged cause and effect accurately defined? (2) Is there a plausible connection between them? And (3), can one rule out other explanations, or at least show that the alleged cause is more important than they are?

Suppose somebody says, "Toxic chemicals in the soil have caused the recent upsurge in cancer cases in this area." Issue number one is: Are the terms accurately portrayed? How are you defining "toxic" chemicals? And has there in fact been an upsurge in cancer? Are we talking about the *number* of cancer cases or the *rate?*

That *first* issue–the accuracy of the description of the alleged cause and effect–is often overlooked. A welfare critic says "the rise" in the welfare caseload is a result of "the epidemic" of teenage pregnancy. There is a tendency for an opponent to accept these alleged trends and go on to argue the causal relationship. That is a mistake, because there may be neither a rise in welfare cases nor in the rate of teenage pregnancy. One has therefore made an unnecessary concession to the welfare critic.

The *second* issue regarding toxic chemicals and cancer is whether it is a plausible connection, that is, does it "make sense?" Yes, it stands to reason that toxic chemicals might do that. Contrast that with the argument that, since cancer rates and medical technology have both been advancing at the same period in history, the latter is the cause of the former. We would reject that kind of argument as preposterous.

Many arguments end right there. Once a believable case has been made, a person may not push on to the *third* issue: Can other explanations be ruled out? That is a mistake. Toxic chemicals may indeed be the villain, but, the lawyer for the chemical company says, a new retirement home was opened at this site, bringing many elderly persons–some terminally ill–into the area. That may be a better explanation for the increased cancer, he says. He may be wrong, but it is the proponent's task to demonstrate that.

This last argument points up an important lesson for the advocate, and one of the major values of analyzing the issues. In order to make one's case, it is necessary to cover all the bases, make sure the arguments are solid on *all* major issues. Otherwise, it is easy to be caught off guard by an opponent.

Arguments for Action

The kind of argument that is involved in advocating a policy change is the most complex of all. It is really made up of a series of arguments by definition and cause-effect arguments. Here there are four basic questions which the proponent must always be able to answer:

1. Is there a need for change? (If not, there is no point in presenting a plan for change.)
2. Will the proposed plan meet the need? (If not, the argument need go no further. It is not necessary to show that the problem will be solved entirely, just that the situation will be materially improved.)
3. Is the plan feasible? (A plan may be great in theory, but if implementing it will cost too much, or it is unconstitutional, or too complex to administer, it should be rejected.)

4. Would the benefits of the plan outweigh any harmful consequences? (A plan may be relevant to the initial problem and feasible, but it might produce side-effects so devastating as to make it worse than no action at all.)

Remember that the advocate for change must make a convincing case regarding every one of the above points. The opponent can overturn the whole case by knocking out one point. Strictly speaking, it is up to the opponent whether to offer a counter-proposal, but to be a nay-sayer without offering an alternative plan can place the opponent in a vulnerable position.

WRITING A BRIEF ABOUT ABORTION

To show you what goes into a brief, I will lay out the basic design of a brief calling for a total ban on abortions. Then I will do a 180-degree turn and argue for total discretion in abortions. These are not simply opposite sides of the same issues. In each case, the definition of the problem will be different, so the issues that flow from that definition will be different. In the first case, that of the anti-abortion proposal, the advocate will focus on the immorality of abortion, the definition of the beginning of life, and the potential harm to the fetus. In the second, the focus will be on the rights of the pregnant woman. At points the issues will overlap.

The Anti-Abortion Brief

"The U.S. Constitution should be amended to prohibit abortions under any circumstances."

The advocate must show that abortions are inherently wrong and that it is a legitimate role of the government to ban them. The *Need for a change* section of the brief will therefore focus on what is wrong with abortion. The strategy will be to show that abortions are wrong legally, morally, and socially.

Need for a Change

1. When does life begin? The advocate must show that from conception onward a human life is at stake in order to argue on the grounds of legal rights, morality, and the social consequences for the fetus. Evidence for this part of the argument will be sought in philosophical and theological as well as scientific literature.

2. Is a fetus a "person" in a legal sense? This is a different question. It could be argued that human life at its earliest stages lacks the legal definition of a rights-bearing person. Unless the personhood of the fetus is established, it will be difficult to claim constitutional rights for it. The evidence for this part of the argument may be found in treatises on constitutional law. However, the advocate will not base his or her case solely on constitutional grounds. The advocate will also argue that abortion is morally wrong, regardless of how the constitution is interpreted by the courts.

3. Does abortion deprive the fetus of its constitutional rights? If the advocate has established that the fetus is legally a person in its own right, it follows that it cannot be deprived of life without due process of law. It is absurd to think that the fetus can have done anything to justify killing it.

4. Is abortion morally wrong? Here the advocate must establish some moral criterion acceptable to the audience. If the audience shares the same religious beliefs, the argument can be grounded in these religious tenets. Or the advocate may cite statements from leaders of diverse religious communities or respected philosophers. Most likely, the appeal will be to broadly shared beliefs in the value of human life.

5. What are the consequences of abortion for the fetus? Not content to rely on constitutional and moral grounds, the advocate now tries to show that abortion is cruel and inhumane. We do not base the humane treatment of animals on their being humans. So the advocate will seek evidence showing that fetuses not only die but suffer in the process. Anti-abortion organizations are the most likely to know where such evidence is. The advocate will seek data from objective scientific studies, rather than rely on dramatic material from interested parties.

6. What are the consequences of abortion for the mother? (The opposition will question the use of the term "mother.") Here the advocate will focus on trauma, stress and guilt, and conflict over the decision connected with abortions. There is also some evidence (mixed) regarding the effects on future pregnancies. Evidence on this will be sought in psychological research and clinical data from psychiatry, social work, and other helping professions.

7. What are the consequences of abortion for society? One line of argument here is the loss of human potential for society. There are the unknown contributions of the unborn to art, literature, and science. Abortion cheapens the value of human life, thus generally cheapening values in society. By focusing on abortion as a solution to the world's problems, we fail to focus on the real problems of hunger, want, and maldistribution of resources. This line of argument relies heavily on interpretation of evidence, which might be drawn from a wide range of sources.

8. Is the problem urgent? The advocate pulls together statistics on the number of abortions being performed and any projections of future trends. Standard statistical sources are the most likely place to find evidence.

The Plan

9. What action is proposed? The advocate must state the plan clearly. Examples of the same or similar kinds of proposed Constitutional amendments could be offered. This also helps lay the groundwork for feasibility. Books on the abortion issue are the most likely place to learn about precedents of this kind. The previous bill in Congress proposing such an amendment could be appended to the end of the brief.

10. Will the amendment remedy the problem? The advocate demonstrates how the plan deals specifically with the nature of the problem as described in the section, *Need for a Change*. Each issue raised in that section should be restated and the case made that the plan will address that particular concern. If similar actions have been shown to be effective in curbing abortions, that evidence should be included here. Evidence is most likely to be found in books on the abortion issue. Anti-abortion organizations can give leads on where to find this information.

Feasibility

11. Is such a plan economically feasible? Such an amendment would automatically preclude expenditure of state funds for abortions, and thus reduce, not increase, direct costs. However, the advocate will have to deal with the question of paying for the care of additional children, many of whom will undoubtedly be at high risk, since so-called "unwanted" babies figure prominently in the aborted pregnancies. It is important to get as accurate figures as possible on the costs of any proposal, so as not to give a misleading impression. Any figures of this kind are going to be at best speculative.

12. Is the plan politically feasible? The advocate should try to show support for such a bill in Congress, state legislatures, and among voters. Evidence can be found in *Congressional Quarterly Almanac* during earlier debates and in public opinion poll data. Books on the history of the abortion issue are a good source.

13. Is the plan vulnerable to challenge on constitutional grounds? It might seem at first blush that by definition the total ban would be constitutional because it would be in the form of a Constitutional amendment. But the Constitution cannot be at war with itself. A new amendment would have to be consistent with the Bill of Rights unless we were prepared to do away with that set of protections, which is rather unlikely. More to the point, having argued that abortion violates the Constitutional rights of the unborn, the advocate cannot now turn around and ignore the same guarantees for the living. There may be articles in law journals dealing with this question. Books on Constitutional law might also be consulted.

Consequences

14. What are the potential benefits of a total ban on abortions? The advocate summarizes positive effects of such a step. Some of these may have been covered previously but would be referred to here.

15. What are the potentially harmful effects of such a ban? At this point the advocate must consider likely objections to be raised by an opponent. Would the ban interfere with the rights of the pregnant woman, or what is sometimes called the right of a child to be wanted? What about the specter of overpopulation? Does a total ban on abortions discriminate against women too poor to travel to other countries for the operation? In response, the advocate might take on the relative priority between the burden to the woman of giving birth and the very life of the unborn child; the unlikelihood that any child would prefer being dead to being unwanted and alive;

the question of whether abortion is the way to solve the problem of world hunger.

16. Do the potential benefits outweigh the potential harm? The advocate must obviously be able to answer this in the affirmative.

Rebuttal

Wearing the other hat, advocates now attack their own case. They may elaborate on negative consequences cited in item 15, but they will also go back and raise questions about the definition of the problem and whether the proposed solution will really do the job. They may propose an alternative solution. They will attack at any and all points where they think a real opponent might. Finally, they will say how they would deal with these attacks on their case.

The Pro-Choice Brief

"The state should make no restrictions on abortion beyond those that apply in any medical procedure."

Our focus shifts sharply now to the pregnant woman and her rights. The alleged immorality and other issues raised in the previous *need* section will have to be dealt with, at the point that this brief engages the potentially harmful effects.

Need for a Change

1. What are constitutional rights? The advocate wants to define these as applying to the living. This will lay the groundwork for distinguishing between the legal claims of persons and fetuses. Evidence might be found in books on constitutional law and articles in law journals.

2. Are women denied their constitutional rights? The advocate wants to place the right to control one's body in the context of equal rights of men and women. The argument will be made that restrictions on abortion are part of overall oppression of women.

3. Should decisions regarding abortion be based on medical opinion? You may recall that in California in the 1960s, abortion restrictions were liberalized to give doctors wide discretion in determining that abortion was appropriate. Under this reform, over 90 percent of women seeking abortions got them. But the advocate will reject this benign domination by the medical profession and argue instead for abortion as a right. As long as women do not have absolute discretion, they are not treated equally. One can think of many analogies such as employees who are treated in a humane fashion but are denied the right to form a union. This issue can be placed in the historical context of sex discrimination. Evidence could be found in the literature on civil rights and equal protection before the law, and history of female oppression.

4. What are the consequences of abortion restrictions for women? Consequences include greater risk of illegal abortion under unsafe conditions, with hazards to women's lives and health. In addition to continuing with the equal-rights-for-women line of argument, the advocate focuses on poor and minority women, linking denial of reproductive rights to race and class discrimination, and feminization of poverty. Teenage pregnancy which cannot be terminated leads to school drop-out and aborted career aspirations. Affluent women will still be able to get abortions outside of the country. Social science literature, especially material used in women's studies courses, may be helpful here. Also, substantial information can be found in popular books and magazines. When studies are cited, see if you can get back to the original.

5. What are the consequences of abortion restrictions for society? Abortion restrictions bring births of unwanted children and overpopulation. Teenage parents have high risks of health problems (for both mother and child) and welfare dependency. A teenager's potential contribution to society is lessened because of dropping out of school and not getting career training. Pro-choice groups may be helpful in steering the advocate to sources of evidence. There is a larger threat to freedom in the anti-abortion crusade: the attempt of one religious group to impose its values on society. This raises question about the basic principle of separation of church and state. Evidence may be found in some books tracing the history of abortion.

6. What are the consequences of abortion restrictions for the fetus? The chances of babies being born deformed, otherwise impaired, vulnerable to abuse and rejection, are greater. Anti-abortionists play on the abortion-as-cruel theme; it helps to show that the suffering is not restricted to the aborted. Again, pro-choice groups are likely to know about supportive evidence.

7. Is the need for action urgent? The advocate focuses on estimated risk of maternal injury and death due to illegal abortions and the continued discrimination against women. Again, the advocate starts with pro-choice groups to find evidence but does not stop there. The advocate wants objective information sources.

Plan

8. What is the proposed remedy? The advocate can simply call for enactment of a statute and not take on the more difficult process of amending the Constitution (two-thirds majorities in both houses and ratification by two-thirds of the state legislatures). The reason for this is the rule of presumption: unless a restriction is enacted, there is no restriction. Until states enacted anti-abortion laws in the nineteenth century, they were not prohibited except for mild and limited common law sanctions. (It did not even take the involvement of a licensed physician.) What the Supreme Court did in 1973 was to overturn these statutes. It said states may prohibit abortions in the third trimester, and under certain circumstances in the second, but it did not declare that fetuses were protected. Therefore, new legislation guaranteeing women the right to have an abortion would challenge existing state laws but not the Court's interpretation of the Constitution.

We can be sure, of course, that such a law, assuming it could get through Congress, would be challenged in the courts by anti-abortion groups. The advocate could go for a Constitutional amendment, a more limited version of the Equal Rights Amendment that failed for lack of ratification by enough states. Pro-choice groups may be aware of model legislation of both the statutory and Constitutional amendment kind.

9. Will the proposal remedy the problem? The advocate takes each issue of need and shows how such a law would help to correct it. Establishing reproductive rights in law will not erase sex discrimination, nor oppression of low-income minority women. It is necessary, however, that it improve the situation significantly, especially as one considers potential negative consequences later on. For a bill to risk causing problems without simultaneously remedying others it was intended to deal with would make it a harmful bill.

Feasibility

10. Is the plan economically feasible? It is hard to see how cost would loom as a major factor in enactment of such a law. It may actually reduce costs of law enforcement. It may also reduce indirect costs of caring for additional high-risk children, birth trauma to women, and women less able to contribute to the economy–although these cost factors might better go in the section on positive benefits, below. One might try to get evidence of these costs. The Alan Guttmacher Institute of New York has issued reports summarizing some of this evidence. Start by checking a university library for these items.

11. Is the plan politically feasible? A bill making abortions totally discretionary on the part of the woman is probably not feasible at this point, but might become so in the future. A case can be made for introducing the idea now, in order to set the political debate in motion. It is not unusual for new proposals to take ten years or more to move to the point of enactment–usually in a form different from the original. National health insurance legislation, discussed as a possible part of the 1935 Social Security Act, was enacted in limited form (Medicare) 30 years later. Evidence on political feasibility can be found in previous votes and opinion polls. (See the *Feasibility* section in the preceding brief.)

12. Is the plan vulnerable to challenge on constitutional grounds? The ambiguity of the Supreme Court's *Roe v. Wade* decision, one that was itself highly controversial, raises a serious potential problem for a law as sweeping as that proposed. As of the writing of this book, the current Court has moved further to the political right on such issues, so it would be expected to take a more restrictive view of abortion than the 1973 Court. For evidence, the advocate should review those court decisions and discussions of the issue in law journals.

Consequences

13. What are the potential benefits of the plan? The advocate summarizes the positive consequences anticipated, including any not covered previously.

14. What are the potentially negative consequences? The advocate must take each of the grounds on which anti-abortionists base their case and answer it. (See the *Need for Change* section in the preceding brief.) Are the legal "rights" of the fetus compromised? The status of the fetus as a rights-bearing citizen is challenged.

Is abortion morally wrong? The Roman Catholic Church, the main proponent of that view, did not always ban abortion. Other religious groups disagree. Most state laws were erected on medical grounds, at the urging of the medical profession which was then seeking professional recognition and wanted to retain control over this sector of health care. Many of the persons doing abortions at that time were quacks. If abortions are restricted, it will drive young women into the arms of quacks, and undercut the original rationale for abortion statutes. Books on the history of abortion are good sources of evidence on this. As far as the lost contribution to society is concerned, there is a much greater loss in terms of the suffering and disadvantage that many of these high-risk children will experience. The alleged trauma of the aborting woman must be weighed against the trauma of unwanted births and back alley abortions. (See preceding brief for sources.)

15. Do potential benefits outweigh potentially negative consequences? Again, the advocate must show that they do.

Rebuttal

Play devil's advocate against the case, as in the previous brief, and say how you would answer the challenge.

NOW YOU TRY PLANNING A BRIEF

Having seen what a brief looks like and how one goes about developing one, you are ready for the next step: engaging in the process yourself. I am not suggesting that you undertake to complete a brief at this point but that you go through the steps required in planning one. Basically, this will be a brief minus the evidence. Below are suggestions for getting started on planning a brief concerned with the funding of community mental health centers.

The proposition: "Federal funding of community mental health services should be expanded."

In the *need for a change* section of the brief, you should ask what was the intent of the current policy. Then ask if current funding allows for the full implementation of that intent. What are the effects of the gap between intent and implementation on (1) the mentally ill, (2) the maintenance of professional services, and (3) the community at large? Finally, why is the need for a change urgent?

In the section on *plan,* what is it that is proposed and what specifically would be done with the money? (You need to avoid being accused of wanting to "throw money at problems.") Does the past track record of such services give us reason to believe that the spending of more money will actually remedy the problems you laid out in the *needs* section?

A major *feasibility* issue, of course, will be economic. Can the country afford the extra expenditure? Do you propose reducing other expenditures? (Avoid simply resorting to global rhetoric about cutting "star wars" spending.) Or would you raise taxes or increase the federal deficit? Do not fudge on the cost of what you are proposing. The figures in the full brief would have to be real figures. Closely related to the economic feasibility question is political feasibility. What leads you to think Congress and the administration would buy your plan?

What are the potentially negative *consequences* of your proposal? Is this plan a way to help the mentally ill, or a donation to the welfare of mental health professionals? Do we get full value out of dollars spent this way? Will this take political and economic support away from other pressing social needs?

In your *rebuttal,* go back to the very beginning, the interpretation of what was intended by Congress. Also, maybe times have changed since 1963. In the same way scrutinize the answer to each issue.

POINTS TO REMEMBER

1. Preparation of the argument begins with an assessment of the target's definition of the situation: focus, presumptions, and values.

2. The task is to create the conditions for the target to change his or her definition by shifting the focus, modifying presumptions, and tapping into shared values.

3. Active allies must be kept engaged and provided with supportive information.

4. With active opponents, the task is to direct one's arguments to the real target, who is usually not the opponent. It is sometimes possible to collaborate with opponents on other agendas.

5. With apathetic targets, the task is to get small commitments as a basis for larger commitments. Focus is used to gain attention. Information is used to dispell the illusion that there is no need for change.

6. Ambivalent targets are harder to assess than others, because their reactions may be similar to those of apathetic targets or antagonists. The task is to get public agreement–the more public and irreversible the better. Focus and information are used to provide the justification for taking the desired position and abandoning the unwanted one.

7. The advocate should presume that targets are sincere, share one's concern for people, and are open to change. Above all, one should never concede the argument, or provoke unnecessary opposition.

8. A brief is a resource for the advocate's own use, not a document to share with targets. Occasionally, however, advocates find it useful to give a copy of the brief to a friendly policymaker or advocacy group.

9. The brief is a presentation of the evidence, with documentation, organized around the set of issues which structure the argument. This makes it maximally useful in preparing a presentation or finding answers with which to respond to questions from others.

10. The advocate first puts together as complete and air-tight a case as possible, then seeks to attack his or her own case in a rebuttal. Finally, the advocate indicates his or her strategy for dealing with the issues raised in the rebuttal.

PART III: PRACTICAL APPLICATIONS

Emphasis on *practical.* The third part of this book translates the basic principles discussed in Part II into tactical guidelines for engaging in advocacy in four different contexts: (1) direct contact with *a* policymaker, the most basic meaning of the term, lobbying; (2) presentations to groups in a variety of settings; (3) testimony before a legislative committee, a special kind of public presentation with its own rules; and (4) what is becoming increasingly important in all facets of political action, the mass media.

This material is more than simple "helpful hints for the aspiring advocate." The specific tactics proposed are at times very explicit: how to practice in front of the mirror before going to testify at a committee hearing, and how to word a news release. The more general guidelines set forth in Part II always serve as the basis for the tactical decisions.

Chapter 8 discusses the kinds of people you will be lobbying and how the process looks from their side of the desk. It takes you step-by-step from preliminary planning to the follow-up letter after your visit. Exhaustive planning and preparation of every step is essential.

In Chapter 9, you will learn how to work *with* an audience. It is only when they become active participants in the process that you can hope to have an impact. As with other parts of the book, I make no assumptions about previous experience on the podium. If you feel you are beyond some of the material, skip it.

Chapter 10 deals with a subject that will terrify some readers: getting up in front of a group of legislators, presenting one's views and, worst of all, fielding their questions. As you proceed through the steps, you should find that much of your initial anxiety melts away. Not that it is any less of a challenge, but it is one for which you can muster your best efforts instead of being paralyzed by fear.

The mass media, the subject of Chapter 11, surround us every waking minute of our lives. Their power to influence decisions is obvious. You will find access to this strategic realm is easier than you might at first think. There are many messengers competing for attention, so skill in presenting your message effectively will be a crucial factor in whether or not the media work for your cause.

Chapter 8

Lobbying One-On-One

The ultimate target of policy advocacy is the person who casts a vote for or against a bill, helps draft or revise legislation, submits a new measure, writes regulations, or vetoes any or all of the above actions. The most direct way of influencing that person is by talking with him or her in person. There are other ways of communicating with policymakers, through letters and phone calls for example, although they have less impact. Sometimes you communicate through somebody else, for instance a staff aide to the policymaker. All these activities go under the rubric of lobbying. We will consider what the process looks like through the eyes of the person being lobbied as well as the person doing the lobbying.

Chances are you have lobbied for or against something at one time or another, although you may not have thought of it as lobbying. A large part of lobbying can be classified as *special pleading,* making a request for a response to one's personal or corporate needs. In this book we are talking about a different kind of lobbying, that directed toward changing general policies that affect many people. Much policy lobbying grows out of the self-interest of various parties. The industrialist who pays huge sums to a professional lobbyist to get a clause inserted into a tax bill is trying to protect his or her firm's interests. But it is a policy change, nevertheless, affecting everybody if only by shifting a certain amount of the tax burden to other people.

I shall assume you are not interested in lobbying in order to tell your friends, "Today, I lobbied," nor to demonstrate that, yes, democracy lives. I am going on the assumption that you have a commitment to specific kinds of policy goals, enough of a commitment to become actively involved in promoting them. That strong investment in the substance of policy is the driving force that can make you effective as a lobbyist. Whatever satisfaction you may find in keeping the democratic process alive, whatever ego gratification in rubbing elbows with power, you should consider fringe benefits; the frosting on the cake, perhaps, but not what we are concerned with here.

LOBBYING AN ELECTED REPRESENTATIVE

Lobbying as an Exchange

When people think of lobbying, they usually have in mind the kind that is directed to a senator or representative. Implicit in this kind of one-on-one activity is an exchange relationship between the advocate and the person being lobbied. The former wants action on a bill, let us say. The latter wants support in the next election. Neither party may state this exchange openly, but both know it is the basis for the relationship.

Several years ago, when "message" posters (i.e., those trying to make a point regarding large issues) were in vogue, one of the favorites had a picture of a series of fish, each about to be gobbled up by a larger one. The message was, "There's no free lunch." The real point was that life is a series of exchanges and everybody pays something for what he or she gets.

Being clear about what you want from the target helps you avoid becoming distracted from your real goal. Recall the plight of Betty and Brad Advocate, whom we met in Chapter 4. They never could decide on their priorities nor what they were willing to settle for. Confusion about that can set you up for failure. If lawmakers can buy you off cheaply, without making any real changes, that leaves them more elbow room for dealing with other interests that know what they are after. If you and your allies cannot arrive at a common agenda, the alliance is doomed, and with it your chances of having an impact. If what you are really after is to show how corrupt or futile the whole policymaking business is, that will yield little in the way of satisfaction in the long run. What it will *not* yield is policy change.

The lawmaker's agenda may not be obvious. It may seem that he or she does not need anything from you. After all, this legislator got elected, maybe several times in a row. Especially if you are a member of the other party or backed the opponent last time, the legislator must have written off your support by now. Do not believe it. Aside from the fact that, as a constituent, you have the right to a serious hearing, the smart politician will never write anybody off. Besides, your support in elections is not the only thing he or she needs from you. Especially if you come armed with good information, you can play a key role in supplying him or her with good arguments for doing what you want done. And, regardless of a lawmaker's private sentiments or those of the majority of his or her constituents, those arguments are important.

A friend of mine used to work in the election campaigns of a U.S. senator. He described what happened when any advocates approached this senator asking him to support a particular bill. He would immediately express skepticism about the bill, no matter what he really thought about it. In that way, he found out if the advocates knew what they were talking about. Even more important, it was a way of getting the best arguments possible on behalf of the measure. Then when the senator lobbied one of his colleagues on the bill, or was asked by reporters why he took the stand he did, he was prepared for them.

Remember that politics is not a solo operation. When you lobby your representative you are not just after that one vote. You want him or her to urge other representatives to support the same measure and to have a good rationale for taking the action. Remember State Representative John Smith, who had to take a stand on the bill requiring parental consent for abortions. A critical task for him was to develop a strong case once he had decided which way he was going to vote. You can help your representative justify the action you are after. For a lawmaker to say he or she is backing a bill only because of pressure does not sound very good. A legislator has to be able to put it in terms of public interest and the needs of his or her district.

Regardless of how important the case for action, without maximizing your power base you will not get very far. So you need to attend to both aspects: the political leverage and the means of justifying the position. We will start with the power base.

Establishing a Power Base

"Negotiators or lobbyists who forget the power of their supporters and the thrust of their goals cannot be effective," writes Maryann Mahaffey (1982:70), long-time elected official and social work leader, "they can even sell out their constituents." It might be added that a lobbyist who sells out his or her constituents is soon a lobbyist without a constituency.

Policymakers are very astute at sizing up your power base. If you approach them as a lone individual, let us say a resident of their district, that will count for something. More than one voter, because they know you talk to other people, and you had to have more than average interest in the issue or you would not have bothered to come see them. But if you are seriously interested in influencing social policy, you need a bigger power base than that.

So your first task as a would-be lobbyist is to locate a constituency, a power base. Naturally, you need allies who share your policy goals. Suppose that in your preliminary research, you have come across the names of various local, state, or national groups that are working on the same set of issues as you are. As you explore different possible alliances, you should try to get a sense of what they can do to help you and what you may have to contribute to their work: for example, professional expertise or strategic information on the topic. When you mesh all your lobbying activity closely with this organization, you multiply your effectiveness. By keeping its members informed of what you are doing, you demonstrate your value to them, thus increasing your leverage with this group.

Congruence of your priorities with theirs, and their potential power to help your cause are two important considerations. These may be in conflict; an organization with which you are in total accord may have little political clout, while a major power broker would demand too many concessions on your part. You must strike some sort of balance between these two factors.

There are definite advantages in becoming an active member of a group. You then have an identity beyond your own, you get the regular newsletter and other materials sent to members, and it may be possible to influence the actions of the total group. In effect, you become one of the regular players. On the other hand, there may be factors which preclude it–ineligibility, high membership fees, inadvisability due to your position, or unwillingness to go along with the overall goals of the organization. Conversely, there may be advantages in joining more than one advocacy group. No matter, the important thing is to combine forces in working toward a common objective.

Carving Out a Specific Action Agenda

Organizations often work on several related concerns. You can be most helpful to them and to yourself if you can define a specific role in relation to one policy area. You then become identified with those issues, and as you bone up on them, you enhance your value to the group and to your own concerns. The more involved you are in the group, the more your agenda will be contingent on what the body as a whole sees as priorities.

Let us say you have settled on a bill currently in committee, one which is likely to be acted upon in the coming months. As you study the bill and do preliminary background searching on the topic, you come up with a clearer idea of where you want to go. What would you consider the optimal outcome? What would be a significant change for the better, short of the ideal? What are your fallback positions? What would you consider so limited that it would be better not to support it?

It is best, of course, to do this in collaboration with an advocacy group so that you and they are working together, thus maximizing your collective impact.

Targets

The next question to ask yourself is, whom should I lobby? And how does that person define the situation? Your approach should be targeted to a specific individual, and you must tailor your arguments accordingly. To help you understand what makes legislators tick and how lobbying looks from the other side of the desk, I shall introduce you to three members of the Pennsylvania State legislature. Together they represent a wide range of individuals and constituencies. One is a liberal Democratic House member representing a blue-collar district in the southwestern corner of the state. The second is a conservative Republican senator from a mostly rural district in the northwestern section of Pennsylvania. The third is the state's first African-American woman senator, a Democrat representing an inner-city district in Philadelphia.

Representative Allen G. Kukovich

Representative Kukovich has been in the Pennsylvania House of Representatives since 1977. He is an attorney by profession. Kukovich represents Westmoreland County, which is a "bedroom" for Pittsburgh and contains several large electronics, steel, and glass manufacturing plants. The district is 60 percent Democratic, but it consistently supported Ronald Reagan, and George Wallace once won here in a presidential primary. The John Birch Society has been active in the area in the past.

There is a large Italian-Catholic population, a majority of which is strongly anti-abortion. Kukovich, a Lutheran (the name is Yugoslavian) and an avowed feminist, says his opponents can count on 2,000 votes on the abortion issue alone in any election. The ultraconservative newspaper in his district has published more than 100 editorials that were critical of him, but he has the support of the Philadelphia and Pittsburgh papers. Among media people based in Harrisburg, the representative has a reputation for being available, willing to talk, and honest.

How does he manage to buck the odds and keep on being returned to office? He says it is because he is a no-nonsense legislator who works hard for his constituents. He has demonstrated that he will go to bat for them on issues of special concern to them. Senior citizens, unions, and feminists have all been supportive. In addition, he has high name recognition.

In 1988, Representative Kukovich's power in the Pennsylvania House took a big leap upward when he was elected by his Democratic colleagues as chairperson of the Majority Policy Committee for the 1989-1990 session of the legislature. Not only did this give him a key position in the formulation of the party's agenda, but it put him in line for further moves up the ladder of House leadership in the future.

Prior to this, he was a member of the House Committees on Consumer Affairs, where he chaired the Subcommittee on Public Utilities; Health and Welfare, as chair of the Subcommittee on Youth and Aging; Appropriations; and Judiciary. When he first came to the House, his main interest was in reform of public utilities and government, but when the support for human services eroded during the Reagan years, that became his priority concern.

Representative Kukovich denies future aspirations beyond continuing to serve in the House. A few years ago he gave serious thought to making a run for governor, traveled around the state and developed a wide network of local support. He had statewide name recognition of 10 percent, high for a state representative. But a combination of poor relations with the state's powerful insurance industry and a realization of what he would have to do in order to garner enough financial support led him to drop the idea. The aborted campaign was not without its impact, however. The representative believes his activity had a significant impact on the administration of Democratic Governor Robert Casey.

Kukovich has the support of a number of public interest groups at election time. His biggest contributions come from the National Organization for Women. He gets substantial support from organized labor, the Pennsylvania Trial Lawyers Association, and the Pennsylvania State Education Association. He also holds special fund-raising events. Major campaign expenses include radio advertising and direct mailings.

He divides legislators into five categories in their dealings with lobbyists: devil's advocates, ingratiating, rude, fence-sitters, and listeners. Which is he? A listener, he says; he tries to decide based on what he hears. If that sounds like a standard politician's answer, in Kukovich's case it appears to be an authentic statement of how he views himself.

Lobbying Allen Kukovich. How do we translate this profile into a lobbying strategy? It is clear that Representative Kukovich is an issues person, drawn to the political scene because of a burning interest in several policy concerns. In approaching him, one should be prepared for some searching questioning. If you are talking about one of his pet topics–consumer protection, women's issues, or children and youth, for example–you will get his attention. Demonstrate that you and he are on common ground on an issue that interests him or that you are speaking for a significant part of his district and you can get his active support. If you cannot show one or the other, chances are you will get a respectful hearing, maybe some practice with your debating skills, but little more.

Representative Kukovich likes to meet with lobbyists personally so there is an opportunity for give and take. He will sometimes play devil's advocate to smoke out the strongest arguments from the lobbyist. Handwritten letters from constituents–but *not* form letters or petitions–get his attention.

How does Representative Kukovich assess lobbyists he does not know? Much depends on how these persons present themselves, how cogently they make their cases, whether they are straightforward. The fact that people take the time to come to see him personally counts for something.

Senator John E. Peterson

The 25th senatorial district, located in the northwestern part of the state, is the largest rural district in Pennsylvania and the third largest in the United States, a fact which John Peterson and his staff often cite to people they are dealing with. This says a lot about Senator Peterson and the way he sees his mandate. He takes very seriously the task of representing the constituency which has been sending him to Harrisburg since 1977, first as a state representative, and since 1984 as a senator. The district, which covers all of five counties and parts of three others, is roughly 55 percent Republican, a clear margin but close enough to keep any elected official mindful of the need to be attentive to the range of interests he represents.

Senator Peterson's roots in the district run deep. He lives in the same area where he grew up and for many years ran a grocery business. He is past president of the local borough council, the chamber of commerce, and the Lions Club, a former trustee of the Titusville Hospital, member of the Venango County Industrial Board, and active in the Pleasantville United Methodist Church.

For John Peterson, politics was one more challenge, not unlike that of building a small business into a successful, profitable operation. Although at one time he gave some thought to running for Congress, he has been content to focus on the job at hand and not nurse larger political ambitions. He ran unopposed in the last election. He relies on his many regional ties to know the sentiments of his constituents. Frequent appearances at meetings in the district offer him another way to tap local views. The geography of his district–5,000 square miles with a scattered population–is reflected in the fact that he has three district offices.

Were one to conclude from this that John Peterson has a narrow, provincial outlook, it would be an erroneous conclusion. The fact that his district includes a portion of Erie County, whose center is an industrial lake port of 280,000, keeps him attuned to urban as well as rural issues. However, it is Senator Peterson's role as chair of the Public Health and Welfare Committee that has done much to broaden his perspective. Its area of concern–health and human services–is the largest segment of the state budget. It involves the senator heavily in urban problems far removed from the place he grew up. He has also taken increasing interest in the substantive issues involved in health and welfare policy. But his greatest commitment is to be the outspoken advocate for a constituency which he feels tends to be overlooked amid the claims of competing factions: farmers, whom he calls "constituents without a voice."

In addition to Public Health and Welfare, he serves on the Senate Committees on Agriculture and Rural Affairs, Game and Fisheries, Community and Economic Development, and Consumer Protection and Professional Licensure. These all suggest areas where he can be expected to have an interest and more than average influence.

Lobbying John Peterson. For Senator Peterson, it is not broad social issues as much as service to his district that is the main driving force. One has to keep this in mind when trying to promote a cause with him. How will it affect the 25th Senate District, and more generally, rural Pennsylvania? This is not all that concerns him, but it is a first hurdle to get past. Peterson takes seriously his responsibilities as head of the Public Health and Welfare Committee, and his mind is open to compelling arguments regarding the questions that come before this body.

When approached by lobbyists for the first time, Senator Peterson wants to know who these persons are, where they are from, and why they want to talk with him. Are these people interested in finding out his views or merely wanting to sell their own? Most important, there has to be some point to the meeting. The senator does not like to waste time on idle conversation, so the would-be lobbyists had better be able to make clear why their meetings are worth his time. The one exception to this insistence that the time be productive is where his own constituents are concerned. They have a right to expect a hearing, he says.

We can imagine Allen Kukovich using a lawyer's principles of tight logic and solid evidence with which to assess people and their ideas. To a much greater extent, John Peterson relies on a knowledge of the person. Over time he gets to know who is most competent, who is to be trusted. He constantly tries to determine what is driving the other person. In considering lobbyists and their appeals, he draws upon his years of experience in retailing. They are *selling* themselves and their ideas. He must be a thoughtful consumer.

There is one important additional thing to understand about Senator Peterson: the extent to which he looks to the expertise of his staff for guidance regarding human services issues. In addition to being knowledgeable about substantive policy questions, they are familiar with the region that the senator represents. When lobbyists want to discuss the details of policy, they are as apt to talk with a staff member as with the senator himself. In the late 1980s, when this book was first published, the likely contact was Barbara J. Gleim.

Barbara J. Gleim

When John Peterson moved into the chair of the Public Health and Welfare Committee, he brought Barbara Gleim along with him. Her official title was Executive Director of that committee. Getting to find her was the first task. She worked in a small cubicle physically removed from Senator Peterson's office suite, and the clerical staff was a buffer between her and the many people who wanted to get her ear.

> One quickly gets the idea that Barbara Gleim is not a person impressed by the trappings of high office. The best way to describe her work area is "spartan clutter." The walls and files are gray-on-gray and, except for a news clipping whose headline reminds us that health and welfare are at the top of the budget priorities, the walls are bare of decoration. Her desk is

piled high with an assortment of documents. She grabs a quick snack at her desk (lunch) and puffs on a cigarette while telling her visitor about the work she did in helping to put together an anti-smoking bill. The apparent incongruity tells us that Barbara Gleim is interested in the process of legislating as much as in the substance of what is produced. Just as Allen Kukovich thinks issues and John Peterson thinks district, Barbara Gleim thinks *workable consensus.* In the case of the anti-smoking bill, she called each person known to have an interest in the legislation–ranging from the Tobacco Institute and the tavern owners to the American Cancer Society–and asked, "What can't you tolerate?" Over a two-week period she gradually mediated the conflicting views down to the point where she felt a common stance could be crafted. Meanwhile, she was in contact with staff aides to key senators from both parties.

She saw as one of her chief functions that of acting as the lightning rod for the various factions on a controversial issue. "If people got angry, they'd get angry at me, not each other." When it looked as if a compromise was possible, she brought together the various interests, including legislative staff, to hammer out the final version of the bill.

What does she do when some person(s) will not budge and the rest are ready to act? She keeps the tone diplomatic, but lets them know that if they cannot go along she is sorry, but the action will go ahead without them. That is often enough to bring the adamant ones around. Underneath the mild manner is a tough operator when toughness is necessary.

Health and welfare is a sprawling area. How does she get up to speed on an issue with which she has had little previous experience? As soon as she senses that the problem will eventually hit her desk, Gleim begins collecting everything she can lay her hands on. When AIDS first began to get national attention, she alerted the news clipping service to send her everything they could find on the subject, talked to people she felt knew something about it, and attended AIDS conferences. She was thus able to write a report on the topic for the GOP caucus. Based on her knowledge of the subject, general attitudes toward it, and the typical response of localities to issues of this sort, she recommended that educational efforts be focused at the local level–for example, through a series of town meetings. She was convinced that the public needed to get its information from personal contact with somebody who was known and could be trusted.

Lobbying Barbara Gleim. In working lobbyists into her busy schedule, Barbara Gleim was guided by three considerations: (1) is this an authentic source of information, preferably from first-hand experience rather than from theory; (2) is this a voice that will need to be included in a future working consensus; or (3) does Senator Peterson want her to meet with the person? As for the third consideration, Gleim understood the first law of politics: loyalty. She would never cross up or upstage her boss. He knew he could entrust major responsibility to her. But it goes beyond that. One way to close the door forever on any further access to a person such as Barbara Gleim is to embarrass her or the senator or others involved in the legislative process. You do not start dealing with her and then go hunt up her opposite number on the Democratic side and share information with that person.

Letters, typed or handwritten, are useful ways to get your views to senior staff aides. They can easily spot form letters and will tend to write them off as orchestrated attempts at manipulation. They need more than just the fact that you are for or against a bill. They also want to know the reasoning behind your position.

Senator Roxanne H. Jones

On one occasion when I was scheduled to meet Senator Jones, she suggested it be at her home, a second-floor walk-up over a fabric shop on a busy street in North Philadelphia. When I arrived she was busy mopping the floor of the shop because a carton of frozen chickens the shop owner had agreed to hold for her had thawed and made a puddle. She was about to cook the chickens for a supper at her church. She once surprised fellow legislators by inviting them to an African-American dinner–prepared in part by none other than the senator herself. Senator Jones treats her staff as "family." The atmosphere is egalitarian, with a sharing of work roles among the members. She has sought to avoid losing touch with the world she once inhabited: that of a welfare recipient struggling to raise a family.

These homespun images should not mislead you. Roxanne Jones is a very savvy politician. She probably has her senate district locked up for as long as her health holds up. Though she was elected to her first political office in 1984, she has been in politics for more than two decades–as an outsider. In 1967, as a recipient of AFDC, she organized a local unit of the National Welfare Rights Organization. The following year she became president of the Philadelphia Welfare Rights Organization.

Roxanne Jones defies other stereotypes. While deeply committed to the needs of the people of her district, and African-American and low-income people more generally, she can as readily relate to Caucasian legislators from rural Pennsylvania.

What is the main moving force for this state senator? First, she is a *people*-oriented legislator. Her natural warmth pervades everything she does. That personal touch and readiness to respond to human needs freely and openly is a must in the 3rd Senate District. There one's value is measured less by espousal of esoteric policy issues than by willingness to answer urgent calls for help and act as an intermediary with an often hostile public bureaucracy.

Roxanne Jones is a living demonstration of the possibilities in people in the meanest of circumstances. She has received numerous awards and is in demand as a speaker at schools and youth group meetings. Her legislative priorities are housing and drug abuse, urgent concerns in her district. When interviewed, she was getting ready to resubmit a bill that would set up rehabilitation centers throughout the state for drug-dependent mothers and their children.

The one-time provocateur who led many a noisy demonstration of welfare recipients in the Capitol rotunda now rubs elbows with some of the same senators who used to be offended by the tactics. She is the ranking Democrat on the powerful Senate Public Health and Welfare Committee.

Lobbying Roxanne Jones. As might be expected in a rather informal operation where roles overlap, lobbyists are equally likely to deal with the senator herself or one of her legislative aides.

When approached by a lobbyist, Senator Jones starts with the assumption that this person has a job to do for his or her employer, be it an insurance company or a public interest organization, and will try to make the best case possible. Rather than get into a debate with the person, the senator will listen to the presentation and then present her own views. Always uppermost in her mind is the impact on her constituents. She then goes into extensive consultations with people she trusts to get their assessments of the issue: ward leaders and other key informants in her district, other legislators, members of the Philadelphia City Council, maybe the Mayor. Her staff shares in this survey of friendly sources. Jones often pleads ignorance, on substantive issues as well as legislative protocol, an approach which can both be flattering to others and assure that she will get maximum information.

If one wants to interest the senator in a cause, it is clear that, above all, it must have meaning to the lives of the people she represents. Demonstrating that understanding increases the advocate's ability to get a sympathetic hearing. But one should be aware that soon after the interview, the senator will be on the phone seeing if what has been told her is corroborated by the people she trusts.

Unlike many of her senate colleagues, Senator Jones sets up few barriers between herself and those seeking her attention. This ready accessibility is one of the reasons for her popularity and growing influence in Harrisburg. The calls that keep coming in at all hours concern public policy issues and personal crises in the lives of constituents. No matter to Roxanne Jones, they are equally what being a state senator is all about.

* * *

We have seen three very different legislators, each with a distinctive style and sense of mission, but for each of whom the interests of his or her district have top priority. To each, then, the would-be lobbyist must be able to say, convincingly, "This will help your constituents." There are state legislators who lack the dedication and energy of these three. Some have given up trying to make a difference but somehow cannot quit. Some can be bought if the price is right. But it has been my experience that the Allen Kukoviches, John Petersons, and Roxanne Joneses are more the rule than the exception.

How Allen Kukovich sees the world in general, his role in it, and people like you will help to decide how he will react to your pitch. More specifically, when he thinks about, say, community mental health services or welfare reform, what does he focus on? What presumptions from experience come into play? How do his deep-seated values *and* those of his constituents color the way he will receive an advocate's message, even before that person has a chance to present arguments? If the subject is abortion, we know that a substantial number of Representative Kukovich's constituents will start with a different definition of the situation from his.

John Peterson's focus, presumptions, and values will be different. Because Senator Peterson is a complex individual with a mixture of definitions, it is important to try to understand how he defines the specific problem one wants to address with him.

Roxanne Jones will have still another definition of the situation. You can be sure that if you approach her about welfare reform, you will have her attention from the beginning. When she hears or reads that phrase, her focus, presumptions, and values will be different from John Peterson's.

Once you have a sense of how your target defines the situation, you can then prepare your case to move that definition where you want it. What follows is the sequence of steps you must engage in, in order to do that.

FACE-TO-FACE MEETINGS

Suppose you have received an action alert from an advocacy group with which you have been working. It says:

> Members of Congress will be on spring recess next week! Now is our chance to tell them what we think about HR 213. Call your congressperson's office tomorrow and make an appointment. His local address and telephone numbers are on the attached sheet. Below are the points we want to make about HR 213.

The moment of truth has arrived. You are going to have to put all that research to work and meet your U.S. representative face-to-face. Actually, it may be a staff member with whom you will talk, but you are still a little nervous about the meeting. What do you do now?

Preparing for the Visit

I shall assume that you have already laid the groundwork by thoroughly researching your subject, including the writing of a brief, and have done an equally careful job of sizing up the representative and his likely definition of the situation. The next step is to call the office and try to get an appointment with the representative. The person on the other end of the line will want to know what it is you would like to discuss with Congressman John Smith: HR 213? Could you tell me what that is in relation to? Services for the chronically mentally ill? Oh yes. Let me see. He's going to be pretty tied up next week. Would you want to write to the congressman about it? That way he could probably be most helpful to you. (No, you are anxious to talk with him in person. Your schedule is fairly flexible.) Well, it looks as if he will have a little time next Wednesday afternoon, say about 1:30? (Yes, that would be fine.)

As soon as you hang up, write a letter to the congressman thanking him for his willingness to see you regarding HR 213 on services for the chronically mentally ill. Specify the date and time of the appointment and include where you can be reached by phone. Do not be too surprised if you get a call Tuesday morning asking if you can switch to a different time. Be willing to change the time but stick to your request for a face-to-face meeting. In writing the letter you are already lobbying. You are beginning to create in the minds of the congressman and his staff the association between you and HR 213. You are demonstrating flexibility, appreciation for his responsiveness, *and* determination to be heard on the issue. You are already not somebody to be stroked a couple of times and forgotten.

The next step is to go back and review your brief and other material. If you can do a dry run with a friend, do it. Does this sound like excessive preparation for a visit to your representative? Advocates would do well to take a leaf from the book of James Baker when he was scheduled to appear before the Senate Foreign Relations Committee in confirmation hearings for the post of Secretary of State. Baker was a very seasoned political operator and it was generally assumed that the Senate would unanimously confirm his appointment to the cabinet position. But Baker took nothing for granted, even though he was down with the flu a few days before he was to appear before the committee. Here is one newspaper account of the preparations:

> Mr. Baker, who has been ill with the flu over the last several days and studying his briefing papers at home, has prepared a 10-to-15-minute opening statement for the hearings. . . .
>
> Mr. Baker, a master of stage-managing political events, sent an advance team to the hearing room on Friday to check acoustics, camera angles and the position of the furniture. He plans to be accompanied to the hearings by his wife and several of their eight children as well as a contingent of policy aides. (*The New York Times,* 1989)

Prior to all this, Baker had held private meetings with every member of the committee. He had thus prepared them and himself for the session. Furthermore, he made no secret of these detailed preparations. He wanted the Senate and the country to know that he took this assignment seriously.

You want your congressman and his staff to know you are every bit as serious about HR 213. That is what will make them take you seriously. In addition to boning up on the substantive issues, you will review your background investigation of the congressman and the staff aide responsible for dealing with mental health issues.

Preparing the Presentation. In putting together the brief (discussed in Chapter 7), you were guided by the inherent logic of the argument, each issue being a necessary building block for the next. The presentation to the target is different, and its organization is based on what is most salient to the person you will be talking to. For example, if your representative is preoccupied with the threat of violence by ex-patients, you may want to begin by addressing that issue head on. Or you may decide to focus attention on the majority of ex-patients who are not violent. If your target has spoken eloquently of the need for services, but has taken a stand against any new programs because of the urgent necessity of lowering the federal deficit, you may decide to lead off with arguments regarding the economic feasibility of the plan–and the costs of doing nothing. Figure on having a very limited amount of time in which to present your case and make every minute count.

Finally, prepare a one-page summary of the major points you want to make about HR 213. This you will leave with the congressman or the staff aide with whom you meet. Like everything else, it should include the name of the bill, its subject matter, your name, address, and telephone numbers. Again, you are building up a linkage in people's minds. The same kind of pains should be taken with the appearance of this as with the rest–neatly typed, not crowded on the page, and limited to a single page, no more.

Tracking down the hard-to-reach target. What if you cannot get an appointment? Do not give up. Figure out a way to meet the target. One good approach is to learn about meetings where the person will appear. Representatives frequently come back to their districts (not just during recesses) to address citizen groups. State legislators are even more accessible. Go to the meeting early and find a seat near the front. If you can get the floor during the question period, state your name clearly, and ask about the progress of HR 213, which would provide services for the chronically mentally ill. Be sure to get that all in. You are reinforcing an association in the minds of the representative and, at least as important, staff aides who will also be there. This is also a way to alert others in the audience, possibly the news media, to the importance of the bill. After the meeting, try to corner the representative to shake hands, state your name clearly and reiterate your interest in HR 213. Do not worry about getting into arguments for the bill right then. Those can come in your follow-up letter. If you cannot get to the representative, who will be surrounded by other people with their own concerns, talk with the staff aide. This will be a senior staff person, and worth establishing a connection with. If it is impossible to get to either, write a follow-up letter anyway, saying you were there, how interesting you found the representative's remarks on such-and-such, and then going into your case for HR 213.

There is not a well-developed set of rules for cornering public officials. A professional lobbyist I know has had to learn by experience. One of her biggest assets, aside from an engaging personality that puts people at ease, is a lively imagination. For example, there was a time when a legislative committee chairman she was trying to see kept avoiding her. Finally tracking him down to a committee caucus from which she was barred, she planted herself outside the men's room, knowing that sooner or later nature would direct her quarry in that direction. Sure enough, eventually he walked right up to her, having no other choice.

Experienced lobbyists have no monopoly on that kind of creativity. One student sat for hours in the outer office of a state representative, whose secretary kept assuring her that the representative would be back "any moment now." Meanwhile, the student knew from a variety of clues that the legislator was right there on the other side of the door taking phone calls. In this case it was the secretary who had to obey the call of nature. As soon as she was gone, the student knocked on the door of the representative's office, was admitted, and got a respectful and friendly reception. She may not have convinced him of her case, but she most certainly managed to impress him with her dedication to her mission.

The Visit

Like dentists, public officials are chronically behind schedule, especially as the day winds on. It is an unfair exchange, in which you should make it a point to be there when you say you will even though you will have to sit in the waiting room for a while. Everything you do from the moment you enter the outer office should convey respect and persistence, regardless of the kind of response you get. Everybody is important, starting with the receptionist. It is a time for authenticity, not cuteness. You are there on serious business.

Do not be surprised if, after all this preparation, you get to talk with a staff aide instead of the representative. No matter, treat her or him as if you were dealing with the official. Begin by making sure the person knows your name, that you are interested in HR 213, and that the bill concerns services for the chronically mentally ill. Your target has to keep track of many things at once and may forget which issue this is.

The individual with whom you meet will be trying to size you up: Who are you? How important are you to the representative politically? What is your interest in this bill? The staff may have checked with people in your local area to see if they know you. If you can make a connection to a known person–such as a local party activist–that will help. But be sure you know that this person is on good terms with the representative, not an old enemy.

Start by saying who you are and why you are interested in the issue. Then tell simply and directly why you favor HR 213. When you make a general statement follow it with a concrete illustration. Assume you are talking to an intelligent person who knows little or nothing about the bill. A good rule of thumb for advocates, teachers, and writers: never underestimate the audience's intelligence, but never overestimate its knowledge of what you are communicating. If the representative or aide is familiar with the bill, he or she will let you know that soon enough. Just be sure he or she has the right one and not some other that sounds the same.

If you want to make a real impression, alert the person to a few of the points he or she will hear from the opposition and answer these. Do not worry about giving ammunition to the other side this way; chances are the representative is already aware of these arguments. But you will come across as really informed, fair minded, and not afraid of open debate. More important, you will be prepping your target to handle such issues when discussing them with colleagues. In any event, take only a few minutes to lay out your case, then invite questions. Here are some of the responses you may get:

- *Target already supports your position.* You are delighted to hear that. You know that some members of the House are opposed to it; maybe cite by name a specific one you know to be opposed. Could the representative speak to that colleague about the bill? If you know this representative has co-sponsored such legislation in the past or has a generally "good" voting record, it would be good to cite that, showing that you are keeping tabs on the legislator's performance. Does the target have any suggestions on strategy? Do you have findings from your research which might be helpful to the target?
- *Target generally favors the bill but has specific concerns.* Acknowledge that the concerns are important and then give your arguments regarding them. If they are issues to which you have no answers, stick to you basic position and say you would like to check the matter out further and will get back to

the target. (It is essential that you do the follow-up, of course.) You must not let the specific concerns overshadow the main thrust of the bill. End the conversation with appreciation that the representative understands the real value of the legislation. In other words, you and the target are still basically on the same side.

- *Target is on the fence or noncommittal.* Present your case. Try to get at the specific issues about which the target has concern. Do not press for a definite answer. Offer to get additional information. Plan to come back to the target in the future with more information supporting your case. It may well be that the target needs information to justify taking a stand either way or simply has not thought much about it.
- *The target is opposed to the basic thrust of the bill.* State your case. Respond to specific arguments against, but do not allow the meeting to turn into a debate, which the target will either "win," no matter how well you perform, or will resent the implicit put-down in being out-argued. Keep bringing the focus back to your issues. For example, when the target cites the horrendous cost of the program, acknowledge the importance of the fiscal issues and then pull out another case history of a person whose life was devastated because of lack of services. Leave the target with some arresting case histories seared into his or her brain. They may come back to haunt the target after you have left. Of course, it is just possible she is playing devil's advocate to see if you (1) are committed and (2) know what you are talking about. You can play a useful role by giving good arguments.
- *The target would rather talk about other things.* For instance, your uncle whom he or she knew many years ago, the fortunes of the Pittsburgh Steelers, or his or her bill to rid the sidewalks of America of jewelry vendors. Play the target the way an angler plays a fish. Go with him or her for a little bit, but then pull him or her back to your agenda. Chances are he or she will get the point after a while, but even if the two of you end up carrying on separate conversations, the target will know that you are serious about HR 213 and cannot be diverted from your mission.

- *The target is impatient or frequently interrupts to take phone calls.* You have been given time with the target and you have a right to be heard, so do not be intimidated if this person continually checks his or her watch. If it gets too bad, or the interruptions are preventing you from making a coherent case, you might suggest rescheduling the interview. If you have to be kicked out, he or she will do so; the schedule is the target's problem, not yours. But when you leave, be sure to express thanks to this person for taking the time to talk with you, and do not allow a note of sarcasm to creep into your voice when you do it.
- *The target is just plain rude.* Model nice behavior and pretend not to notice. You may be surprised to learn later that you made a good impression after all.

In any of the above cases, remember to leave your one-page summary with the target. Leave the door open for future contacts regarding HR 213. And *always* make your exit gracious, so that the final impression is positive–on the office staff as well as the target.

After the Visit

As soon as possible, write a letter to the representative expressing thanks for his or her time, making sure once again to include the magic words: HR 213, for services to the chronically mentally ill, your name, address, and telephones where you can be reached. If you have run across any friendly editorials, news items or the like, enclose a copy. If you have talked with a staff aide instead of the boss, address the letter to the representative–Attn.: the staff aide. You should tell the representative how helpful the aide was.

If you are working with an advocacy group on HR 213, be sure to send them a copy of the follow-up letter, with a cover note telling about the response you got. This will help them get the greatest mileage out of future contacts and multiply your own impact.

Remember, you have had not one contact with your target system, but four–the initial call, the confirming letter, the visit, and the follow-up letter. It is five if you count the one-pager which is likely to be passed among different system members. Given politicians' natural ability to remember names, yours is by now well known to the target, linked indelibly to what? Yes, to HR 213.

GROUP VISITS

Going to see a policymaker as part of a delegation has several distinct advantages. Also a few hazards. We should consider both.

The Advantages

The impact of numbers. Politicians, as the old saying goes, may not be able to think too clearly but they all count exceedingly well. You and the target know that five constituents do not amount to much in terms of votes, but, psychologically, facing several people at once is vastly different from meeting a lone individual. Depending on the composition of the group–for example, reflecting a diversity of interests or including big contributors or known political heavyweights–the effect can be substantial.

It is usually easier to get an appointment. Not unrelated to the first point, delegations can command a piece of the target's time in a way that one individual, especially an unknown, may not. Do not expect to walk in unannounced and find the target sitting around waiting for visitors. The meeting should be scheduled ahead of time, just as with the individual visit.

There is comfort in numbers. Even the shyest among us feels safe in going to see policymakers as part of a delegation. Especially when you are trying to recruit other people to lobby, the knowledge that they will have company makes the job many times easier than it would be if they thought they would have to face the target alone. However, do not overwhelm the target with a mob. Five is probably the maximum number–two or three is better.

The Hazards

Internal dissension. Nothing will wipe out the effectiveness of a delegation quite so fast as a disagreement within the ranks in front of the person you are trying to impress.

"Don't everybody speak at once." The opposite problem: the group settles down in the awesome presence and nobody speaks up. Eventually things will get unplugged, perhaps with the help of the host, but the impression is one of an unprepared delegation.

Generally sloppy planning. The increased sense of security, cited above as an advantage, can turn into a minus factor if it lulls everybody into assuming the task will be a piece of cake. Not only is the delivery of the pitch weak, but the impression can be that the folks just wanted to be able to tell their friends back home that they met with the Great Person. Autographs, anyone? And let me have my secretary give you tickets to the gallery. The paintings in the rotunda are really. . .

Putting the Delegation Together

If your goal is to maximize your impact on policy decisions, then who goes can be as important as how many. One sign that the target is taking this seriously: the secretary asks for the name and address of each person who will be attending. She may put it in terms of security, but the real reason is to check out the political potential of the meeting. People with political clout or generally respected in the home district are an asset *as long as they understand the purpose of the meeting and are known to be supportive of the agenda.*

It is not just that they are present in the room. In all likelihood the target, being naturally attuned to political influence, will turn to a known quantity and ask him or her to state the case for the group. As soon as that happens, you have no control over where the discussion will go. You can chime in with corrections along the way, but that may simply create the perception of internal disagreement mentioned above. So if you decide to take along such a person, be sure he or she is well prepared.

Open-ended invitations to members of allied groups to come along are risky for the same reason. If they cannot be avoided–for instance, feelings will be bruised if people are told to stay away–at least take pains to prepare the group in advance.

Preparing for the Visit

This is one place where you should be very forceful in stating your opinion. Stake out a firm position at the outset as the group defines the situation. The purpose is to influence the decisions of the policymaker, and everything else should be subordinated to that goal. Team players only, and anyone wishing to attend the session with the target should be expected to attend at least one prior session in preparation.

Briefing materials, both on the subject matter and the target, should be distributed before the warm-up meeting. People should bring their questions to that session. Have it understood that if questions are not raised then, people will keep them to themselves and not bring them up midway through the visit to the target.

You should spend some time at the beginning of the meeting helping first-timers deal with their anxiety. Emphasize the kind of positive awareness of strengths discussed in Chapter 5, then on to the business at hand. Spokespersons should be chosen. It is well to have one person act as chief of the delegation and lead off the presentation. Allow time for role-play and discussion of what happened in the mock exchange.

Conducting the Visit

If possible, have the group rendezvous near the target's office 15 minutes to a half-hour before the scheduled appointment. Coffee shops have the advantage of allowing delegates to put something in their stomachs to relax them, but they do not allow privacy in case there must be a final briefing. Bars are a definite no-no, not because the fortifying will get out of hand, but you do not want to walk in smelling like a distillery. Alcohol on one person's breath may be noticeable. In a group it can be overpowering, especially if nobody else in the room has been imbibing.

Assume that anything that can go wrong will go wrong and plan accordingly. Have more than one person ready to take the helm, in case the designated hitter is down with the flu or held up in traffic. The same goes for the one-pager. Have two people charged with bringing it in case one falters. Perhaps most important, be ready to step into the breach in case others forget their lines or decide to use the opportunity to lobby for a controversial measure that is not on the agenda.

After leaving the target's office, the group should go somewhere together to reflect on what has happened. If it has gone well–for some the fact of having been able to carry out the mission at all will feel like a success–you will want to celebrate. If things went wrong, people need to be put back together. In any event, this is an opportunity to assess what did happen and make clear this one visit was not the end of the process but only a beginning. Members should look forward to continuing work. This time the setting matters very little. Maybe that bar would be a good idea. At the least a coffee shop so the group can reward itself.

Follow-Up

In addition to making sure the thank-you letter gets sent soon afterward, send your own thank-yous to all members of the delegation. Let them know they did a good job. If you have any additional news regarding the target's subsequent action, be sure to include that. Helping delegates feel they have accomplished something and are appreciated will assure that they will have an appetite for more. Remember, it is awareness on the target's part that the advocates are serious and will stay around for the long haul that gives the group real power. Policymakers count on people to lose interest in an issue. You want to be able to demonstrate that *this* group of people is different.

WRITING LETTERS

Next to in-person contacts, letters are the most effective way to lobby. They have the advantage of being part of the permanent record, available for future reference. We are talking here about letters that are substitutes for in-person visits, not the follow-up notes after a visit. Keep in mind that the target's only way of sizing up you as well as your message is through the written word. Meaning: take every bit as much care in preparing to write a letter as you take in preparing for a face-to-face encounter, because whatever is on the paper is *it.* There is no chance to elaborate or modify the message.

Letters have considerable impact. You bothered to write. The target knows that for every letter writer there were maybe a hundred other constituents who would not or could not do so. Your letter counts for much more than an expression of the views of a single individual.

Letter writing is becoming a lost art. In this age of instant communication via everything from telephone to computer, who needs to go to the work of writing things out? I may be showing my age in suggesting that something really is lost in the transition, and that letters will continue to play an important part in the political process for a long time to come.

Tailor It to the Task

There are few standard rules for writing to a policymaker except the ones concerning grammar and spelling. Those, incidentally, are supremely important. Through your handling of the mechanics you speak volumes about yourself and the importance you attach to the letter itself. Take the time to proofread. It is a good idea to get somebody else to go over the letter, too. Word processors, though not necessary, facilitate the job, both of writing and of correcting errors.

Having another person or persons look at the final product is good for another reason. They can pretend they are the legislator receiving the letter. How does it hit them? It will be easier for them to spot problems than it will be for you because by that time you will be too wedded to your own words.

Remember what was said about the exchange between you and the target. What is that person looking for? How will your opening sentence trigger off a definition of the situation inside the target? What will convince the target to modify that definition?

When lobbying in person, you begin by saying who you are, why you are concerned, and establish why you are worth listening to. Use the same principle in starting your letter. In the opening sentence you identify what the letter is about (for example, *in favor of HR 213, concerning services to the chronically mentally ill*). Then establish who you are. Then go into your argument.

Providing Ammunition

Arguments are a way of persuading the target to do something. They can also supply the target with supportive evidence, as does the following excerpt from a letter to a senator urging support for health care legislation:

> My four-year-old son has had recurrent bouts of bronchial asthma, and needless to say, his high fevers wheezing, along with numerous (and expensive) trips to the doctor and pharmacy are stressful for my husband and me. However we are blessed that we have both the cash flow to pay the doctor and pharmacy bills as they occur *and* a good medical insurance policy (my husband's employer pays the full premium) that reimburses us a full 80% of all outpatient and hospital and prescription expenses. . . .
>
> But my friend E______ , a 35-year-old divorced mother of six children, is not that lucky. She works at least 40 hours a week as a secretary in ______ , but her $13,000 salary doesn't stretch that far. Until a year ago, she received Medicaid, but she always had difficulty finding a doctor who would accept her card. Now . . . she is no longer covered under Medicaid. Instead, she has a pretty pitiful health insurance policy offered through her employer: She pays $520.00 a year in premiums, but the policy pays for *hospitalization only,* no doctor's visits or prescriptions. As a result, her kids don't always go to the doctor when they're sick nor get the prescriptions they need, because sometimes E______ simply doesn't have the money. Also, the kids don't have regular eye and dental checkups. . . .

How Long Should It Be?

The length is important. In general the briefer the better, but it must be long enough to make the point you are trying to make, including the concrete illustrations and other evidence. One page or less is best. Anything more than two will probably not be read past the first couple of paragraphs to get the drift of the message. On a highly controversial issue, even this amount of detail may be a waste of time; they may be reduced to the point of counting the yeas and nays. On a very few issues, a person with a large constituency (for example, a U.S. senator from a big state) may actually weigh the piles of pro and con letters, though that is rare enough that you should assume otherwise.

Chances are that the target will not read your letter but will assign this task to an assistant. This is not important. Your opinion will weigh just as heavily regardless. Ditto answering your letter. You may wish to frame the personal letter you get from your U.S. senator, but be aware that it was probably churned out by a machine. Occasionally, your letter will get into the wrong pile and you, a devoted foe of abortion, will be thanked for expressing your pro-choice opinion. That is least likely to happen with issues that are not highly controversial, so that the letters are a trickle, not a torrent.

Typed or Handwritten?

Guides for letter writers to public officials often warn against using the typewriter. Some lawmakers say the same thing. It is claimed that handwritten letters will get their attention, whereas typed letters will be dismissed as part of an organized effort. Some organizations go to great lengths to disguise their efforts by supplying different colors of stationery on which members can write out the message in longhand and even supply the stamps so the letters will be sure to be mailed.

The concern strikes me as excessive. Experienced politicians and their aides can spot a canned message, regardless of how it is written. Fifty handwritten letters, each starting with, "I am opposed to HR 213 because of the danger to my children," or some variant on that theme are an orchestrated campaign, easily recognizable as such. A single handwritten epistle that goes into substantial detail, showing knowledge of the intricacies of the subject, citing evidence, etc., does not ring true. That is not the way people present detailed arguments these days.

A thoughtful message, produced on a typewriter or word processor, stands a good chance of getting a thoughtful reaction. One thing to be said, finally, for the typed variety: they are legible. That should count for something with the people who have to read them.

Opinion Wires

Back in the 1960s, Western Union came up with a cheap way to register an opinion with official Washington. For less than a dollar, one could send a brief message to one's senator or representative. For a little more, the same message could go to one's representative and both senators, also to the President if one wished. In the early 1960s I was involved in a peace group, one of whose members happened to see a tour of the White House, including the mail room, on television. The mail clerk told the interviewer that President Kennedy personally read everything that came in within the first 24 hours following a major policy address or incident. After that, we alerted our members via a telephone network to send in opinion telegrams immediately after any major event concerning peace issues, on the theory that they would get the personal attention of the President. I am sure dozens of other groups of activists around the country did the same thing. I am equally sure that in a short time the tactic became obvious and the White House staff did more screening, for example, sending the President every 100th wire that came in.

You can still send opinion wires to your representatives in Washington, but the price has gone up. As of 1995, the cost was $9.95 plus tax for a single 20-word message; multiply that by four if you decide to wire your representative, both senators, and the president. You may also find yourself ordering your own confirmation copy for $5.95 plus tax unless you are careful. There may be better ways to spend close to $50 for your favorite cause–for example, telephoning the offices of the same officials plus a few dozen of your friends around the country and asking them to make additional calls.

Petitions

Petition drives, except for those designed to get somebody's name or a referendum question onto the ballot, have very limited impact on policymaking. They have all the disadvantages of the obviously orchestrated letter-writing campaign with none of the virtues. Politicians know that many persons who sign petitions are doing a friend a favor, or are flattered to be asked or just have a hard time saying no when somebody shoves a piece of paper and a ballpoint pen in front of them.

Petitions have one important function, of course: they provide names and addresses for mailing lists. If you signed a petition on the abortion issue, you are a prime target for an anti-abortion or pro-choice organization's direct-mail campaign. Depending on how the computerized lists are sorted out, you will also start getting mail on everything from banning handguns, to saving the whales, to attending a rock concert for the benefit of children in the Sudan. The causes are worthy, but we are into a different kind of lobbying.

LOBBYING BY TELEPHONE

It is painless. Sit at home, pick up the telephone and dial your representative. You can call the local district office and convey the message that way. You will give your information to a staff aide. If the issue is hot and they are down to counting the yeas and nays, you will be asked to identify yourself and state your position. If you are not asked to identify yourself, they are probably not even keeping score any more.

It is the easiest way to register your views. It does get recorded, and therefore has an impact. But, it is just as easy for everybody else. As compared with in-person visits and letters, telephone calls are a relatively weak form of lobbying unless you have a personal relationship with the target or somebody else on staff. As a stranger, calling cold, you will have some impact but not a lot. Between that and doing nothing, of course, there is no contest.

LOBBYING APPOINTED OFFICIALS

From everything that was said in Chapter 5, it is clear that appointed officials are much harder to lobby than elected ones. They are not looking for your vote. They are specialists who are very well informed, have heard all the arguments, no doubt, and start off by assuming that you know less about the subject than they do. However, they handle that all-important phase of policymaking, turning enacted laws into regulations, so they are worth trying to influence.

The Action Agenda

Work on regulations is detailed work, not a matter of broad, general principles. You are most effective if you carve out specific points to focus on rather than a total piece of legislation. Needless to say, it should be something with which you are very familiar. You are not going to try to play one-upmanship with the professionals, but you at least have to demonstrate that talking to you is not a total waste of time, because you do have something to contribute.

It is probably especially important in this kind of lobbying to work closely with advocacy organizations that have already established working relationships with certain administrators. As was suggested in Chapter 3, this may affect your precise position on the subject matter, because now you are not the only one setting the agenda.

The Target

Here again, experienced insiders are necessary allies because the general public does not know the people who churn out regulations. You may be dealing with a cadre of persons rather than a single individual. Ordinarily, there is one key individual who, either because of strategic position, old friendships, or professional affiliations, is the link to the system. It is very likely that this person is looking for feedback from trusted sources, which can only help the advocates to make their input. The key word here is *trusted.* A stranger offering advice may get a polite, even cordial reception, but is unlikely to register much impact on the decisions being made. In addition to representatives of advocacy organizations, staff aides to legislators considered friendly can also open the door to the regulation writers.

At the beginning of Richard Nixon's ill-fated second term as president, he decided to carry out a major shake-up in the Department of Health, Education, and Welfare (now the Department of Health and Human Services). The HEW secretary was Caspar Weinberger, an old Nixon ally from California who shared the president's fiscal conservatism. Weinberger installed James Dwight, another California conservative as head of the Social and Rehabilitation Service, which oversaw the allocation of federal funds to states for social services. Unlike many key aides in the Department, Dwight was an unknown quantity (Richan, 1981:165).

His major mission soon became clear: to sharply restrict such expenditures. Under his direction, the regulations governing these expenditures were rewritten in such a way as to carry out the mission. Not only would many consumers of services be cut off, but so would social workers staffing these programs. Even the universities training social workers would feel the pinch. The social work professionals–and with their encouragement, consumer groups–immediately mobilized for a fight. They had to act during the period in which the draft regulations would be out for public review. At the end of the period, the regulations would become the law of the land.

James Dwight made clear he was no friend of social workers. When the American Public Welfare Association tried to set up meetings with him, he flatly refused to attend. Experienced social work lobbyists received a chilly reception. The civil servants who worked under Dwight were told to have no contact with the social workers, the National Governors' Association, and other groups seeking to protect social services funding (Richan, 1981:167). For the time being, at least, the door was closed.

An intense campaign of public pressure generated a record number of letters to Dwight's office calling for revision of the regulations. Congressional Democrats picked up the cry, adding still more pressure. Technically, the administration could simply refuse to budge, but realistically they had to be concerned about the political fallout.

It was an underling of Dwight who finally broke the impasse between the Department and the social service advocates. John Young, commissioner for the Community Services Administration, made the first tentative overtures to the staff of the National Governors' Association, knowing that he did so at considerable risk. This might never have happened if the latter had not established a sense of trust. A first exploratory meeting was held without Dwight's knowledge. Mike Suzuki, an aide to Young and a social worker, helped facilitate the process. In time, the federal officials, lobbyists, and congressional staff hammered out a compromise agreement that resulted in new legislation for the funding of social services (Mott, 1976).

There are several lessons for would-be advocates in this case history. One is the delicate nature of relations between administrative staff and outside interests. Another is the critical importance of developing relationships over time, so the insiders know they are dealing with outsiders they can trust. The appointed official who fails to return your phone calls may not want to be bothered, or may be convinced that he or she knows more than you do, or may want very much to talk but be afraid to do so. Clearly, trust involves not only good intentions but also the perception that the outsider is competent and thoroughly informed. Those are attributes you can cultivate, but it will take work.

Another important lesson from the above incident is that one cannot stereotype departmental staff. James Dwight was not a human services professional. Neither was John Young, but his definition of the situation was different from Dwight's. Mike Suzuki, a social worker, had still another definition. Depending on which of these the advocate wished to approach, then, it was necessary to know as much as possible about where that person's attention was focused, his presumptions about human services and the people who used them (also the social workers who delivered them), and his value orientation. Only then could one decide how to try to modify that definition and, thus, how to prepare the case.

Preparation of One's Case

Assuming you have gained access to the bureaucracy, how do you maximize your impact? It is clear from what has been said that an exhaustive grounding in the details of the legislation is necessary. Beyond this, since legislative intent is an overriding consideration–the touchstone that everybody will use to justify a particular interpretation of policy–the advocate must research what led up to the final enactment of the bill. At the federal level, *Congressional Information Service* will lead you to transcripts of committee hearings and committee reports. *Congressional Quarterly Almanac* and *National Journal* have background information on major policy issues. These three periodicals can be found in university libraries and some large public libraries. At the state level, you may have to rely much more on personal contacts with the people who lobbied the legislature before final enactment. Staff aides to friendly legislators are another potential source. Aside from legislative intent, your case needs the same thorough investigation required for any brief. The fact that you may be dealing with an expert on the subject–though not necessarily–should not daunt you. The worst that can happen is that your message will fall on deaf ears.

Presenting One's Case

All the rules that apply to lobbying elected officials are equally relevant here: making the initial contact; writing a confirming letter; finding out everything you can about the person you will be visiting; making sure to get to your destination on time, but being prepared for a rescheduling or talking to a person you did not expect to; being short and to the point; being gracious, whatever the response; providing a one-page summary before leaving; writing the follow-up letter.

Lobbying by letter may be the only way to get your message across–for example, if the target is in Washington, DC, and you are in Salem, Oregon. Because the appointed official has less need than an elected representative to curry your favor as a potential voter, it is easier to ignore a letter. At least if you see the target in person you know you had his or her attention, if only for the moment.

Letting People Know

Because of the hidden nature of this phase of policymaking, it is doubly important to let others know you made the contact. Your representative and senator should be informed. Having a say in the agency's budget appropriation, they have a kind of clout you lack. Remember that fear of having the agency's budget cut is the first concern of an appointed official. Friendly advocacy groups also need to know, though as was said previously, the foray into the bureaucracy should be planned in conjunction with such groups if at all possible.

POINTS TO REMEMBER

1. Lobbying involves an exchange between you and the target. Be clear about what you want from the target and try to figure out what the target wants from you.

2. Your power base determines your potential ability to influence decisions. Coordinating your work with allied advocacy groups multiplies your power base.

3. Get as much information as possible regarding the target and his or her constituency. In particular, what forces affect the target's political fortunes? What are his or her special concerns and biases? How much weight does he or she carry with colleagues?

4. Careful preparation, prior to any kind of lobbying, pays off many times over.

5. Your presentation should be organized around the issues that are most important to the target.

6. Take along a one-page summary of your case when you visit the target.

7. Everything you do, from the moment you enter the outer office until you leave, should be with an eye to maximizing the positive impression on the target and all staff members, including secretaries.

8. Follow up the visit with a letter of thanks, with copies to all advocacy groups with which you are involved on the issue.

9. Group visits have several advantages over solo visits, but they also have risks. To minimize the latter, insist on careful selection of the delegates and thorough preparation of everybody involved.

10. Letters can be an effective alternative to in-person visits. At least as much care should be taken with letters as with visits.

11. Petitions have little value. Opinion wires are expensive; there are probably more effective ways to use your lobbying resources. Telephone calls are relatively weak but are far better than not lobbying at all.

12. It is harder to gain access to appointed officials than elected representatives. Do not feel insulted if somebody seems to be trying to avoid you.

13. Thorough knowledge of legislative intent and of the details of policy are essential when one is trying to influence the drafting of regulations. Keeping the agenda sharply focused maximizes your impact.

14. It is especially important to alert your congressional or legislative representatives as well as allied interest groups that you have been in contact with the appointed official, and the of nature of your input.

Chapter 9

Working with a Live Audience

In Chapter 10, we will look at how testimony is presented in a hearing. That involves speaking in public before a live audience with its own culture and rules of procedure. First, however, it is necessary to cover basic principles of all public presentation. That is the subject of this chapter.

The title means exactly what it says: working *with,* which means actively involving the audience in the work. I have talked about the approach in this book as being audience-centered. Audiences are not so many open jars into which we pour our arguments; they are active participants in the process. The basic task is to *create the conditions for self-persuasion.* A critical issue, then, is the kind of audience one is dealing with and how it defines the world; more specifically, the subject matter under discussion. And there are all sorts of audiences.

So this chapter will talk a lot about audiences and much less about public speaking. Thinking more about the audience and less about yourself may help to calm any jitters you might have. To paraphrase an old observation, 90 percent of all Americans are nervous about speaking in public and the other 10 percent are liars. If you do not feel at least a slight shudder when about to address a strange audience, maybe something is not happening that should be. The nervousness is what sets the adrenalin flowing and thus is essential to doing an effective job.

The first time I felt very uncomfortable in front of an audience was when I was 11 years old. I was the master of ceremonies for a YMCA presentation to an auditorium full of adults, and I froze in my tracks for what seemed like an hour while the audience tittered. Somebody in the wings whispered my cue and off I roared. But I went home miserable that night, sure that I had ruined the entire program.

The last time I felt very uncomfortable in front of an audience was about a year ago. While introducing another speaker I had the sense that it was not going smoothly. This time I did not freeze. One learns how to get unstuck. But that feeling is never too far away. Which is a good thing.

AUDIENCES

If possible, you should do a thorough analysis of the audience long before you make your presentation. You want to know not only what will sit well with them but also their potential for influencing others. If you are asked to speak to a community group, the person who invites you can tell you a lot about the group. Size and general characteristics, of course, but also what they are likely to know about the subject and their basic orientation to it. Who else has spoken to this group, what was the content, and what was their reaction? Program planners are usually happy to share this kind of information, but the fill-in may be on the vague side.

Now comes the real research. If you know somebody who knows this group, ask for his or her impressions. Again, push past the abstractions. Obtain a recent list of the officers of the organization, assuming there are officers. If you will be talking to a subgroup within a larger body–for example, the social action committee of a church or temple–who are the key members of the subgroup and do they have the support of the larger organization? Churches and temples have pastors and rabbis. Who are they, what is their relationship to the members, and what is their orientation to your subject matter?

Rieke and Sillars (1975:164) suggest in-person interviews with audience members beforehand. If this is not practical, telephone interviews are a reasonable alternative. If this seems excessive preparation for making a presentation, consider the case of Garrison Keillor, the well-known radio personality.

A few years ago Keillor brought his program, *A Prairie Home Companion,* to the college in my community. He spent the preceding week on location, getting a feel for the place and the kind of audience he would encounter. Prior to that, his staff studied a wide assortment of documents including back issues of the student newspaper and the local weekly. By the time of the show he knew a great deal about the college and the community and sounded that way.

Being able to demonstrate a familiarity with the audience says to them that they are important, worth the effort it takes to know them. Having names to connect with helps you establish rapport with them. But the primary purpose of the research is to know how to help them define the subject the way you want them to.

What to Look For

1. Are you dealing with one audience or several? If the latter, are some more important to reach than others?
2. What concerns are uppermost in members' minds? It is these concerns you want to tap into right at the beginning, to draw the audience into your orbit. You and they need to be working on the same problem together.
3. What do members know about the topic, and what do they "know" (presume) in advance? What they really know is important, because it is what you build upon in furthering their understanding. What they *presume* to know may pose a barrier to further learning. Nobody gives up presumptions easily.
4. How do they feel about the subject? This is different from asking what is uppermost in their minds. If the subject involves a particular risk population, are members of the audience positively disposed toward that population? If a government program, is the audience inclined to favor such a role of government? (Research is particularly important here because of your own tendency to stereotype audience reactions.)
5. How do they feel about you or people like you? You have an identity–age, sex, race and ethnic, class, religious, educational and occupational, even height and weight. It will influence how your message is received. Without other clues, audience members will use intellectual shorthand to size you up and decide how they should receive your message. That does not mean you should try to be someone you are not. For example, I would not shave off my beard to please an audience, but I

would want to know what the group is likely to feel about people with beards.

6. How do you feel about people like them? Honest answers only. After all, you do not have to tell anybody else your secret dark thoughts. If you have a problem with elderly people or Asians or Caucasians or African Americans or macho men or Catholics or Jews, admit it to yourself. More on what to do with that bit of self-insight later.

I once worked in a rural area where I was *the* professional social worker for miles around. As luck would have it, the night I was supposed to speak to a service club in a distant part of the county about child welfare work, the roads decided to coat up with ice. I arrived only a short time before I was scheduled to speak–meaning the dinner I was getting for my troubles was bolted down in a hurry. I had assumed that this group was counting on me for its program, and if I canceled at the last minute their evening would be ruined. Not exactly. It turned out that I would be going on right after George told about his experiences working for the rural telephone company. Just to put his listeners at ease he told a racist joke. It went over just fine, of course. Oh yes, said the person in charge after George finished, we have invited the new county child welfare worker to speak.

I was sure they hoped I would say, "Well, in view of the weather and all, I guess there won't be too much point in spending a lot of time hearing from me," and let them go home. Instead I decided, "No way. You and I are going to go through with this." Hating service clubs, rural anything in general, and this group in particular, I then gave them the same stock speech I had been giving to church groups and PTAs around the county.

There were no questions after I got through, I received a polite spatter of applause and we went our separate ways. At least by then the roads were a little more navigable.

My point in recounting this horror story is that, having grimly decided to see the thing through, I could not get past my mindset to really work with that audience. I should have decided either to bow out after a brief response and write it off as a lost occasion or to treat it like any other opportunity to educate a group of people who needed it. It so happens that service clubs in that part of the world were extremely interested in children, and their members regularly volunteered in various youth-oriented projects.

But I "knew" there was no hope of reaching this audience. Take away the icy roads, the rushed meal, and George's speech. Would my judgment have been all that different? I am not sure it would have, because I already "knew" about this kind of crowd, and the events of the evening simply reinforced my preconceptions.

Talk to a Caucasian who has just had a negative experience with an African American, or vice versa. You may hear: "I'm not a prejudiced person. My whole life I've been open-minded, but you see what happened when I trusted one of them." Ask what the person knew about "them" before the incident. Chances are, down deep, the person really expected this sort of thing all along. The bad experience simply confirmed what he or she always "knew," canceling out many good experiences that did not fit into expectations.

The basic point to remember: When probing your presumptions about your audience, dig deep and do not be afraid to acknowledge what you find lurking below the surface. If you cannot get into the right frame of mind, cannot accept the audience as somebody worth working with, better look for another speaker. I am not saying you have to love every audience any more than you have to love every legislator you lobby, but you have to believe there is something to work with. Hostile audiences are discussed in the following section.

Kinds of Audiences

Your research should give you a fairly good picture of how much the audience knows about the subject, how involved in the issue it is, and whether friendly or hostile. Each type of audience requires variations in approach.

Informed Audiences

These tend to be the most intimidating but are actually easier to work with than those who know nothing about the subject. You need to have done your homework on the subject, but you do not have to be the all-wise expert. Remember that you and the audience are sharing responsibility for the communication process, and you are creating the conditions for them to persuade themselves. Put your listeners' knowledge to work.

You have been invited to speak to the administrators of community mental health centers about a bill that would change the state formula for reimbursement and require additional paperwork. Your mission is to get these administrators to actively oppose the bill. These are the experts on running mental health centers; you are not. How can you tell them anything they do not already know?

Begin by not assuming they know anything about the particular legislation. Most of them have been too busy running their centers to pay much attention to state politics, even where it concerns them. Fill them in on the basic components of the bill and its status. Then ask *them* to tell *you* what this would mean for their centers.

Silence. Do not worry, the anxiety is going to work on them as much as on you. Eventually somebody will speak up, and others will pick up the baton from there. If nobody responds, you can ask specific individuals to do so. I like to pick people whose body language and interaction with others suggests they are active listeners.

As they tell you, they are telling each other better than you could what a mess this measure would make of their operations. Now you and they are working together. You have created the conditions for them to persuade each other to go to work and defeat the bill. You have not tried to lecture to them.

Suppose one member of the audience who spends a lot of time traveling to the state capital says there is no point in fighting this bill; he has got it from his sources that the majority party wants it passed. At this point it is important to understand the limits of expertise. Regarding mental health center operations, you should defer to their knowledge; regarding what is happening in the legislature, you are on at least as solid ground as the audience, and are likely to be accepted as such. On that subject, do not defer but agree to respectfully disagree. Remember why you were asked to come in the first place–because somebody or maybe most of the group *is* ready to get involved. Let others in the audience deal with the naysayer. Again, work *with* them.

Uninformed Audiences

The problem here is that it is easy to confuse an audience that is not familiar with the subject. To confuse them is to lose them. If listeners cannot follow the music, they get bored and want out of the situation. The solution is not to be pedantic or patronizing, surely a temptation when you are feeling insecure, and suddenly discover you know more than the audience does.

The basic task is the same as with the roomful of experts: work with them by tapping into what they *do* know. Let us suppose you are trying to mobilize people against that same bill that would alter the state reimbursement formula for community mental health centers and create additional paperwork for agency administrators. This time, instead of center heads, you are to speak to the Junior Chamber of Commerce (Jaycees). You have surmised in your initial research that its members probably think mental illness is something that happens to somebody else. They have been seeing more "crazies" hanging around the public park in the center of town and understand this is somehow connected with the fact that the state hospitals have been discharging many patients. Your audience is only dimly aware of community-based mental health services and totally unaware of any pending legislation affecting them.

It will not make any sense to start by talking about House Bill 1234 or even the struggles of being a mental health center director. That is a foreign country to this group. They have to understand the local language before they can know what is going on. Skip that step and you have lost them. They will not say, "We did not understand what you are talking about," because nobody likes to acknowledge that. They may smile at each other or look bored. Somehow they will let you know it didn't work. Wasted evening–maybe worse than wasted if you have made them feel a little more alienated from the world of mental health.

Start by talking about what they *do* know–for example, people with whom they are already familiar. Tell about Joe, the salesman who starts having run-ins with his boss. Anybody here ever had a run in with your boss? (The heads nod and a few members of the audience smile in recognition.) Sure, we have all had days like that. But with Joe it was not just a few days here and there; it began to be every day. Customers, too. They would complain to the company or simply stop placing orders. What neither Joe nor anybody around him realized was that Joe was sinking deeper and deeper into a severe mental illness.

By this time your audience is drawn in, thinking about a believable individual instead of a mysterious abstraction called mental illness. Let us say your agenda is to move on into a discussion of the pending legislation, but in the question period audience members start swapping stories about individuals they know. This is where your audience is. When you see an opening, help them see the connection between the individual cases they know about and the policies that can have such a devastating impact on those individuals and others like them.

How do you actively involve the audience in the work? Ask them what they think about the situation and what people like themselves can do about it. You may have to come up with answers to your own questions, but the important thing is that they are actively thinking about the problem. One reason groups do not get involved is that they have too little information to connect with the issue. When you supply that information, make sure to start where they are and move with them step-by-step through the learning process. It will not happen all at once.

Audiences with High Involvement

If you sense that the group has a lot of interest and concern about the topic already, you do not have to waste time and energy getting their attention or stirring them up. But, you do need to make sure that you and they are talking about the same thing. Let us say you have been invited to talk to a junior high school parents' group about teenage pregnancy. They are obviously very concerned about their own children. After letting them know you share their concern, you start to discuss the need for more sex education classes in the schools. At some point you notice that these parents have become very silent. They are not laughing when they are supposed to.

The question period comes and a mother asks if you believe it is right to allow children to read the kind of filth the school has been sending home with them. Another says they did not have this kind of course when she was in school and she is just as glad they did not. As the discussion progresses, it becomes clear that what these parents are really looking for is confirmation of their belief that society has become too permissive, and the schools must be a bastion against that sort of thing. Sex education is the last thing they should be teaching.

There is nothing wrong with speaking to a group that holds this opinion, even challenging their preconceptions about sex education and the role of the schools. But you should prepare accordingly, not be caught off guard and put on the defensive. With a highly involved group whose concern runs counter to your own–for example, the parents who connect sex education with sexual license–avoid challenging their underlying fears. They are real, certainly not something that can be disposed of in an evening's confrontation. On the contrary, you may simply harden the attitudes. Instead, bypass the debate and keep focusing attention on examples of kids who got into trouble because of ignorance. They will remember those human stories hours later, when they are not feeling defensive.

When you sense that you and an audience *are* on the same wavelength, you can move on into working together on your shared agenda. We sometimes settle for too little in talking with an involved audience. You and they agree that the issue is vital to the future of the world, the meeting ends, and everybody goes away with a warm feeling. Instead, you should push to test their readiness to convert their intellectual awareness and concern into specific action.

Audiences with Low Involvement

This can be the most unsettling kind of audience to deal with–worse even than an outright hostile group. Mental health? Teen pregnancy? They are too engrossed in their own music to listen to yours. What you have to do is break up the mellow ambience and make them pay attention.

You have been invited to talk with a high school social studies class about Alzheimer's disease. They did not ask to come to class, or to hear from a guest speaker, or to hear about Alzheimer's. You walk in and immediately the glazed looks and easy distraction and horsing around tell you they are turned off. The teacher, who may have been having his own problems in involving the group, introduces you and it is time to go into your routine.

What to do? One way to hook them is to put them inside the skin of an Alzheimer's patient. Spot somebody who seems to be a natural leader and call her up to the front of the room. Tell her she is an 85-year-old woman with Alzheimer's. Tell her how the world looks to her and how she should behave.

What will be the response? Giggling. Great, you are beginning to hook them. "Why the giggling?" Shrugs, a few embarrassed expressions. Persist until somebody answers. Chances are the answers will be serious and revealing. Ask Sarah (the one you have asked to act out Alzheimer's) how she's feeling.

"Stupid."

"Why stupid?"

"Because you're making me do all this dumb stuff?" (Laughter.)

Ignore the laughter. As you model serious behavior it will help them get serious.

"What else are you feeling, Sarah?" Keep on until Sarah gets serious. Tell them that some percentage of them are going to be Alzheimer's patients. The parents of some before that. Grandparents even sooner. At some point the reactions may turn from giggles to anger. They will not like having to deal with this sort of thing. Nor should they be left to struggle with it alone afterward. Help bring them back down by the end of your presentation.

I once was asked to talk about the federal budget to a group of college students who had no particular interest in the subject. I called one student up and made him the federal budget and I showed how much of him went for interest on the national debt, defense, social security, etc. Each time I added an item, I pretended to hack several inches off of him, starting by decapitating him.

In another presentation on the federal budget I stood up on the teacher's desk so they could see me slice off parts of my body. It got their attention. Throwing one's notes over one's shoulder is a great crowd-stopper, unless one is dependent on being able to refer to them during the rest of the presentation.

There are things you can do with high school and college students that you cannot do with potential contributors or senior citizens. Some tactics that work with young people come off as demeaning with some audiences. But the basic approach is the same:

forcing yourself into the middle of their attention so they have to listen.

With members of an agency's board of directors you might ask the audience to imagine what it would be like to be on the receiving end of a particular policy. Sketch in enough details so they can place themselves in the situation. Even the stodgiest audience will tolerate a fair amount from a speaker. At the very least, put them to work.

By and large, then, the best way to hook an uninvolved audience is to get it actively involved by asking questions or having the members engage in some kind of activity. Your ultimate aim is to work with them, not entertain them.

Friendly Audiences

Like informed and involved audiences, these are the most gratifying to work with. Being able to dispense with having to overcome barriers to work, you and they can move ahead rapidly. Here the challenge is getting everybody into a working mode. If they like your jokes and cheer when you say abortion is good/bad/better than/worse than the alternatives, you will feel a surge of exhilaration. Next question: What are they ready to do about it? At that point the mood may shift as their natural resistance to committing themselves comes to the surface.

The biggest problem may be inside you, hating to dispel the nice friendly atmosphere and make demands on such a cordial bunch. There is a seductive quality to love fests between speakers and audiences, with neither party wanting to think about the morning after.

Hostile Audiences

They may not be informed but they are very involved, though not in a way you would like. There is a prior question to ask, of course: Why are you speaking to an audience you expect will be hostile? The answers may range from the fact that nobody in your camp is willing to, and to fail to show will be interpreted as lack of conviction about your position, to the need for this audience to know there is another viewpoint, even if they do not like it.

Begin by figuring out what the hostility is really aimed at: You? People of your ethnic background? Your position on the issue? What is mistakenly believed to be your position? Second, assess the audience's actual knowledge of the subject. They may be woefully uninformed. They may know a lot about it but have come out at a different point from where you came out. You can make a wrong reading of their level of knowledge if all of your knowledge has come from biased sources that agree with you. That should not happen if you have done the kind of preparation discussed in Chapter 7.

You are scheduled to speak on abortion. You are pro-choice and the audience is anti-abortion. (We will skip the question of why you are making this presentation.) You must understand how the audience is defining the situation *and you.* You will not sell this group on your position. You can, however, achieve two things: Sell yourself as a reasonable and thinking person and, therefore, your position as one that reasonable and thinking persons hold. Why bother? Because it may make future policy dialogues on this most emotional issue a little more reasoned, allowing for a meeting of minds on some issues. After all, if Gorbachev and Reagan could do it, you and the anti-abortionists ought to be able to.

Your task in the presentation itself is to break up a fixed perception of you. If you can honestly say, "I personally hate abortion," that will help. They then have to deal, not with a stereotype of a baby murderer, but with the specific reasoning behind the position you have taken. It can be a risky strategy unless you are crystal clear on how you moved from your hatred of abortion to your policy position which says they should be allowed.

Let us make it harder: You believe the woman has an absolute right to choose, regardless of whether it is a matter of conscience or convenience. You are a pro-choice hardliner. Actually, you have one distinct advantage: You can be totally consistent. The woman is a rights-bearing citizen. The other party is not until it emerges from the womb, and it therefore cannot be considered a bona fide party at interest. That is a great position from which to win debates, but not for selling yourself as a reasonable person. Pro-choice advocates range across the spectrum, and many of them have real difficulty with an out-and-out categorical option for women under any circumstances.

In any event, how do you sell yourself as a reasonable and thinking person? One way is to trace the evolution of your thinking. Since so much of the opposition to abortion has a religious base, you might tell about the way your religious philosophy developed. Either you once thought little or nothing about the abortion issue and gradually became drawn into it, or you once felt the way your audience did but have now shifted to the other side of the question. What influence did your parents have on your developing philosophy of life?

Regardless of how you present yourself, you should be prepared for questions. If you believe such-and-such, how can you hold a pro-choice position? It is essential that you have thought all this through carefully in advance. You should avoid coming off as someone who has arrived at your position without having thought things through.

In the question period, stay cool. Be very sympathetic, understanding, and respectful of their right to hold their view; they will be more likely to respect you for yours. To some questions, you may have to answer simply, "That's a tough one. I don't know the answer." As long as you are not conducting a debate against the audience–and I am suggesting you should avoid that–it does no harm to acknowledge there are some questions you do not have a good answer to, and people will just have to arrive at the conclusion that makes sense to them.

MAKING DEMANDS

What we have been talking about in the preceding section is getting an audience to work with you, and that means making demands on the audience right from the beginning. We are often willing to settle for a one-sided relationship with the people in front of us–I will put on a show for you; you let me know if you like what I did. But one-sided relationships are failed relationships, whether between a speaker and an audience, an employer and employee, family members, lovers, or neighbors.

Do not expect the audience to understand that right away. After all, we live in an age when people merely have to push a button to be entertained. If they do not like the show, they push another button. We should not be fooled by this apparent one-sidedness.

Even in television there is an ongoing exchange. Take the commercials. The most effective television ads get the viewer to participate by supplying the punch-line. The comic scene ends with somebody making a wry face or the plate of spaghetti about to tumble onto the floor. The viewers tell themselves what is going to happen: "Hey, the husband has to turn around and drive them back home for the suitcase he forgot," or "Now the spaghetti is going to mess up the floor she just cleaned." Then of course comes the real punch-line, also supplied by the viewers: "They should own a Zapmobile," or "She should use Lemon Peel on her floors."

The movies you talk about for days afterward are the ones that end ambiguously. You are not quite sure whether the central figure did go straight or whether the lovers made it back together, or it is not clear why the woman betrayed her friend at the end.

The late Marshall McLuhan (1964) asserts that a basic problem for Richard Nixon when he debated John F. Kennedy in that famous television debate–and possibly set the stage for his own political demise–was that he was too well-defined. Kennedy left the viewer something to wonder about.

If the "passive" medium of television demands that the viewer participate, an active audience is many times more important in a live presentation. From the moment you arrive on the scene, you should convey a sense of shared responsibility. It is not necessary to say in so many words, "I expect this to be a two-way process." You demonstrate by your bearing that you want a response.

You arrive early enough to work out arrangements with the woman who will introduce you. She already has your biographical information. If she asks you if there are certain things you want emphasized in the introduction, you have an answer: "I think, considering this group, they might be most interested in . . . " You are not usurping her role, merely responding to her question in a way that says you know what you want.

When it comes time to speak, check to see if the audience is scattered around the back of the room. If so, you can suggest they move up closer to the front. Give them time to do so. Ordinarily, some people will come forward. If they continue to hang back and the acoustics allow it, you might consider wading into the audience–for example, standing in the center aisle. If there is a public address system, tap the microphone to see if it is on.

Make sure you have their attention when you begin to speak. Take a few moments before starting. One deep breath will settle you down and also bring the audience fully alert. Then talk to them, not to your notes or the ceiling. If you need to check your written material, do so, then bring your eyes up to look at your audience as you speak. Above all, do not be rushed. Take time after each major point to let it sink in, before moving on to the next.

If you are on a panel including a number of speakers, make sure to use your allotted time. If it is 15 minutes, use your 15 minutes. If you are the second speaker and the presider asks you to be brief because speaker number one went way overtime, ignore the request. You have been asked to take 15 minutes, not solve the presider's scheduling problems.

You have completed your presentation, and the presider asks if there are any questions. There are none at first. Give them time, undoubtedly there will be. If you are on a panel and you have some added thoughts about a question which another panelist has answered, do not hesitate to volunteer your ideas. But do not be upset if all the questions go to other panelists. It may mean there are specific things the audience is looking for, which are in the special bailiwick of the others.

But we are getting ahead of ourselves. We need to go back to the point before the meeting when you are preparing your presentation.

GETTING READY TO SPEAK

Preparing the Speech

Every college or university library, and most public libraries, have books on public speaking, including how to put a speech together. I will not try to duplicate those, but instead relate speech preparation to what has already been said about involving the audience in the work.

Connecting with the audience. Your beginning should tell who you are and why this audience should listen to *you.* Are you a kindred spirit? Tell some things about yourself to make that point. Maybe instead they have never met a person like you. There are common experiences between you and the audience that help them make the connection with you.

Preparing them to work. What should they look forward to? What are you going to tell them? Does the formal title of the presentation really capture what you will be saying, or do you need to elaborate? What do you want them to do? It may be that you want them to pay particular attention to something about the speech, or to be ready to revise their thinking, or "I don't want you to accept everything just because I am saying it. Really think about what you are hearing, and if you have any questions I'll be happy to talk with you about them at the end."

A few major points. Always keep in mind that you are familiar with what you will be saying, but they are coming in cold. It is better to nail down two or three major points than to overload the audience so people go away confused. State these points succinctly at the outset, illustrate them with plenty of concrete examples that have meaning to this audience, then reiterate them at the end.

The concrete illustrations must be very concrete. The audience should *see* Mary X being stuck in her room in the boarding home because there is no drop-in center available for ex-mental patients. They should *see* the harrowing experience of the woman seeking an abortion at the community hospital.

Visuals. Flip charts, placards, chalkboard diagrams, slides, videotapes, hand-outs–all of these can help your audience literally see what you are talking about. It takes practice to coordinate your delivery with the displays, but it is well worth the effort. The added advantage of hand-outs is that people take something with them that can act as an added reinforcement afterward.

Think of how you want to use visuals. Should you give out the material in advance? If so, will that distract them from what you are communicating at the front of the room? Or will you need them to have it in front of them while you speak, to guide them through it?

The ending. A good ending gives the right snap to a presentation and sends the audience off ready to go into action. It pulls together the major thoughts you want to leave them with and gives the whole thing a lift. Maybe a final quote with emotional impact or an ironic twist. Maybe a joke, depending on the mood you want to create. If you are pressed for time, drop out other material from the speech so you have a chance to do the ending properly.

Script or Notes or Memory?

Should you read a paper, speak from notes, or wing it without anything in front of you? While the last of these can be rather impressive, it is too easy to lose one's way, go off on digressions, or simply get stuck if you do not have anything to cue you.

The basic rule is, do what is most comfortable. It is better not to read directly from a text if you can wean yourself away from it. If you do read, come up frequently to look at the audience. As you do, be sure to put your finger where you left off so you can quickly resume the delivery.

An approach I often use is to write out the whole speech, including sidebar comments. I then read it as if I were presenting it to an audience, timing myself. That way I know if I have to cut out major parts. About three o'clock in the morning of the day I am going to present I wake up with all kinds of ideas as to how I ought to change the paper. I then handwrite either on the same pages or on extra pages the various alterations I want to make. By then I am very familiar with the content. Depending on the kind of presentation, I may go with the full text or brief notes covering the major points I want to make. I usually take the text along, regardless.

In the meeting, a comment by the presider or another presenter touches off additional thoughts and I simply jot down a note at the top of the first page. When it comes time to speak, I begin with those last-minute thoughts, as a hook to what has already occurred in the meeting, then launch into what I had intended to say.

ON THE PODIUM

This can be unnerving if you have not done many presentations to audiences. Remember that the responsibility for making this work rests on the audience as well as you. You know your material thoroughly, better than they do. They expect you to be successful in making your presentation and are usually supportive. They feel more comfortable if they sense that you feel comfortable.

They will probably not see your knees shaking. If they do, they will forget it when you start to speak. Speak to individuals in the audience, aiming for people toward the rear. If they can hear you, the ones in front can. Do not focus on just one individual. Look at people in different parts of the room. Above all, take your time. Remember that you are familiar with the material and they are not. They need to be able to absorb what you are saying.

Asking Questions

A good way to get an audience working with you is to pose questions. If the size of the group lends itself to it, have them volunteer answers. Do not just jump in with the "correct" answer but show them you have listened to them. If possible, weave their answers into your presentation. This way they see this is a serious dialogue, not a gimmick.

Experienced presenters will ask people their names when they offer their opinions, then refer to them during the exchange. "Yes, Betty, you're agreeing with Sylvia. You both feel social workers should be able to offer abortion as an alternative. What do other people feel about that?" Sylvia knows she is really being heard, not just talked at.

Perhaps the size of the group does not allow for this kind of exchange. If not, you will have to answer your own questions. The more provocative the question, the more they will actively struggle. Act as your own devil's advocate. "Am I really saying that chronically mentally ill persons should be empowered to make decisions about their lives–even whether to take medication or not? That is precisely what I am saying. This is why. . ." "Tell pregnant teenagers where they can go for information on abortions? Absolutely, because if I don't. . ."

DEBATING

A debate is one kind of argument. It involves two or more parties in a dispute who seek to resolve their difference through reasoned discourse. Debates are conducted according to agreed-upon rules. Courts of law, deliberative bodies, and academic settings each have their own ground rules. One or another party may be convinced by the other's arguments, but often the arguments provide justification for accepting a solution based on other considerations, such as a difference in power between the parties.

Most of this book is about argument but little of it has to do with debating. Ordinarily, the people you debate with and the people you want to persuade to act are different. You should avoid debating with an audience. If you are debating another panelist before a group of people, be clear that your real audience is not the other panelist but the people watching. You want to give them the justification for supporting your position. When you prevail in a debate, it is easier for the audience to respond to your message. Even if you lose the debate, the audience may be strongly enough committed to your position that it will redefine the debate for itself, or find other means of justifying the position. Then again, the audience may be so committed against your position that it will ignore your superior arguments in the debate.

So accept debates as a useful process without over-estimating their significance. It is worth remembering this point because of the importance most people attach to the winning of debates.

Keeping the Audience on Board

Avoid allowing yourself to be maneuvered into debating with the audience. Once in that position, you must either lose, in which case your position is undercut, or you must win, which forces the audience on the defensive and may increase its resistance to your message.

You may, on the other hand, find it necessary to debate a member of the audience during the question period. You can win that debate without making the rest of the audience become the losers. But as you do this, it is important to try to focus on that specific person and his arguments and not allow him to claim to speak for "everybody in this room." If he tries that, ask him to speak for himself; you know that the others are capable of speaking for themselves.

I once spoke to a church group about school and housing desegregation a few days after a shoot-out in which three Caucasian police officers and four African-American civilians were killed. It had apparently been started by the civilians, who were members of an extremist group. A local newspaper carried a cartoon showing the three slain police officers.

When I finished speaking, a clergyman in the back of the room asked me how I could call for integration when three people had just been killed. That sort of thing did not happen around their neighborhood, he said, implying it was because there were no African Americans there.

I said he had just made my case. It was not three persons who had died but seven, I said, but we tend to be aware of what happens to white people and not black people. That is what happens to a society that lives in two separate worlds. I was not attacking the clergyman. More important, I was dealing specifically with him and his question, not generalizing to the rest in the audience. What if he had not given me the opening by asking the question in that way? I think I would have made very much the same point: that the ones who had started the shoot-out had done something no one in his right mind could condone, but that the seeds of this kind of madness lay in a divided society.

On another occasion, I spoke to a group of social work students about becoming advocates for their clients. From the audience, a self-styled radical whose body language had told me he was not buying any of this, said it was irrelevant to the struggle for social justice. His conception of social justice sounded rather abstract to me. I said that to some extent I agreed with what he was saying. Certainly, advocacy of the sort I was describing could not do it all. Then I mentioned a few other things of a more political nature that social workers were involved in. I wondered what he had been doing for social justice lately. He said he had been to a conference in Tennessee. I shrugged and moved on, the other students moving with me.

Formal Debates

If you are invited to participate in a formal debate, insist that it be under conditions that allow for a fair contest. If the proposition to be debated calls for action, the burden of proof is on the proponents. Sometimes program planners pose a question instead of stating an assertion, in the belief that it will attract more interest. If this is the case, attend carefully to the way the question is asked.

"Is abortion murder?" sets up an impasse. If you take the negative side you are probably licked before you start. Conversely, "Should a woman have control over her own body?" is a losing proposition for a speaker on the other side. "Should abortions be limited to cases in which the woman's life is in danger?" is a fair question, one which can be debated. In a strict sense, the question should be stated as a positive assertion–"Abortions should be limited to cases in which the woman's life is in danger"–in which case the burden of proof is on the party agreeing with the statement.

Debate questions that open up new territory, expose the issues, and force the audience to think in new ways are much better. For example, one might want to stimulate creative thinking about the funding of mental health services. "How can government assure a sound financial base for community mental health services?" has already fixed the parameters of the discussion. Government should deal with the problem. "How can a sound financial base for community mental health services be assured?" leaves open the possibility of private as well as public solutions. "Resolved: that government should be the provider of mental health care," pushes us in the direction of a yes/no answer, as well as inviting vagueness regarding the form of support which is desirable. "Resolved: that House Bill 1234, known as the Community Mental Health Funding Act, should be enacted" is very clear, moves us into talking in concrete terms, and allows the negative the opportunity to offer one of any number of alternative schemes.

Defining

The statement of the proposition to be debated merely sets the framework within which the parties will then seek to define what is at issue. You should base your defining strategy on your analysis of the audience and its prior definition. You should also anticipate how your opponent will try to define it.

If you speak first, try to establish the definition. Your opponent may feel it necessary to argue on your terms, which will give you a significant advantage. If the opponent goes first and presents a definition you do not like, be sure to present yours. If the opponent's position seems vulnerable even using his or her definition, you might add, "Let us say, for the sake of argument, we were to buy this way of looking at the problem," and then show its weakness. But do not stay there. Argue on the ground you have previously chosen.

Issues

Focus attention on the issues where you are strongest. You will have to respond to the opponent's issues in some manner, though if several are presented, you can pick the ones to spend the most time on. But get in, get out, and move the argument back to the turf you want to fight on. The longer you linger on the opponent's issues, the more the audience will focus on those.

Rebuttal

Challenging your opponent's case begins with your first opportunity to speak after he or she has spoken. If your opponent speaks first, take note of any vulnerable points and then raise and answer these briefly when you begin. Then move the focus to the issues you want to stress. Prepare a rebuttal in advance, but use it as a resource list rather than as a set speech. Canned rebuttals sound that way.

Instead of straight rebuttal presentations, the format may call for cross-questions between the panelists. You should be clear about the exact format well in advance and prepare accordingly.

Formulating Questions for Cross-Examination

These are questions designed to expose weaknesses in your opponent's case or underscore points in your own. Do not give the opponent an open-ended question with which to launch into a long speech. Do not ask obvious questions; your opponent will be prepared for them. The most effective questioning technique is a series of questions in which the opponent is led into a contradictory position or forced to acknowledge the wisdom of your argument. The opponent has three options:

1. "I am not sure what you are asking. Could you state it a different way?" If the meaning is obvious, say no, you cannot make

it any clearer than that. You may want to give a concrete example, but beware of blurring the point you are trying to make.

2. "I do not accept the premise of your question." If you have prepared well, the premise should be one the audience will accept. Say what the premise is and ask, "You really do not accept that?" This should push the opponent to an extreme position, one the audience is unlikely to buy.
3. The opponent answers something you did not ask. Point that out and restate the question. It is tempting to back off and simply drop the line of questioning or shift ground. Do not do either. The pressure is on the opponent, not you.

Whenever the opponent concedes anything, state, "Well, it appears at least we agree on. . ." And remember the cardinal rule of cross-examination: *Never ask a question to which you do not know the answer.* Cross-questioning in a debate is not a search for knowledge but an attempt to establish your position and undermine your opponent's.

You must retain control of the questioning when you are asking the questions. If the opponent seems to be using the occasion to filibuster, cut in and say, "Thank you," and go on to the next question. Keep the questioning coherent. Do not jump around.

Being Cross-Examined

I shall assume you have prepared both your case and that of your opponent, an essential step if you are going to debate. You have already prepared the cross-examination for your opponent. If possible, you have also gone through several dry runs with friends (whom you have instructed to be merciless).

Try to place each question in your opponent's strategy: Why is he asking this? Is he leading *me* down a logical one-way street? If you sense that is happening, challenge the context within which he is proceeding (not just the premises of the questions themselves). Do not vacillate, whatever you do. If he says you are taking an absurd position, say that is his opinion–there happen to be a lot of people who agree with your absurd position, such as (followed by a list of luminaries whose views you share). If he says you are disagreeing with some heroic figure, say good people often disagree. If the heroic figure has been dead a long time, say times have changed since then.

If the opponent scores a point and says, "Well, I guess we agree on . . . ," say, "Not at all. Perhaps I did not make myself clear," and launch back into your own case.

Maintaining the Dignity of Everybody

If you feel you are getting the upper hand in a debate, it is tempting to go for unconditional surrender. Resist the temptation. Leave the other side something, as long as it cannot be interpreted as support of their argument. Always show genuine respect for the opponent, no matter how offensive to you his position. He may even be nasty. No matter, be gracious in victory or defeat. Extending a handshake to the opponent at the end makes clear that this is a contest between ideas, not personalities. Even audiences looking for a strident confrontation appreciate this kind of civility.

The Non-Debate Debate

There are debates that are not billed as such. If you are going to appear on a panel and other presenters have a different perspective, be prepared for a debate. You may want a free-ranging exploration of ideas, searching, but open-minded. If that is what ensues, fine. If it does not, be ready to respond accordingly. You may have to point out that you are really involved in a debate. You may have to do a little educating regarding what constitute ground rules for a fair contest. As long as you are prepared, you should have no problems in making the adjustment.

The Impromptu Debate

In the midst of an informal discussion about a range of topics, you suddenly realize that this is really a debate and you are defined as being on a particular side. Be sure that is the side you really want to take, even if only to play devil's advocate. Refuse to let somebody else define your position for you. That leaves only the problem of handling arguments you did not specifically prepare for in advance.

Check out the audience. This is whoever is witnessing the encounter. Is it leaning one way or the other? Is it worth convincing? If the cards are stacked the wrong way, you may decide to bow out at the beginning. That way the only damage is likely to be to your ego, unless this audience is important for future issues and you need to come across as somebody who knows what he or she is talking about. In any event, do not rush into one of these ad hoc confrontations blindly. Above all, do not get angry or give into the temptation to draw blood. This is like any other except that it is without prior planning.

Connie Paige (1983:89-91) describes am impromptu debate that took place in a hotel lobby during a Right-to-Life convention. A pro-choice activist who had been participating in a demonstration outside wandered in to escape the afternoon heat–and found herself in the heat of verbal battle with, of all things, a nine-year-old. They were surrounded by 15 pro-lifers and a corps of reporters with tape recorders.

> "Legalized abortion does not mean that every woman will have to have an abortion," Braine explained slowly and patiently. "If it did–"
>
> "I know that," Maggie interrupted excitedly.
>
> "–then," Braine continued, "something would be very wrong with our society, because–"
>
> "I know that," Maggie repeated.
>
> "–because it would mean that women would feel there was no need or purpose to having children."
>
> "Yes, I know that. But the people who are for abortion, and the women who are for abortion, will have them, and then there will be only a few people around the world left, and even less people who are pro-life."

At this point Maggie's adult sister, Olivia, joins in, and Braine realizes that she is not just arguing with a nine-year-old child. She is asked questions to which she does not know the answer. When she asks Olivia whether she has ever had an abortion, the latter says she has, adding that it was a horrible experience. Meanwhile, nine-year-old Maggie joins the discussion from time to time, sowing confusion as she goes. Braine is clearly rattled by the experience. At one point she loses her temper, further conveying the image of an adult being bested by a mere child.

> "*I say I don't know and I don't think you know any better than I do!*" By this time, Braine was practically yelling in frustration.
>
> "There are millions of people waiting on line to adopt babies," Maggie persisted. "You don't have to have an abortion."
>
> "What about all of the little black babies who are left at adoption centers and bounced from one foster home to another and don't have parents who care about them?"
>
> "It's not true."
>
> "It is true. It is true."
>
> "Well, I would adopt them," Maggie replied smugly.

Anybody who has been cornered in an encounter like this can sympathize with Braine, the pro-choice activist. Taking on a nine-year-old probably seemed easy enough. Clearly she was not taking on a nine-year-old, but her adult sister as well, surrounded by a crowd of supporters. There may be a point to pursuing a debate under such lopsided circumstances–for example, smoking out the opposition's arguments for further references. But this was not what drove Braine on. So one has to question the advisability of even beginning the dialogue in the first place.

Assuming one does get caught up in such an exchange, what can one do? The first thing is to stay cool, not allow oneself to be provoked into anger. That way you have the best chance of figuring out a good course of action.

Keep the argument focused on your issues, not theirs. Braine was drawn into territory with which she was not familiar, and so had to acknowledge she did not know, when asked certain questions. For all she knew, she may have been conceding untrue statements. Just keeping the argument focused on *something* would have helped in this case. The debate went all over the map, a new issue being brought up before an old one was disposed of.

Avoid asking set-up questions that are well known by everybody. "What about the many women who will get abortions, even if they are outlawed, who will get them in back alleys with coat hangers . . . ?"

You know before you start that any anti-abortionists worth their salt have a pat answer to that question. You simply provide your opponents an opportunity to trot out their punch lines.

If she were going to get into this kind of debate, Braine should probably ignore Maggie altogether and insist on arguing with the adult sister. Allowing a nine-year-old to rattle you–however absurd the arguments–means you have lost the debate in the eyes of the surrounding supporters, and more important, in the eyes of the reporters with their tape recorders on.

Do not ask a question you do not have the answer to. "Have you ever been a mother?" Suppose Olivia says yes, and starts telling what a joy it is and how she shudders even to think of the idea of murdering sweet little Mary. Olivia has a better answer than that: She has actually had an abortion. It thus turns out she has a kind of firsthand knowledge Braine lacks.

At that point, Braine might have said she was sorry and shift the focus to empathizing for Olivia and her unfortunate experience. Instead, she was sufficiently locked into the debate that she could not respond as one woman to another.

In the next chapter, we turn to public presentations of a different sort: testimony in a legislative hearing. This calls for the same careful analysis of audience and preparation of arguments as in any other work with a live group. But in this case there are additional demands on the speaker.

POINTS TO REMEMBER

1. Working with an audience means actively involving it in the process.
2. A crucial first step is to do a thorough analysis of the audience and how it is defining the subject-matter.
3. As important as knowing how the audience perceives you is to know how you perceive the audience, including prejudices you may be harboring.
4. Audiences differ widely in how well informed they are, how involved they are, and whether they are friendly or hostile. Find out as much as possible about the audience in advance.

5. To involve the audience actively, you must be prepared to make demands on it.

6. Effective speaking to an audience requires careful preparation, beginning well before the event.

7. In a debate, the target is the audience, not the opponent. One should avoid debating with an audience.

8. Before entering into a debate, be sure it is the right debate, happening under the right circumstances. Impromptu debates are the most risky.

Chapter 10

Testifying in a Hearing

Public hearings before legislative committees can be very exciting. The witnesses, sometimes well-known public figures, give their testimony, then are exposed to a withering barrage of questions from committee members. Exciting like a television drama—and often about as spontaneous and unrehearsed. At the very least, everybody involved is acutely aware that this is political theater.

The official purpose of committee hearings is to provide vital information to committee members, but opinions on the extent to which this is true vary widely. Especially in Congress, the information gathering function tends to be secondary. Committees have staffs of experts who spend months researching the subject, briefing witnesses, and preparing questions *and answers* for committee members.

As for the interest groups that provide the testimony, if they were interested only in imparting information they would send their technical experts. Instead, they are likely to send high-visibility spokespersons, who are often colorful public figures.

Historically, state legislatures have lacked strong technical staff support, compared with Congress, so they have relied to a greater extent on committee hearings for an understanding of policy content. "The committee hearing is generally the most important source of information for legislators," wrote two political scientists in 1969, "and lobbyists tend to flock to the committee rooms as the focal point of their contact with legislators" (Zeigler & Baer, 1969:162-163). But in recent years, legislatures, particularly those in large states, have developed technical capacity rivaling that of Congress.

Then why has this venerable institution persisted all these years, if anything taking up more of lawmakers' time and energy? Obviously, they must serve a purpose for committee members or they would have been abandoned long ago. If we broaden our conception of information to include the political as well as the substantive, their significance becomes clear.

This is one way for legislators to hear directly from the range of viewpoints on a given issue. Staff tend to screen out certain information in response to what they perceive their bosses want to hear. In the space of one or two days, a committee member has paraded before him or her all the major players in the game. Furthermore, the actors are talking policy more than politics. This is a great way for the lawmaker to hear the major arguments that constitute the debate on the question. He or she has an opportunity to challenge or support witnesses.

It is not only those giving testimony who are on stage. Elected officials, whose careers depend so much on public exposure, have a fine opportunity to look wise and statesmanlike. The news media are willing partners in this process.

Beyond the purely political aspects, by holding public hearings a committee chair can generate support for a bill or expose it to public outrage, speed up or delay action. Particularly as legislative staff, administrators in the executive branch, and outside interest groups work in concert, they can do much to orchestrate support for a course of action through the hearing process.

There is a more subtle use of committee hearings: providing a safety valve for strong emotions. Given its "day in court," a vocal faction may be more inclined to let the movers and shakers have their way. Clearly, that can subvert the democratic process, but it also allows action to proceed on some issues that could produce a gridlock if every faction insisted on being actively involved every step of the way.

But as an advocate you do not have to decide on the socially redeeming value of legislative hearings. They are an integral part of the process and there is every likelihood they will continue to be in the future. Your task, then, is to see how to make the most effective use of them.

YOUR AGENDA AND THEIRS

In Chapter 4, we saw the importance of knowing where you want to go lest you discover you are in somebody else's tour book. The first thing, then, is to see whether you want to testify at all. You do not want to be a set-up or a punching bag for a hostile legislator. You may, however, decide to represent "the other side" in a hearing tilted in the wrong direction, willing to allow a biased chairperson to look fair-minded as the price of getting your own views out to other committee members and the public via the news media. The media like controversy, and newspapers in particular look for quotes from the opposition. This prevents the majority from creating the illusion that people are all of the same mind on an issue.

Try to figure out why the hearing is being held on this subject at this time. Assume the scheduling has been carefully thought out by the chair and majority committee staff to get maximum mileage. (Each party has staff, but the committee staff director is always in the employ of the majority party.) Friendly lobbyists and advocacy groups can help you understand the reasons behind the scheduling.

You will not automatically have a chance to testify. As you are trying to figure out their agenda, they will try to figure out yours. If you think the committee chair and his staff will want to keep you off the roster, you might try the minority staff, who will have some slots available. Your chances of testifying are best if you can go as the representative of an organization identified with one or another side of the question. The more powerful the organization, the better the chances, but then you have to find a way to interest the group in having you represent it.

Check the list of committee members. Is your representative or senator on the committee? That may be a way in. You will not be invited just because you are a constituent, of course. Somehow you will have to convince somebody that what you have to say is vital enough that they should hear you instead of one of the dozen other would-be witnesses anxious to speak.

If you are not allowed to testify, you can still submit written testimony. By circulating copies to the news media you can have nearly as much impact as if you appeared in person. If you have material worth sharing with the committee and its staff, your written information may be used in the deliberations.

Keep focused on what *you* want out of the hearing. Does it appear to be mainly an opportunity for a legislator to feed a gigantic ego? So what? You are not there to build character or give lessons in modesty. Keeping focused is even more important in the hearing itself. It may be tempting to score points in a debate with a committee member. The news media will of course eat it up. However, winning arguments with a committee member in a hearing is a little like a teenager's winning a debate with a cop on the street. It rarely happens, and winning may be worse than losing. Your opponent will insist on somehow having the last word.

Neither should you be put in the position of conceding that your viewpoint is wrong or of coming out looking beaten. More on that later. Testifying in a hearing is different from one-on-one lobbying in one crucial respect: It goes on in a goldfish bowl. Maintaining one's own dignity and allowing committee members to keep theirs is a must.

It has been said repeatedly that policy advocacy is not a solo activity. Particularly since hearing testimony is public and may become part of a permanent record, it is important to find out in advance who else is testifying and touch base with allies. In this way, your approach can be consistent, if not coordinated. It may be possible for two or more witnesses to divide the territory in order to cover all the important points. How do you find out who is scheduled to appear at the hearing? The staff director (who can be reached through the chairperson's office) will be willing to share that information. Knowing who the friendly *and* unfriendly witnesses are to be will help you decide where to focus your own remarks.

AUDIENCES

While figuring out why you should testify and what you want to achieve, you will have been thinking about where you want to aim your message. Are there issues on which you can educate the committee, say, out of your work experience or personal situation? If so, why are you using the hearing route, since you could share this content with staff members directly? Are you interested in providing ammunition for friendly committee members? If so, you will want to alert them in advance, so they can be prepped to ask helpful questions.

One potential audience for any public hearing testimony is the news media and, through them, the public. They may or may not be someone you specifically want to reach, but you should take them into consideration. Sometimes they are the *real* audience. You will need to prepare enough copies of your written statement (discussed below) so they can be distributed to all committee members, with additional copies for reporters, allied advocacy groups, and your own representative and/or senator.

Not only do you want all these to see your material, but you want them to be aware that you presented testimony. In the eyes of your representatives you cease to be merely one more vote. Elected officials always pay attention to constituents who are informed, articulate, and willing to express their views in public. Your potential role at election time is not lost on them.

Your main pitch will be to the priority audience, but you must keep in mind the secondary ones as well. Regardless of your priorities, there is one group of people who warrant particular attention—the committee members. By being thoroughly familiar with them, their biases and concerns, and especially the make-up of their districts, you are in the best position to anticipate the kinds of questions you will get from them.

In Chapter 8 we looked at ways to case an individual lawmaker. The process is essentially the same for committee members. Be sure to check beforehand and find out if this is to be a meeting of the full committee, a subcommittee hearing, or an inquiry conducted by a single legislator. As you gather information on the committee members, keep in mind that they will be in the public eye, not talking with you in the privacy of an inner office. Everything is on the record, and they are keenly aware that they are performing in front of an audience.

PREPARING TESTIMONY

You have two tasks at the outset: establishing your credibility (you are knowledgeable and sincere) and focusing the audience's attention where you want it. As in the case of one-on-one lobbying, your aim is to get your audience to define the situation the same way you do. The task is complicated by the fact that you are communicating simultaneously with several audiences, and what you say is likely to become part of the permanent record. From the beginning of your testimony, you must seize the initiative and focus attention where you want it. You must also establish your own credibility.

The Written Statement

Although, as we shall see, some witnesses submit no written statement, there are several good reasons for doing so. As Sharwell (1978) points out, the document states very clearly that you have approached this task in a professional manner; in short, you mean business. With such a statement, you can provide a more extended discussion of the issues, with added evidence, than is possible within the time constraints of the hearing itself. It is the written material the news media are most likely to use, unless you are sufficiently good theater to warrant live coverage on television. The statement will become part of the permanent record, which committee members and others can consult later. Most important, perhaps, in writing the statement you are forced to be very disciplined in formulating and expressing your ideas.

Great care should be taken in preparing the written statement. You will draw heavily on your policy brief (see Chapter 7), but the statement for presentation to the committee will be different in several respects. You will not present the opposition arguments, unless to set them up to be knocked down. Initially, you will want to establish who you are, whom you represent, and basically why the committee should listen to you. In the main body of the statement you should organize the major points specifically for the audience to which they are directed. If the need for action is generally conceded, you may even bypass that portion of the argument entirely. If feasibility questions are paramount, you may decide to lead off with those.

Sharwell (1978) suggests starting and ending with the strongest points, leaving the less crucial ones for the center of the paper, the idea being that a strong start and finish leave the best and most lasting impression on the audience. Kleinkauf (1981) says the written statement should be short, no more than two typewritten pages, and should focus on broad principles rather than be too specific. Her reasoning is that in the constant jockeying that goes on in the legislative process, one should have maximum flexibility.

It may be desirable to think in terms of two written documents: a basic position paper that one's sponsoring organization can support (one couched in generalities), and a statement prepared explicitly for a particular hearing. However you decide to go, the most important thing is that your reasoning be tight and your evidence convincing.

In 1979, Senator Daniel P. Moynihan held hearings in Buffalo, New York, on toxic waste cleanup in Niagara Falls (U.S. Senate, 1979). The announced reason for the hearings was to gather information to assist ongoing deliberations on a proposed Superfund for cleaning up hazardous materials.

We shall see how three witnesses representing different interests approached the task of giving testimony. The first was Bruce D. Davis, a Hooker Company official. The second was Lois Gibbs, president of the Love Canal Homeowners' Association (LCHA). The third was Dr. Glen Haughie of the New York State Department of Health.

I shall present excerpts from their testimony and look at what they were trying to do and how they went about it. Both Davis and Gibbs provided written statements, prepared with the help of experts. The experts could have done the testifying, but the impact of a senior official of the company and the woman whose name and face had become well known was important. We are always selling two things: our content and our credibility. First, Davis of the Hooker Company:[1]

> Hooker is deeply and vitally concerned with the problem of the disposal of wastes–what we as individuals and a society no longer want, no longer need or no longer use–not just locally, but nationally, for this is indeed a problem national in its scope. I understand that various Federal legislative proposals have been brought forward, and I am pleased to see the beginning of discussion for possible national solutions to this problem.
>
> [Davis describes the work of Hooker cleaning up toxic wastes and developing new technology for that purpose. The testimony is detailed and at points technical.]
>
> Finally, I will share with you some thoughts and concerns about legislation dealing with the disposal of hazardous wastes. In developing legislative approaches . . . we believe it

[1] See U.S. Senate, 1979: 12-18, 33-38, and 48-53.

> essential to keep in mind that in both origin and scope, these problems run far more broadly than Hooker, or the chemical industry, or even industry as a whole. They run far more broadly than the Niagara Frontier and New York State.
>
> The recommended approach in the bills introduced in Congress thus far is a super fund or ultrafund. We believe this is a viable financial solution. However, it does need considerable refinement. . . .

Davis ends his testimony with a set of recommendations for limiting the uses of the Superfund, for example reserving it "for emergency and imminent hazard type situations and not as a monetary source for total reclamation of the land." He also proposes a limit on total payouts "to prevent abuses of the fund."

This witness has two audiences to deal with. One is Senator Moynihan, who as chair of the Subcommittee on Environmental Pollution has a pivotal role in shaping the federal government's toxic waste policies. The other is the citizenry of the Buffalo-Niagara Falls region. The local news media are sure to report extensively on this hearing. Davis must rely on media representatives to carry his message to the public, possibly adding their own editorial "spin" in the process.

He begins by addressing the latter audience. Rather than dwell on who did what at Love Canal—a debate in which Hooker is bound to lose, no matter how valid its arguments—he focuses on his company's image as a concerned and responsible member of the community. He defines the problem as national, not local. In fact, the local waste disposal sites are not even mentioned until well into his testimony, then only as illustrations of certain types of pollution problems.

We are all culprits when it comes to toxic waste, says Mr. Davis. Note the early reference to what "we as individuals" do. Later, "I urge you not to let the focus of recent public attention, or the focus of my remarks today on the chemical industry, lead you to believe that the problem of hazardous wastes is limited to industry alone."

The terminology is carefully chosen. Never does the word "toxic" (poisonous) appear. Wastes are at worst "hazardous," which puts them in the same category as cigarette smoking.

For his other audience, Senator Moynihan, Davis is more specific, at points technical. He knows enough not to oppose the proposed

Superfund legislation outright—another losing debate, given the public mood. Instead, he urges a number of "refinements," mainly aimed at limiting the potential cost to companies like his own.

The witness is defining more than the problem. Throughout, he is also defining himself as a trustworthy source of information. He does this partly by going into technical matters in some detail, in effect becoming the patient teacher of the senator. Rather than be affronted by this implicit role reversal, Senator Moynihan, a former university professor, appears to welcome Davis's testimony and even submits to him a list of questions for further elaboration after the hearing.

Bruce Davis has the company's counsel, Thomas Truitt, at his elbow during his testimony. Lois Gibbs, the Love Canal Homeowners' Association (LCHA) spokesperson, brings along Dr. Beverly Paigen, a cancer researcher who has been a consultant to the citizens' group.

> First of all, my name is Lois Gibbs and I am president of the Love Canal Homeowners' Association (LCHA). The LCHA is a citizens group consisting of over 1,000 families, representing more than 90 percent of the residents of the area. LCHA was formed to deal with the problems of living near the Love Canal dumpsite.
>
> I would like to address the issue of the adequacy of present local, State, and Federal Government response to hazardous waste emergencies. At the start I would like to say that upon learning of the situation at Love Canal, the State moved very quickly to begin health and environmental studies. They also put into effect a remedial construction plan which would attempt to reduce chemical migration from the Love Canal. Although there are many problems which I could discuss, I will limit my testimony mainly to the experiences I have had in dealing with the different State agencies involved at Love Canal. . . .

Midway through her testimony, Lois Gibbs is asked a question. Dr. Paigen, who has been sitting with Lois Gibbs, then interjects a comment and from then on questions are directed to her instead of

Gibbs. Clearly, Dr. Paigen rather than Gibbs is seen as the real party to deal with.

Senator Moynihan's staff has filled him in on what Lois Gibbs will say. They may have even given her suggestions on what to say. She is not there to instruct him on toxic waste disposal but to give him leverage. Even within the Buffalo area, the senator is no doubt receiving conflicting messages. Environmentalists and members of the LCHA are telling him to take strong action, maybe to crack down hard on companies like Hooker. But chemical companies are big employers in that part of New York State, so there is bound to be a sizeable faction telling him to go slow. Graphic descriptions of the plight of Love Canal residents, picked up and amplified by the news media, make it easier for the Subcommittee on Environmental Pollution to act.

Lois Gibbs may or may not have calculated this, but a U.S. Senate subcommittee hearing in her own backyard is a banner opportunity to get out her message. She does not have to fight for media attention–a chronic problem of grassroots organizations. The senator, being an experienced politician, knows how to maximize the media coverage of an event. He thus helps Lois Gibbs in her task of getting exposure. The hearing is sure to get good play in the local press, but in addition the wire services may air her remarks nationally. Her task is simpler than that of Bruce Davis. She has a single, straightforward message: The little people, having been the unwitting victims of industrial carelessness, are now suffering unnecessarily from bureaucratic callousness and incompetence.

This is the same message she has been presenting in state hearings, television interviews, and news releases. Everybody in the news knows what she is going to say, but it still has a freshness and authenticity that means it will make the headlines again. This is not unlike the stock campaign speech that becomes boring to reporters accompanying the candidate on the campaign trail but still sounds new when it is shown on the six o'clock news on the Hometown, Illinois television channel.

The introduction is probably something she says in her sleep by now: "[M]y name is Lois Gibbs and I am president of the Love Canal Homeowners' Association . . . a citizens group consisting of over 1,000 families, representing more than 90 percent of the residents in the area." Senator Moynihan already knows that, but there could be reporters around who do not.

She then goes directly to the theme of her presentation: Official foot dragging and incompetence are disrupting and in some cases endangering human lives. The Hooker Company is ignored. The real villain, she says, is the New York State bureaucracy.

By this time, Gibbs herself is news. Beverly Paigen could just as readily say, "This is especially alarming since on March 9, 1979, thick, black, oily leachate was found running off the north section of the canal onto the street. . . . " The word "leachate" would probably seem more natural coming from her–she may in fact have written all or part of the statement. But when Lois Gibbs says it we can visualize *her* children being exposed to the demonic brew, *her* house slowly sinking into the morass. It is effective theater, which in large part is what this hearing is about.

Dr. Glen Haughie, a New York State health official, uses a different approach. He brings no written statement and will rely on the questions and answers to bring out his message. As long as the focus is on the appealing housewife from Love Canal, the state officials are on the defensive. When it is Dr. Haughie's turn to speak, he tries to shift the ground of the dialogue by emphasizing what Lois Gibbs lacks, professional credentials.

> *Dr. Haughie:* Yes, Senator. My name is Glen Haughie. I am a physician. I am a graduate of Harvard College, Harvard Medical School, and I have a Master's in public health from the Harvard School of Public Health. I believe this is a university dear to you, sir, as it is to me.
> *Senator Moynihan:* Particularly that school of public health, if I may say. We will call you an epidemiologist.
> *Dr. Haughie:* Well, sir, I do not carry that title easily. I have spent a couple of years with the Center [sic] for Disease Control serving as an Epidemic Intelligence Service officer.
> *Senator Moynihan*: In Atlanta?
> *Dr. Haughie:* Yes. I was assigned to the State health department in Albany in the late 1960s. I have served as director of the Monroe County Health Department of Rochester, N.Y., for a period of time. For the past 3 years, I have been employed . . .

Senator Moynihan: We will accept your credentials, Doctor.
Dr. Haughie: I have no written statement, Senator. I am prepared to answer questions that you may have for the department. I may offer a couple of comments concerning the discussion of the definitional terms requisite nexus. They are definitional because from an epidemiologist's point of view, I think what we are saying is, is there a causal association between exposure for a given chemical, or group of chemicals, and an adverse health effect. This, of course, has been the concern on our minds in the investigation of the Love Canal situation.

* * *

If I may, sir, I respectfully disagree somewhat with the comment you made earlier regarding the department's apparent lack of effort to obtain information from residents of the area about their health status.
Senator Moynihan: Doctor, I do not recall myself saying that.
Dr. Haughie: I think the issue has related to our blue-ribbon committee. You may or may not be aware that we have convened a blue-ribbon committee on four occasions. This group of experts to which I just referred were gathered together in order to obtain their best expert advice on our data.
Senator Moynihan: I am going to exercise the right of the Chair to say again, what was it I said? I do not recall . . .
Dr. Haughie: I think, Senator, in response to a comment made by Ms. Gibbs concerning the closed door policies methods by which the department has . . .
Senator Moynihan: Oh, I did say something to the effect I wondered about the question of excluding persons who were not professionals. I meant not in the least an aspersion on anyone who is professional. You go ahead and correct the record.
Dr. Haughie: I am intimately familiar with the concern Ms. Gibbs raised. I am also intimately aware of the numerous efforts we have made to conduct public meetings and to try to explain to a lot of very anxious people the nature of our studies, the progress or lack of progress, and the efforts I think the department has made in trying to unravel a most difficult problem.

Senator Moynihan: Let me, then, correct that record to show that no aspersion was intended and that none remains.

Explain that blue-ribbon committee to me. Did you have a question of data analysis that you wanted a jury to say is this the way to go about it?

Dr. Haughie: From time to time, Senator, we asked physicians, toxicologists, statisticians, chemists, geneticists and epidemiologists, and others to give us advice on the design of studies, methods of collecting our data and also sought their advice in trying to interpret our data.

Senator Moynihan: Would you tell me for this record–and we are trying to get a record here–what you have done in the way of data collection in the Love Canal?

[Dr. Haughie goes into an explanation of current steps being taken by his department and the difficulties involved in carrying them out. Senator Moynihan continues to interject questions for clarity. He ends by urging cooperation between the state's efforts and those of Dr. Paigen.]

One gets the sense that Dr. Haughie knows where he wants to go but is not always sure of how to get there. His attempt to distance himself from the embattled housewife via professional credentials, his strength and her weakness, is a sound strategy, but he appears to have overdone it as Senator Moynihan in effect says, all right, we accept your professional credentials, let us move on. One basic rule of thumb is never to gratuitously irk your inquisitor. It is his show, not yours.

Dr. Haughie then proceeds to remind us of what is the state's most vulnerable point, its failure to sufficiently inform and consult the Love Canal residents. The question is one of indifference to the plight of ordinary citizens, not limitations in scientific expertise, which could perhaps be justified in the arcane world of toxic waste disposal. This is a classic case of focusing your audience's attention on the wrong issue, forcing yourself on the defensive. If Dr. Haughie wants to set the record straight, he can simply describe in detail the exhaustive attempts his department has made to involve the people affected.

Even assuming there is good reason to raise the issue, Dr. Haughie should direct his fire at Lois Gibbs. Instead he quarrels with something Senator Moynihan is supposed to have said, putting *him* on the defensive. Some committee chairs would have made it a point to administer their own put-down at this juncture, basically nullifying anything else the witness had to say. But Moynihan is not about to be diverted by this nonissue and the hearing proceeds. His final admonition to the two sides to work together could be interpreted as a subtle downgrading, since Dr. Paigen has no official standing and the state officials have tended to dismiss her work as lacking in scientific credibility.

Dr. Haughie may have in fact prepared a written statement and practiced delivering it several times, but one gets the impression that he has relied on his general expertise to get him through the presentation. Even if one feels comfortable in operating in this way, lack of a written statement means one is relying solely on the committee to bring out the points one wishes to make. Given the fact that the purpose of holding such a hearing has a large, if not exclusive, political component, it is wise to bring a written statement and spend a little time laying out one's position. The news media may or may not be interested in the content, but the chances are good that by the time you get to testify they have left the hearing room, with or without a document from the presenter.

GETTING READY TO TESTIFY

Especially if you have never testified before, you will probably die a few deaths on the way to the witness chair. The nice part is actually going through the experience and discovering that you did not die. Generally, the more anxious you are going in, the more of a high you will feel afterward.

The first thing to do is have a little conference with yourself. Mirrors are good for this sort of heart-to-heart. Look yourself in the eye and say (out loud), "I am scared." At this point you have taken the most important step of all: admitting to yourself that you are afraid. Next, say (also out loud): "I can do it." Not just once, many times–preferably with increasing volume. When your roommate gives you a strange look afterward you can say, "And I'm not afraid of you, either."

Now practice a little focusing, as in definition of the situation. Get your mind off yourself and onto business. If there is any information you lack about the hearing set-up–time, place, which committee members are likely to be in attendance, who else will be testifying, where you come in the order of appearances, how much time you will be allotted–get it from the staff director's office.

Have you done your research on the members? Have you decided how they are likely to define the situation? How you want them to? Now you are ready to plan your presentation:

1. Open with who you are. If your work or past personal experience is pertinent be sure to spell that out clearly. This is where you will establish your credibility as a witness. If you state your position title, be sure to make clear whether you are speaking on behalf of the organization, another group, or merely on your own behalf.
2. If you plan to speak about a particular issue, state that.
3. Make your major points concrete by using illustrations, preferably from firsthand experience, but do not neglect to state what it is you are illustrating.
4. At the end, summarize briefly what you have said and offer to answer any questions.
5. Practice delivering your testimony several times. Having a friend listen and make suggestions can be useful, but only if the friend does not have so many ideas that you begin to get rattled. A more useful role for your friend is to act as devil's advocate, raising questions both of you think the committee members might ask. Practice answering those, too.

GIVING TESTIMONY

On the day of your actual appearance, try to reduce stressors to a minimum. Give yourself extra time to get to the hearing room so you will not feel rushed. Cecilia Kleinkauf (1981) suggests going in time to listen to others testify and see which legislators ask what kinds of questions. The last thing you want to do is arrive in the hearing room out of breath, while everybody else looks mellow and bursting with self-confidence. If you know any friendly witnesses who will also be testifying, you may want to link up beforehand and go together.

Friendly co-testifiers are like friendly roommates. Avoid getting a lot of last-minute suggestions from them. It will only tend to confuse you. But they can point out who is who among the committee members and opposition witnesses if any are scheduled.

When your turn comes, take your time walking to the witness table. If you are shaking, chances are nobody else will notice–least of all the committee members. If there is water at the witness table, take a sip. It will help clear your throat and give you something to do with your hands. Avoid fidgeting, rattling papers, and other distractions. You can always fold your hands in front of you.

The chair will introduce you. If your name has been mispronounced or wrong information given about your job title, etc., quietly state the correction. It will be appreciated. Assuming there is a microphone, speak loudly enough so you hear yourself coming back through the sound system. If it is too soft, move closer to the microphone. If it shrieks at you, move back a little.

Initially speak to the chairperson. Thank him or her by name for inviting you to speak. If you are reading written testimony, bring your eyes up periodically to meet the eyes of the chairperson, then other committee members.

Above all, do not allow yourself to be rushed. If the chairperson asks you to wind up your presentation, jump ahead to your closing paragraph. If any vital details have to be omitted, say you can pick those up in the question period. Remember also that the committee members and the news media will have access to the full document

When you have finished, say you will be happy to answer questions and sit back. Take a deep breath. Wait–there may be silence for a few seconds while the committee members digest what you have said. You do not have to worry about the silence; that is the chairperson's problem, not yours.

FIELDING QUESTIONS

When a committee member asks a question, take a moment to be sure you understand what is being asked. If it is not clear, ask to have it restated or clarified. Naturally, that can be overdone.

Address your answer to the person asking the question, preferably by name. Make your answers brief and to the point and bring in concrete illustrations wherever possible. Do not ramble. If you have not fully answered everything asked, the questioner will probably follow up, asking for more.

Many questions will be friendly or neutral–at least you should start with that expectation. People really do want to know what you have to say about the subject. But there may be some questions which are not friendly. Below are a few problematical kinds of questions. In all cases, keep cool, treat the questioner with utmost respect, regardless of how abusive or off-the-wall the behavior.

Legitimate Debate

When you take a position on a controversial issue, you can expect to be challenged at points. That, after all, is an important function of public hearings–to air opposing points of view and expose them to critical evaluation.

Response

Chances are if you have done your homework, you are already aware of the major criticisms of your argument and have prepared a response. Plug in your answer and see if it holds. The questioner may persist. If so, see if the further questioning really advances the argument or is simply a rehash of what was already answered. You may want to restate your position on that issue, possibly adding an illustration, then let it go. If the committee member will not give up, shrug and say you guess the two of you agree to disagree and drop it. Below is an excerpt from a hearing on welfare reform in which two representatives of a public employees' union try to respond to questions about mandatory work requirements. They are opposed to making them mandatory. Some committee members feel otherwise. One in particular, Representative Brown, persists in focusing on that issue. The witnesses must respond to this, like it or not.[2]

---

[2] See U.S. House of Representatives, 1987: 404-406 and 409-410.

Mr. Brown [Committee member]: Thank you, Mr. Chairman. Mr. McEntee [witness], I appreciate your coming this morning and look forward to working with you to develop a bill in this area.

I noticed you indicated a concern about making jobs mandatory. Does this same concept transfer over to mandatory education and training? Do you feel it would be inappropriate to make those mandatory?

Ms. Meiklejohn: Well, I think again you have a problem.

Chairman Ford: Pardon me. Would you state your name for the record? I do not know whether you did earlier, but . . .

Ms. Meiklejohn: I am Nanine Meiklejohn, and I am in the legislative department of the union.

I think while that may be theoretically a desirable thing, again you have the problem of trying to do something with the limited amount of resources. You would be choosing to cover everybody and diminishing the quality of services that you are providing, and that is unavoidable in this current fiscal climate.

So, again, we think it is better to start off with motivated people who do well in the program, and as the program gains credibility with the welfare and the general public as a whole, that, in turn, produces more support for program expansion.

Mr. Brown: So, you think it is wrong to require people to attend a work program or a training program or an educational program as a condition of receiving welfare?

Mr. McEntee: I think it would probably be one of the worst things in the world to give them the training and the education and no place to go. I think it would just be tremendously frustrating and, once again, that is why the scope should be limited.

* * *

Mr. Brown: Well, that was not really my question, but I appreciate your comment on that area.

I wonder if you share my concern for what happens to people when you provide them with welfare benefits and ask for nothing in return.

Ms. Meiklejohn: I think that presumes that the recipients are not motivated to improve themselves, and I think that most . . .

Mr. Brown: No, no. I am sorry. I am not presuming anything. I am simply asking you what happens when you provide welfare benefits and do not require something in return.
Ms. Meiklejohn: Well, I think you have to look at what is involved in, for example, requiring a young teenage mother with a child to finish her education. We have to be prepared then as a society to make sure that her children are in a decent child care arrangement while she participates in the program. We have to make sure that she has transportation that does not involve her spending two hours going back and forth. We have to make sure we cover her other needs.
Mr. Brown: Yes, but if I understand your statement, your position is that even if we provide adequate child care and transportation, you are still opposed to mandatory participation in work, training, or education programs–is that right?
Mr. McEntee: Go ahead.
Ms. Meiklejohn: I think our concern is that we will write a law which will have the mandatory participation requirements and not in the end be able to follow up with the dollars to provide the services, and, so, when you are left with a range of activities that includes workfare and job search, it will draw the system into these activities because they are not as expensive.
Mr. Brown: I am not trying to put words in your mouth, but am I hearing you say now that if there is money available in a particular program, then you feel that mandatory participation would be appropriate?
Ms. Meiklejohn: No. I do not.
Mr. Brown: That is still a concern for others.

[Later another committee member picks up the mandatory v. voluntary issue.]

Mrs. Kennelly: Let me ask the legislative person something. Mr. Brown asked you about, did you still have reservations–did you have reservations about mandatory education as well as mandatory taking of a job.

How many children do you think would go to school if it was not mandatory that they go? How many people do you think; I do not know if you have got children. I had children.

Unless it was mandatory for that person to get educated, to become literate, to be able to get a high school equivalency, would go unless it was mandatory. Let us talk about who we are talking about.
Ms. Meiklejohn: It is hard for me to believe that a person who has a dependent does not want to seek a way to be self-supporting, and it is hard for me to believe that if she was given an opportunity, a real opportunity with a real promise to it, that she would not take it.

[Further along in the hearing another committee member comes back to the mandatory work issue.]

Mr. Chandler: I think that it is fair then to ask if we are sending a negative message to a person by requiring a work element of their asking for and receiving assistance from society, what kind of a message we are sending when we do just the opposite, provide assistance without any requirement for anything, for any contribution in return?
Mr. McEntee: I guess we just keep going back to the same situation. If we had a situation where we could provide all of these things with the promise of a job, then that most certainly is one set of circumstances.

* * *

We are trying to deal with the realities here. That is what we are trying to do, and not with a theory or what could happen or what may happen. We are trying to deal with the reality that the Federal government only has so many bucks, only have [sic] so many dollars, and to get as many people as we can in a voluntary way off those rolls, and let the American people see it as an unqualified success then maybe down the road a little bit, we can do other and more things.

The congressman then picks up on something McEntee has said about defense spending, and the focus shifts away from the mandatory/voluntary participation issue. The two union representatives have been queried by three different committee members on the mandatory/voluntary issue. In assessing the witnesses' argumentative strategy, we should begin by looking at their initial posture, which defined the battleground in the first place.

McEntee devotes about two-thirds of his opening statement to the mandatory participation issue, so he is inviting dialogue on that issue. His basic argument is that success is more likely if one starts with those who volunteer to participate; mandatory participation without sufficient investment of government funds in day care and other support services would end up hurting the children; and there would be a temptation to stress workfare, to the detriment of real job preparation.

Representative Brown asks if the witnesses' opposition is to mandatory education and training as well as mandatory jobs. Ms. Meiklejohn responds by reiterating the points laid down in McEntee's statement. Brown persists: What if you were assured of adequate education and support services? Would you still be opposed to the mandatory feature? The witnesses appear to be on the defensive, Meiklejohn saying the congressman implies that recipients are not motivated to improve themselves.

Brown will not be put off. He wants them to address the mandatory feature head on. He does not say, but might have, "Can you think of any circumstances under which you would favor mandatory participation?" The witnesses continue to skirt that central issue.

What should one do in response to this line of questioning? The most important step comes *before* the interrogation. Decide in advance where you are ready to draw the line in the dirt. Either you are categorically opposed to mandatory participation, in which case you simply say so and agree to disagree, or you decide under what circumstances it would be acceptable. Above all, avoid seeming to waver.

McEntee could have said under no circumstances would he support mandatory participation. He could have said, yes, if you will guarantee adequate education and training, or guarantee a job at the other end, then I have no problem with mandatory participation. Instead, his strategy is to keep focused on the circumstances themselves and say we must deal with reality, not some hypothetical wonderland.

Representative Kennelly raises the question of mandatory education. Is that really a problem? We have compulsory education for children. Do you think children would go to school if they did not have to? She has challenged the witnesses' stance at perhaps its most vulnerable point: not wanting to require people to enroll in educational programs which presumably can only help them escape from poverty, and which in any event are akin to apple pie and motherhood in this country.

Meiklejohn detects an underlying message in Kennelly's comments, a view of welfare recipients as unmotivated, and seeks to meet that head-on, as she did with Representative Brown. The exchange ends on an inconclusive note.

It is possible to challenge Kennelly's underlying assumption that one can isolate a particular part of the total package–education–and ignore the rest. But what about her comparison of school attendance laws and mandated participation in educational programs by AFDC recipients? When presented with an analogy–in this case between schoolchildren who might prefer to play outside than go to school and AFDC mothers–it is important to consider whether it is an appropriate comparison. Is making your teenager abide by compulsory school laws which apply to everybody the same as requiring female heads of households in poverty to attend programs with a dubious record of achievement?

Representative Chandler voices a common concern: You send the wrong message to the poor when they can get something for nothing. McEntee could have challenged the underlying assumption that the poor pay nothing for their status as recipients. That, of course, would not satisfy the congressman and could simply lead to a protracted argument about whether welfare recipients are motivated–an argument in which the witnesses would remain on the defensive regardless of how good their evidence. Instead, McEntee stays with his theme that the questioning assumes a world removed from reality; the reality is too little commitment of resources for services and no assurance of a job at the other end.

The respective parties to a debate want to score points and show that the opponent's position is wrong. But this airing of honest differences is an essential part of the winnowing process in policy making. We now turn to argumentative tactics that resemble legitimate debate but really are distortions of it. There is nothing unethical about them. They may seem unfair, but in the policy arena fairness is an elastic notion. Like beauty, it tends to be in the eye of the beholder.

The Outright Attack

Understand that in this case the quarry is not your arguments, but you. You can tell the difference by the fact that reasonable responses meet a deaf ear, the questioner shifts the ground, always in a way that makes you personally look bad. You can usually tell by the tone of voice and the facial language, although your judgment of those qualities may be too subjective, especially since you are under attack.

Response

First, make sure it is an attack, not simply difficulty in understanding what you had in mind. If you are asked, "Do you really expect us to believe that . . . ?" and that *is* what you intended to say, stick to your guns. People can disagree. Chances are it is *not* what you intended but has been pulled out of context, taken to absurd extremes or simply distorted. State what you did intend to say, possibly adding an illustration. Do not get into a debate–it is probably one you cannot win, given the hearing format and the fact that you are on their turf.

The Extraneous Issue

You get a question about something entirely unrelated to your testimony. Often this is an oblique attempt to raise doubts about your credibility as a witness. Again, the issue is not the subject matter but your image. Or it may be an attempt to put words in your mouth–a statement instead of a question, using you to corroborate the committee member's biases.

Response

Answer briefly and get the focus back to the main track. Do not try to spar with the questioner. If it *is* your image he or she is after, demonstrate your image by treating the questioner with respect and maintaining your own dignity.

On one occasion I testified before the state senate Public Health and Welfare Committee on a welfare reform proposal. I had a general knowledge of the make-up of the committee but had not done my homework on the individual members. Unfortunately, the ranking Republican member of the committee knew who I was. When I had finished my testimony and invited questions, he asked me if I had previously been the chairperson of the board for one of the State Department of Public Welfare's county assistance offices. (Yes.) And was it true that the State Auditor General's office had found a particularly high rate of suspected fraud in our caseload? (Yes. Implication: How could I be trusted as a witness since obviously we had not been sufficiently concerned about protecting the taxpayer against welfare cheats.) It so happened this senator and the Auditor General had issued a series of reports on fraud in the state welfare rolls.

I knew he was shifting the focus away from my testimony and on to me, but I had no choice but to respond to his questions. Rather than get into a major argument with him–for example, by pointing out that many cases of "suspected welfare fraud" are really staff errors and in most such cases outright fraud is not proven–I decided to try to keep the exchange brief and get back to the main thrust of the testimony.

Then I got a break. He asked me what we did when we were informed of the suspected fraud cases. We did two things, I said. The first was to tighten up on procedures in the office to minimize the risk of fraud. The second thing we did was remind the State Department of Public Welfare that our county had the highest ratio of cases to staff of any in the state, because of limited allocation of staff positions by the state. (Implication: If we had more staff, we would be in better position to monitor the caseload.) We were soon back on track with the discussion about the proposed welfare reform legislation.

Questions You Cannot Answer

These may be friendly, neutral, or hostile. They are sure to be unsettling. Here you have come before this panel as an expert and suddenly you can feel very awkward and unsure.

Response

Rule Number 1: *Never fake it.* Legislators can detect phony responses, and if you are caught in a misstatement, however innocent, your credibility will plummet. Say you do not have that information and you will try to get it for the person who asked. Then be sure to follow through promptly (and accurately!).

This should not be seen as negative. You now have an opportunity actually to extend your influence with members of the committee. As you acknowledge that you do not have all the answers, you come across as authentic and trustworthy. Information supplied to the committee staff later lacks the dramatic punch of testimony in the hearing, but it can actually have more impact, since it is not vying for attention with everybody else's testimony.

While testifying on welfare reform before a legislative committee, I mentioned in passing the economic impact of suddenly cutting tens of thousands of persons off general assistance–the certain result of the bill under discussion. I referred to a reverse multiplier effect. In economics, the multiplier effect is the tendency for additions to spending to have an impact on income greater than the original increase. Even small increments in spending can thus multiply their effects. (See Heilbroner & Thurow, 1975:384-387.)

According to the multiplier effect, placing a dollar of public assistance in the hands of a consumer generates more than a dollar's worth of economic activity. I reasoned that cutting back on the assistance would have a greater *negative* impact on economic activity than the original amount withdrawn. I called that a reverse multiplier. Actually, it is a multiplier, regardless of whether it is an increase or decrease, but to say reverse multiplier sounded more dramatic.

In the question period, the staff director of the committee asked me if I had any evidence regarding the reverse multiplier as it applied to public assistance. I said I did not but would try to get that information for him. I am not an economist, had only a general notion of the concept, and had no idea whether anybody had ever applied the principle to assistance payments.

A few days' research in the library produced an obscure study done a few years before for the U.S. Department of Commerce (Stein, 1975). Its author, an economist, had found that AFDC had a multiplier effect of 2.05. That is, every dollar in AFDC payments generated on the average $2.05 worth of economic activity. Other assistance categories had an effect between 1.90 and 2.00.

General assistance, a nonfederal program that varies from state to state was not included, but it stood to reason that its multiplier effect would stand somewhere between AFDC and the others, since it included some families with children and some adults. In round numbers, every dollar in assistance payments produced two dollars in economic activity. The greatest impact was on (1) rents and real estate and (2) wholesale and retail trade; that meant a predominantly local impact.

With the help of the staff of a poverty law center, I put together a report which described the reverse multiplier that would result from a sudden reduction in general assistance. We broke it down for each county in the state, so individual legislators could see the potential impact of welfare reform on their local economy.

Articles describing these findings found their way into six different newspapers in the state. None of this would have happened if I had not been asked that question I didn't know the answer to, or if I had failed to follow up.

JUDICIAL TESTIMONY: THE AMICUS BRIEF

There is nothing in the U.S. Constitution to suggest that the courts have the power to create new policy, yet we know that many of the most important policy changes in this country have come about through action of the U.S. Supreme Court. Potentially, lower federal courts and the state judiciaries have the same power. For this reason, class-action suits have become one means by which interest groups have been able to initiate change. During the 1980s, the opportunities to use the courts for social change were narrowed, but such suits still play an important role in reforming social institutions.

If you are involved in an action of this kind, you will be working closely with lawyers. Decisions regarding the content of policy will follow the same principles as apply to other kinds of advocacy. You may participate, along with other supporting organizations, in deciding what you want to achieve. The process of getting there will involve technical knowledge of the legal system.

One way you may become involved in action through the courts is in helping to put together an *amicus curiae brief. Amicus curiae* means, literally, "friend of the court." The original concept was of "a bystander . . . without . . . an interest in the case . . ." (Krislov, 1963:694). But there is a long history in this country of using the amicus brief to advance the interests of a party to the dispute. Sometimes the initiative has come from the bench, to assure that all relevant interests were represented, but increasingly in modern times, advocates of a particular cause have filed briefs (Jenkens, 1981:146). In recent decades, the widespread use of class-action suits by advocacy organizations has resulted in a growing number of amicus briefs on behalf of policy change.

Who may file an amicus brief? "[A]nyone who thinks a decision might one day have a personal effect on him or her" (Faux, 1988:224). That is different from saying anyone should. In any event, the actual task of constructing a brief should be directed by attorneys. In some cases, poorly drafted briefs have set back the cause they were intended to help (Faux, 1988:271). The basic strategy is the same as that discussed in Chapter 7.

A series of issues forms the skeleton of the brief, just as is true with the policy brief. The argument must be logically tight and supported by solid evidence. The lawyers know the legal language and the conventions of the court–they are the experts regarding the audience–but you may well have crucial information they are not familiar with. Aside from factual knowledge of, say the welfare or mental health system, you know the critical issues in that field. It is sometimes easy to be cowed by attorneys, who are trained to be assertive and present themselves as knowing what they are talking about. This is all the more reason to look closely at the way they develop the case. You are not dealing with a personal crisis but a matter of policy, one in which you have done exhaustive research. Each partner–the lawyer and the amicus–brings his or her own kind of expertise to the endeavor.

In 1987, several mental health advocacy organizations sought the release of a woman from Bellevue hospital in New York City, where she was being kept against her will. The case, which came before the New York State Court of Appeals, was an appeal of a lower court decision which upheld her continued hospitalization. A coalition of five organizations of mental health consumers filed an amicus brief on the woman's behalf.

In the brief, they first established their interest in the case–i.e., their right to be heard on the matter. (Technically speaking, the amicus asks permission to file a brief, but permission is routinely granted.)

> *Amici curiae,* the organizational members of the Coalition for the Fundamental Rights and Equality of Ex-Patients (hereinafter the "Coalition for the FREE") are all groups whose primary interests and activities concern the promotion of public understanding of mental health issues and the protection of the rights of the mentally ill and of present and former mental patients. Members and clients of these organizations include many present and former patients, their families and friends, as well as advocates for the mentally ill. (State of New York, Court of Appeals, *Brief Amicus Curiae*, 1988:1-2)

The brief goes on to state the coalition's concern about the involuntary commitment to mental hospitals of persons who are not a danger to themselves and others. They make it a point to say they do not categorically oppose any and all involuntary commitments, but want to assure that it is "used as the last resort of a system favoring treatment by choice in the community wherever possible" (p. 3). This is not a class action suit, but clearly the petitioners see it as setting a precedent affecting many other persons in similar circumstances.

In subsequent sections of the brief, the main argument is summarized, then presented in full with supporting evidence. The argument is based on three points:

1. The lower court decision violates the U.S. Constitution, New York statutes, and court precedents.
2. There is no clear and convincing evidence to support the allegation that lack of personal hygiene posed a danger to the woman–a major basis for the lower court ruling. In fact, says the brief, sanitary conditions in institutions in New York and elsewhere involve serious health risks; in other words, the cure–hospitalization–could be worse than doing nothing.
3. There are no grounds for another finding by the lower court, that by verbally abusing others on the street the women posed a danger to herself.

Theoretically, the brief could refute the lower court's ruling by successfully establishing only one of these points. Instead, it addresses all three in order to maximize the possibility of persuading the appeals court to overturn the previous ruling.

The evidence used to support the three-part argument comes from several sources: previous Court rulings, scholarly articles in professional journals, and newspaper items. As was said in Chapter 6, the quality of these different sources varies greatly. In law, previous court rulings are one of the most powerful kinds of evidence. Newspaper items, on the other hand, are much weaker. But all have a place in the strategy of the authors of the brief. It is the consistency of the evidence from different sources that helps to give the brief its cogency (persuasiveness).

The contents and format of this amicus brief are very similar to most such documents. The writers of the brief begin by establishing their credentials and interest in the case, then summarize their case, then present the full argument, heavily documented by citations from legal precedents, the social science literature, and other relevant material on substantive issues. It is in relation to this latter kind of evidence–for example, research reports and articles in the journals in your professional field, along with your personal experiences–that you can be particularly helpful to attorneys writing an amicus brief. You may also need to help the attorneys understand the relevance of certain kinds of information–for example, the special needs of young children and other vulnerable populations.

An amicus must stand up to searching scrutiny. Preparation of such a document thus demands exhaustive research and tightly reasoned arguments. While the standards in legislative hearings are not so rigorous, the same principle holds there as well. Any testimony worth presenting is worth presenting well–a good thing to keep in mind if you are going to try to persuade a legislative committee. Not coincidentally, lawyers constitute a large percentage of the members of any legislative body.

POINTS TO REMEMBER

1. Decide in advance what you want to achieve by testifying, and to whom your remarks are really directed.

2. Do your homework: Analyze all targets thoroughly and figure out how they are defining the situation. Be sure of hearing time and place and any special rules to follow.

3. Prepare your testimony carefully and practice delivering it until you are comfortable with it.

4. Stay calm. You *do* know what you are talking about.

5. In fielding questions, be sure you understand what is being asked. Be honest. Keep your attention and that of your audience where you want them.

6. If you do not know the answer to something, admit it and offer to get more information on it. Then be sure to follow up promptly.

7. *Amicus* (friend-of-the-court) briefs require tightly reasoned arguments and strong evidence. They should be drafted with assistance from an attorney.

Chapter 11

Using the Mass Media

Question: What is it that has the power to make or break aspiring presidential contenders, that large corporations pay millions for, but that you can get at no cost?

Answer: Media exposure. That is the subject of this chapter. To a large extent, as far as you are concerned, media exposure means news exposure.

Why are Americans such news addicts? Why do they keep buying newspapers that are primarily rehashes of old news *and* watch the television news show while getting ready for work *and* listen to radio news on the way to and from work *and* catch at least one and maybe two television news programs after they get home?

According to Paletz and Entman (1981:16-18), the answer lies in the fact that we are driven by two complementary forces: threat and the need for reassurance. News keeps telling us about threats to our safety and well-ordered world, and then holds out reassurance that things will be all right or will get better. It is clear that we are never satiated. No amount of reassurance is enough; there will always be new threats tomorrow.

That we are so obsessed is not surprising, considering the wrenching crises this country has been through over the past half-century. Economic collapse in the 1930s, World War II and the advent of the nuclear age in the 1940s, Cold War in the 1950s, civil strife in the 1960s, our first acknowledged military defeat in the 1970s, and AIDS, environmental hazards, terrorism, and drugs in the 1980s.

No wonder we are so hooked on potions to calm our nerves–and on news. That helps to explain the power of news and news organizations, but also the intense competition from all the people wanting to get their messages out to the public.

If you are to use this potent tool to full advantage, a major part of your task, then, is getting the attention of the people who gather and transmit information. It is also important to be aware of certain risks in dealing with the media. One is that once you share information, you have no control over how, when, or whether it will be transmitted. An innocent off-hand comment can touch off a furor with some injured constituency. A reporter can garble a statement and give it an entirely different spin from the one intended. There are ways of cutting down on such errors but the risks cannot be eliminated.

Then, too, one is always at the mercy of totally unrelated events. When General John Murray, the highest ranking U.S. military officer in Vietnam, publicly denounced congressional cuts in military aid to Saigon on August 8, 1974, he probably expected to make a splash in the news media that would generate pressure back home on wavering members of Congress. He could not know that his remarks would be virtually eclipsed by the resignation of President Nixon.

Similarly, when the British Labour government lost a vote of confidence in the House of Commons on March 28, 1979, setting the stage for Margaret Thatcher's becoming the prime minister, it would normally have been page-one news. But the fact that the crisis at Three Mile Island happened that same day relegated the fall of the British government to the inside pages of American newspapers.

The Blather Corporation holds a news conference to announce that it is underwriting low-income housing to the tune of a 1.5 million. The event rates 15 seconds at the end of that evening's newscasts and an item on page 12 of the next morning's paper. Five activists with so little capital among them that they could qualify for some of that housing hold a prayer vigil at city hall and get a full 60 seconds at the beginning of the evening news and a three-column photo on page one of the morning paper. Why? Because a band of terrorists seized an American jetliner with 100 passengers aboard on the day of the Blather Corporation's announcement, while the city hall prayer vigil happened on a very quiet weekend.

Audience size means just about everything to the news media. Every day *something* has to make headlines or that audience will shrink. But it can be a matter of feast or famine: some weeks everything breaks loose at once. Except on rare occasions, the coverage will be limited to the same newscast format and the same headline type size. Some weeks very little happens and reporters have to scratch for a newsy angle.

Some material–for example, features on a human services organization–can be put on hold; the interest is essentially timeless. The item may be shown days or even weeks later, or not at all, depending on what else is vying for attention then. That can be frustrating to the agency staff members who took valuable time to be interviewed and photographed. They need public support now, not some other year. They should understand it is equally frustrating to the news staff who wrote the story.

News is a callous and fickle master. The task of the advocate is not to wish it were otherwise but to learn to work with it and use its maximum potential. That is the purpose of this chapter. We shall start with the print media, then move from there to the broadcast media. The order is not accidental. While a majority of Americans get a majority of their news via the tube, the people who bring it to them get *their* news from printed sources primarily. If we can understand the newspaper business, we have the key to the news business.

But first, a word from the sponsors–the people who buy time on the air and space in the papers. The power of advertisers to control what is aired is legendary–and in large part legend, not fact. Advertisers need exposure. It would be suicidal for them to boycott the means of getting their message into the homes of potential customers. So, except for an angry reaction to a perceived slight–one which is unlikely to last very long–advertisers do not "take their business elsewhere," partly because there is no elsewhere to go. Cities that used to have several dailies competing for a place in the sun are now likely to have one or two major general-circulation newspapers, often under the same ownership.

Television and radio, which are more diverse, may thereby be more vulnerable, but decisions about what ads to place where are under the control of the marketing department, and these days marketing is a scientific operation.

Major news sources–specifically, the federal government at the national level, police at the local level–do have considerable influence over what goes out. That is because reporters are dependent on them for news. Not only are they able to put their own spin on a story, but reporters are hesitant to cut themselves off from a good news source. (See Paletz & Entman, 1981:20.)

Thereby hangs an important lesson for the would-be advocate: become a good news source. Help reporters do their job, by steering good tips to them, letting them know when an event is coming up, educating them on the issues, spending time in developing rapport with them, and they will help you do yours. Above all, do not treat them as the handmaidens of an oppressive social order or as dangerous people to be avoided at all cost. Obviously, you must also be an accurate news source; we will get to that a little later.

DECIDING WHOM TO REACH WITH WHAT

As with lobbying and testifying in hearings, the advocate's first task is to determine what he or she wants to say and to whom. While the shotgun approach may yield some fleeting benefit, you can make more efficient use of your time if you target your message to specific populations. There are large daily newspapers and small weeklies limited to a certain neighborhood or ethnic group. Just about any organization has a monthly newsletter. There are radio stations that specialize in music for a particular age group or musical taste. There are radio stations that are all news. (Much of the time is devoted to content that could be characterized only loosely as news.) There are ethnic radio stations, likewise a variety of television channels.

Your local chamber of commerce may have a directory of media outlets. The Yellow Pages are another source. You can ask somebody in an advocacy group that shares your interest. Think who is likely to be sending out news releases; chances are they can give you a media list.

From time to time in this book I have emphasized the importance of working with friendly advocacy organizations. That is especially so when it comes to the mass media. Unless you are rich, famous, or a recognized expert on the policy question, the media are not likely to be interested in what you as an individual have to say. That does not mean you cannot get into print or on the air by yourself. Radio call-in shows love to hear from you–the more off-the-wall the better. Letters to the editor are from individuals, by and large. But your input begins to have real impact when it is part of an orchestrated campaign involving allies.

SEEING THE WORLD THROUGH THE PRINTED PAGE

There is one way in which advertisers do rule the roost: the make-up of the newspaper format. Except for page one and the editorial page, the news department fits its material into what is left over after the ad department gets through with layout. Look at your own daily newspaper. Turn past the first page and notice how much space is taken up by actual news. *The New York Times* is looked upon by many as a textbook example of a good newspaper. In a typical weekday edition, the majority of space in the first news section (which includes the editorial and op-ed pages) is taken up by ads. Sunday editions are worse, with many pages filled with ads except for a single column of news. In the period between Thanksgiving and Christmas the domination by ads is even more extreme.

So your first task is to fight for a piece of that shrunken space. What will make the news editor decide to use your material, as opposed to all the other worthy messages he or she is bombarded with? Is the issue sufficiently controversial to peak readers' interest? Is there a man-bites-dog angle to your story? Where is the human interest? A person recently released from a mental hospital, telling about conditions there, has a better chance of getting the editor's attention than an expert reciting alarming statistics. How will the issue affect the average readers? Is this going to show up in their tax bill? If so, can a comparison be made between the tax bite and the payoff for kinds of people they care about?

You should get over your fear of reporters. They can be a tremendous asset to you. You should seek opportunities to be interviewed. Are you bringing in any high-visibility people for a meeting? Depending on how widely they are known, whether they have published books or are recognized experts, they may make excellent copy. More on this later.

News Releases

Newspapers are deluged with news releases, so do not count on much coverage, especially in the large dailies, unless there is a very newsworthy angle. The dailies will rewrite (and condense, usually). The weeklies, which run on a very small staff and are hungry for news that has special relevance to their readership, are more likely to print the release, probably verbatim. Because they go to a specialized constituency, it is best to prepare a release specifically aimed at that audience.

One thing about the neighborhood and ethnic weeklies that is not true of the dailies: they are read from cover-to-cover by a good percentage of their subscribers. Your story will, therefore, hit that audience, and that makes these unsung heroes of the news business an excellent target.

One major caveat: Do not overdo the news releases. Make sure there is potential news value in anything you send out. I once ran the newsroom of a small radio station. A cancer research organization used to send us "bulletins" almost daily, sometimes two or three in the same day. After a while, any envelope with the magic logo was dumped without being opened. As it was, the wire services already carried the more newsworthy items. I will not say that the experience has made me any less ready to make donations to cancer research, but it certainly has not helped the cause.

Writing a News Release

It is beyond the scope of this book to teach you how to write. The writing should be impeccable. Editors will not take time to give a course in Composition 101. A poorly written piece will go directly into the circular file. But some people whose English mechanics are flawless do not know how to write news English. If you can find a news reporter who is willing to help, that is probably the best way to be sure of getting copy that grabs the reader's attention and therefore the editor's.

Above all, avoid jargon and initials like the plague. Assume that the editorial staff as well as the readers have no understanding whatever of your subject matter. Take the time to explain what is meant by "base service unit" or find other language with which to refer to it. "AFDC" *may* have crept into the popular language, but do not assume it. At least some of the people who use it do not know what it stands for. They are just told they do not like it.

An editor is a reader with a very short attention span and an intuitive sense of what the public wants. Some editors will stop reading your news release by the end of the headline, more after the first sentence, still more with every succeeding paragraph. That means your "lead" (beginning) must be arresting and punchy. Punchy but not cute. A lead such as, "I wonder if you've ever thought what it would be like to be seven years old and mentally ill and have no opportunity to meet friends," will make a quick trip to the waste basket. "Susan Martin says seven-year-old Billy has been a new person since he started going to the Grant Street Mental Health Center," has at least a fighting chance.

Writing with excessive words is bad writing. Excessive words in a news release are worse than bad. Here are some suggestions for putting together a news release:

1. Start with a headline. Your release should have one anyway, and putting the headline down first will help you focus you on what you really want to say. Keeping focused is a must.
2. Write the release as if you were writing a news item for the paper you are sending it to. It would be good to look at a few copies of the paper and see what style they prefer, then follow it.
3. Set the release aside overnight, then reread it. You may be shocked at what you wrote. Squeeze out every word you can without losing the meaning. Then go back and squeeze again. Try to keep it to one-and-a-half pages maximum, including the heading.
4. Ask somebody to look at it and make suggestions, but *do not commit yourself to follow any of the advice unless you are mandated to by your organization.* You can specify that you merely want to check for accuracy. Above all, do not let a group write the release. News items written by a committee come out sounding that way.
5. The final copy should go on letterhead or be clearly labeled as to source at the top. In the top left-hand corner, write "For Immediate Release" or "For Release By _______." In the top right-hand corner, write "For further information:" followed by your name and telephone number or numbers.

6. The headline should be centered, boldface and/or all caps and/or underlined. Everything should be double-spaced. The typed or photocopied contents should be crisp black-on-white paper.
7. If the release is earmarked for a particular newspaper–for example, an ethnic weekly–you should make that clear at the top, where you say "For Immediate Release."
8. The chances of getting the release published are greatly enhanced if you can send it to a specific individual. Unfortunately, there is a lot of turnover in the news business, and editors' names on media lists soon become obsolete. It might be wisest to call the organization and ask to whom to send the item, as well as checking the address and the news deadline.

If possible, have someone monitor the publication to see if your release appears. If it does not, you can call and ask why. Either that will remind them to run it or let you know why they turned it down. If it does appear, drop a note to the editor, thanking him or her for publishing it.

If your organization is sending out a news release to several publications, send an extra copy to each representative and senator in whose district the organization is located. It is an inexpensive way to let them know you are alive and are communicating with their constituents.

A SAMPLE NEWS RELEASE

FOR IMMEDIATE RELEASE

FOR FURTHER INFORMATION:
Jo Potter, President
Green County Mental Health Association
(215) 555-1234

COUNTY MENTAL HEALTH UNIT BLASTS GOVERNOR'S PLAN

The Governor's proposal to dismantle 300 drop-in centers for the mentally ill is "cruel and usual punishment," according to Green County Mental Health Association (GCMHA) president Jo Potter.

"This will set us back 30 years in this state," Potter declared in a statement released today. She pointed out that five centers in Green County alone serve an average of 160 clients a week.

"For many of our people this is literally the only thing keeping them out of the hospital," Potter said. "That's a lot more costly than keeping the centers open," she added.

Last spring the Legislature voted extra funds for the centers, only to have the measure vetoed by the Governor.

The GCMHA president cited the case of Mary X, who has been a regular at the Pine Street Center in Middletown since it opened two years ago. "When Mary first came to the center she was afraid of everybody around her and wouldn't take part in any activities. Now she serves on the client advisory committee and helps plan parties and other activities."

Jack Y had his first taste of politics when he joined 60 other mental health consumers in lobbying state legislators last spring. The bus caravan to the state capital was sponsored by the GCMHA. It was only a short time ago that Jack was getting into repeated altercations with the police because he neglected to keep up his medication. But an outreach worker from the Uptown Center began visiting Jack and eventually got him to come in. Now he is a member of a group of six men who help each other remember to take their medication.

"I do not know what is to become of people like Mary and Jack if the drop-in centers are closed," said Jo Potter. "It is important for people to let their legislators know how they feel about this crucial program."

The Green County Mental Health Association is a coalition of concerned citizens, agencies, and organizations interested in promoting mental health.

The lead in this news release is intended to catch the reader's attention. The implied conflict with the governor and the unexpected phraseology "cruel and *usual* punishment," make the reader (and editor) want to read on. Personal stories of two clients add to the interest and keep us reading.

Interviews

One use of news releases is to announce a public meeting with a featured speaker. The same approach can be used to promote a street demonstration. Follow the same procedure in preparing the release. Chances are the release will not appear in any form in a major newspaper. Announcements of future meetings are probably at the very bottom of the list of non-news. Occasionally a community calendar will pick it up, but do not count on it.

The real value of this kind publicity is that it increases the likelihood that somebody will show up to cover the event. If you are listed on the release, the person will look you up. A reporter may call you on the day of the meeting and try to cover it by phone. Tell only what you know with accuracy. You may not, for instance, know what the main speaker will be saying in his or her presentation. Do not be drawn into speculating about it. Do be prepared to recite the person's credentials; that might just induce the reporter to come to the meeting.

Public Events

You should welcome these as opportunities to get the message out, but you must also be on your guard. If possible, get the chief spokesperson for the organization to do the talking. If you are interviewed, limit what you say to what you feel it is safe to say. Prefacing your remarks with the fact that you are only handling arrangements and cannot speak for the organization is meaningless. You may still find yourself being quoted as the president or a spokesperson and your statements treated as official.

It is probably best to huddle with the official spokesperson in advance and prepare him or her in two ways: help to figure out the key point to get across–the phrase that will catch the reporter's attention–and get him or her ready for possible questions.

If the mountain will not come to Mohammed, then by all means Mohammed should make the rounds. I have walked into some city rooms, handed over my news release, shaken hands, and walked out. I have also been asked to stick around and answer questions. In both cases, our story has appeared in the paper. It is not a bad idea to visit a newspaper city room anyway. You get a real feel for what it is like on the other end. A news release and an offer to be interviewed will get you inside, whereas just a social call may get you turned away at the door.

Ideally, a reporter should prepare for an interview by researching both the subject and the interviewee in advance, but time pressure rarely allows this kind of preparation. You will endear yourself to the reporter if you provide the background material. In that way, you also have a chance to influence what kind of material the reporter reviews beforehand.

Do not ask to review the story before it is published. There is usually no time for that if the story is to be current. Also, reporters are very sensitive about being censored or even having their work reviewed by interested parties. You can ask the reporter to call you if he or she is unclear about anything or needs further information.

Then go home and pray (1) that the material is used, and (2) that it is reasonably accurate. Anything beyond that, in terms of prominent location, large headlines, etc., is pure gravy.

News Conferences

Having your guest speaker hold a news conference is a wonderful idea, but full of potholes. First, the speaker must be willing to do it and be given a graceful opportunity to decline. So clear it with him or her well in advance of the event. The biggest risk is that nobody will show up to interview your speaker, an embarrassment to both of you. It might be well to call around and find out if news organizations have any interest in coming before scheduling this event-within-an-event.

There is also the in-house news conference, in which your organization plans to announce its position on a bill, or its reaction to a report or to election results. Here there is no embarrassment risk. It is important to have a short written statement available for distribution at the conference. Do not hand it out in advance or you will end up with no conference. Reporters are under pressure, as are the rest of us, so if they can get a story without leaving the office they will do so.

We will consider television and radio coverage of special events and news conferences later in the chapter.

Photo Opportunities

If you want to know how powerful news pictures are, watch how eager politicians are to be photographed. One picture may not equal a thousand words, but it can pay back for the effort a thousandfold. Even small organizational newsletters include pictures. When planning any kind of event, be sure to alert news organizations to picture possibilities. Obviously, street demonstrations and famous people have the greatest interest. But newspapers also like to feature hometown folk. The more localized the readership–for example, a neighborhood or an ethnic or professional group–the more interest in pictures of members. You may find the ever-present straight-on group photo boring, but readers love to see themselves in the newspapers and have something to send to the relatives. One caveat: Do not overdo the offers of photo opportunities; they can sound like part of a highly orchestrated effort, and that may become the focus of interest rather than the subject matter itself. Reporters and editors have a constitutional sensitivity to being used.

Weeklies and specialty papers will often accept your photos, but be sure to ask ahead about requirements such as print finish and whether color or black and white and what size.

Letters to the Editor

One of the most avidly read sections of the newspaper is the letters-to-the-editor column. Writing a letter is also the easiest way to get into print. The ones most likely to be published are hooked to something that has already appeared in that paper, short, to the point, and well written. You can get a good sense of what the letters department looks for by reading a sampling of what does get printed.

Do not worry about writing too many. Some newspapers have regulars. Occasionally, you will see a letter from outside the local area, one which is obviously part of an organized campaign. It probably means the newspaper was hard up for letters that day.

To find out how to submit your letter, check the box on the editorial page. If you lack information of this sort, call the city desk and ask. Some newspapers ask you to include a phone number so they can verify that you really submitted the letter.

That is what to do if you want to get your name and your opinion into print. That is not what this section is about. This section is about using letters to the editor to influence policy. There is a vast difference. Because access is relatively easy and the readership so high, letters are a superb way for a group to advance its cause. And lest you think this open forum for everybody is somehow too open, merely an opportunity for the riff-raff to vent their spleen, be aware that high public officials and corporate executives use this medium as well.

Letters are most effective when they (1) are part of an organized effort involving several persons but (2) do not look that way. Once having settled on an issue, each group member commits to write a letter within a given time frame. Every letter begins with a reference to something that has appeared in the paper, citing the date it appeared. When one of the letters appears, it can be the hook for succeeding letters.

I once heard of an organization in New Jersey that organized a letter-writing campaign on the subject of stopping prison construction. They had this down to such a fine art that different letter writers would argue with each other. For example, one writer might say prison construction was bad because it was too expensive. This would then be responded to by another writer who expressed disagreement with writer number one because the expense was not the issue, the real problem was that prisons were self-defeating because they turned first offenders into hardened criminals.

In the same way, pro-choice letter writers might argue with each other as to whether the real issue was women's right to choose or equal rights of rich and poor or the fact that tight abortion laws would lead to a rise in the number of back alley abortions.

Most letters columns strive for balance, so you may find your letter followed by one on the opposite side of the argument. Good. That increases public interest. There is nothing to prevent you from writing another letter in response to that letter. Or a few weeks later when one appears criticizing your stance, do not hesitate to respond with still another letter. Each time be sure to cite the letter that triggered your reply.

Writing a Letter

All the rules of good argument apply here. Know your agenda, and decide what audiences you want to reach and how you can change their definition of the situation. Concrete illustrations of general points are a must. Absolute accuracy is also the rule, although you will see many letters that violate this canon. Keep it short.

A cardinal principle of argument is to seize and hold the initiative. You want others to respond to *your* issues, not the other way around. So one thing to avoid is reminding people of the opposition's strong points. Your letter will appear several days, probably weeks, after the news item or letter that caused you to write in the first place. The readers have long since forgotten the original argument. The trick is to connect with that earlier statement without restating the other side's case.

Here is an example of this technique. A previous letter by the writer called for the defeat of a harsh welfare reform proposal (House Bill 2044). That provoked a response from another reader who asked, if the poor were out of work why did not they go to the Sunbelt where there were plenty of jobs? The letter below is a reply to this reply. Note how it merely picks up the hook but does not dwell on the previous writer's argument.

> To the editor:
>
> One can sympathize with _______ for wishing that the welfare problem would "go elsewhere"–e.g., the Sunbelt–in her response to my earlier letter. But with the whole country looking down the barrel of the worst recession in more than a decade, there is really no place to hide. In the face of the economic realities, Governor

Thornburgh's plan to deprive 81,000 poor people of General Assistance is as foolish as it is cruel.

General Assistance employables are no strangers to work. According to testimony of the Secretary of Welfare before a House Committee last August, 92% have been employed previously. Three out of five stay on the welfare rolls for less than a year; four out of five for less than two years. And, reports the Secretary, when they are able to find work, "employables leave the General Assistance rolls."

As the recession deepens in the coming months, many more employables are going to find themselves out of work. This has dire consequences for them and for the rest of the people of the Delaware Valley. Shutting off income from thousands of destitute persons means removing a cushion for the region's entire economy–at the worst possible time to do so.

There is still time to prevent this monstrous and ill-timed action. Readers should urge their state senators to defeat House Bill 2044.

In effect, the opponent's letter has been used to further the original argument against the legislation. If this newest letter provokes additional reactions, they will simply be used as hooks for one more exposure of the writer's position.

It is not only readers who look at the letters column. Editorial writers, local columnists, and reporters do as well. Occasionally, an editorial will refer to a letter to the editor. Like anything else, letters are a tool of policy advocacy. Their use must be seen in the context of an orchestrated campaign, in which other media and direct lobbying and testimony all play a part. That is the way they become more than simply an opportunity to let off steam and see your name in the paper.

Getting Extra Mileage Out of Printed Matter

News items and letters to the editor should be routinely copied and sent to allies and elected officials. It is a cheap way to spread the word on an issue and let people know you are *actively* interested. This is one more way to remind your legislator that you are alive, well, and still in there pitching.

RADIO: THE EVER-PRESENT VOICE

When television became popular in the 1950s, there were dire predictions that radio would go the way of vaudeville and the horseshoe. It did not happen. Instead, radio adapted to no longer being the chief home entertainment medium and is now more intrusive and influential than ever before. It has become our constant companion, the background music to our lives—music, literally, but also information about the world around us. Everybody from the lawyer commuting to work on the train to the teenager hanging out in a shopping center to the weekend jogger wears headphones. An automobile without a radio is an oddity.

How does the advocate tap into this powerful tool of communication? By understanding radio, especially radio news, from the inside. Today radio stations are very specialized in their target audiences. You can often get a pretty good idea about the audience by listening to a station at different times of day.

Some stations do not do regular newscasts. At some stations, "news" is whatever comes in over the wire service ticker. But every station must allocate time to public affairs and allow the presentation of opposing views, although they may interview you Wednesday afternoon and play the tape at 2:00 a.m. Sunday. Call-in radio, which is a special breed unto itself, is discussed below. We will start with the basic staple of the advocate— the news release.

News Releases

Everything that has been said about releases for newspapers applies here. Keep in mind that radio works by the quarter hour, not the day. You may want to aim for a particular time of day when your target audience is most likely to be listening. Use dates, not days of the week. If the news release is not about a specific event and is "For Immediate Release," you may want to say "today" to give the story immediacy. That is perfectly acceptable, even though you do not know when "today" will actually occur. Radio stations often have community calendars, an excellent means of promoting a coming event.

Many organizations simply send the same release to everybody and count on station staff to do the editing. Such releases-for-all-occasions may just as simply be tossed in the wastebasket. They are sometimes read verbatim on the air. In most cases this is too bad, since radio writing has its own requirements. I shall assume that you want to write a news release specifically for broadcast.

Writing for Radio

The first difference to note between print and radio is what it takes to get audience attention. Since radio is background to other things going on at the time, most people half-listen most of the time. What catches their attention is a word or phrase that links to something they are interested in. If I hear "social workers" in the middle of a newscast or ad, I suddenly start listening, because that is me they are talking about. But already the speaker has moved on to the next sentence. I cannot ask that it be repeated. Radio writing thus must not only use words that will hit listeners hard, but it must give the message *after* it has caught their attention.

So a second, even more fundamental difference between print news and radio news is that the audience has to catch the latter the first time around. You can be a slow reader but not a slow listener. No going back to reread what you half understood. No finding a quote from "Haliburton" in the tenth paragraph and checking paragraph one again to see who Haliburton is.

To a great extent, newspaper items follow a formula in which the *who, what, where,* and *when* come in the lead sentence. Try to cram all that into the lead sentence of a radio news item and you will confuse your listener; a confused listener is going to tune out.

The trick is to break up sentences into short, digestible pieces. Do not lead off with, "Dr. Susan Martin of the Heywood Institute, Buffalo, New York, will speak on childhood autism at the annual meeting of the Green County Mental Health Association at its annual meeting, December 8. Dr. Martin is a world famous expert on the subject, according to GCMHA President Jo Potter."

Instead, you might start with, "A world authority on autistic children will be speaking in Green County next month." (We are interested, especially if we have an autistic child, and ready to receive more information.) "Dr. Susan Martin will address the County Mental Health Association's annual meeting December 8. Dr. Martin, a staff member at the Heywood Institute in Buffalo, New York, has written many books on childhood autism. . . . " (For those who half-caught the term the first time around.)

The third point to remember about radio news writing is brevity. Audience attention fades fast. Commercials, with all their use of gags, sound effects, and appeals to self-interest are typically 30 or 60 seconds in length. Except for audiences with a special interest in the subject matter, 15 to 20 seconds is a long time to hold the listeners. How many words is that? Forty-five to 60, or three words per second (Yorke, 1978:38).

Does that sacrifice depth? Indeed it does. If you have more material than can be contained in such a brief format, you might consider enclosing a background piece along with the release, making clear it is not part of the release itself. A better way to have in-depth coverage is to arrange to be interviewed.

Radio Interviews

Many reporters start by working on a newspaper, then move over to radio or television, at which point they have to learn interviewing all over. While everybody is under time pressure, newspaper reporters have the luxury of, in effect, having a conversation with the interviewee. The discussion need not be grammatical or logical. There can be backing and filling as a later comment reminds the reporter of something he or she forgot to ask that does not work in radio.

Regardless of the medium, your message should be focused, with you choosing the points to emphasize rather than leaving it to the interviewer to try to pluck a lead sentence out of the morass. Ned Potter of ABC-TV News puts it this way:

> In most media, you get to make one point–just one. So decide what it is, and make it abundantly clear. A reporter is looking for the quintessence of your argument. I've inter-

> viewed plenty of confused people in my time, and gone on endlessly, desperately, trying to coax one fifteen-word summation out of them. I am sincerely trying to give them a good hearing, but I cannot put words in their mouths. Worse yet for them, I may instead use one of their digressions to illustrate an issue in my story that has little to do with their cause. So know your argument well enough to give ten one-line versions of it. The reporter will pick the most concise one. On a talk show or in some letters, you may get to make secondary points, but if you are part of a reporter's story you generally won't get more words into print than you will on the air. (Potter, 1987)

Increasingly, radio tries to put the listener at the scene of the action through a live or taped interview. So the reporter becomes a performer. There may be general discussion of the interview beforehand, but reporters and commentators do not want a canned performance, nor any implication that the interviewee can veto a question in advance. (See Yorke, 1978:110-113.)

If you are interviewed by phone, ask whether the call is being taped and how it is to be used. You do not want to blurt out some state secret for background, only to hear yourself on the late evening round-up.

Handling Questions

Some of the points made in previous chapters about responding to questions are relevant here. We shall assume that you have had a chance to prep the interviewer and have a general idea of what is to be asked. The reporter wants your help in putting together a story. An experienced interviewer will avoid questions so wide-open they invite the respondent to ramble, or so narrow as to call for a simple yes or no answer.

The reporter has something you want: public exposure of your views. You have something the reporter wants: accurate information which will be of interest to listeners. As in most such relationships, the respective interests are intersecting but not identical. If there is something you prefer not to have aired, better not say it in the first place. Once you are on tape you are on tape. The reporter is then not bound to delete any of the material. What to you may seem like common courtesy may look like censorship to the interviewer.

Normally a great deal of the interview will be edited out before it is broadcast. You know your subject. The news department knows its audience, which as we have said is the paramount consideration for them. You may have definite ideas about what ought to be used, but what you think is important may not be seen that way by the news people. If you think a particular point should be stressed–for instance, the demoralizing effects of funding cuts on staff–explain why that is important in terms the reporter can understand.

Language

I talked earlier about jargon in relation to writing news releases. Avoidance of special language is triply important in radio because of the half-listening and once-by-and-never-again. Good interviewers will ask for a translation of obscure terminology, but you are way ahead of the game if they do not have to.

We all fall into the habit of using inside language–in some settings it is impossible to operate without doing so. It is well worth the effort to break out of that habit, whether one is being interviewed on talk radio or visiting a senator's office. There are usually simple and understandable ways of saying the same thing.

On-the-Spot Interviews

These are great opportunities to get licks in at a point of high interest in the subject matter. They are also hazardous because nobody–interviewer or interviewee–has time for preparation. In general, try to stay factual. Opinions uttered while standing on one foot are unlikely to be as thoughtful as those coming out in a planned interview. Regardless of how you define yourself, you will *be* defined as speaking for your organization. Because the reporter is under pressure to find somebody to interview and under time pressure to get in and get out, the questions may seem more curt and provocative than they are intended. But on-the-spot interviews are still a wonderful way to be heard.

Call-In Radio

Before you write off this form of diversion as no more than a haven for neo-Nazis, sick people, and elderly shut-ins, you might want to listen a while. Between all the off-the-wall clatter you will discover lucid people making lucid comments, some of which you may find yourself agreeing with. That means somebody is out there listening–a lot of people as a matter of fact–and it is one more way of getting the word out.

The individuals who conduct these adventures in arms-length intimacy run the gamut, from obnoxious and abusive know-nothings to sharp minds with a social conscience. By and large they tap directly into the modal outlook of the station's listening public, which is why they continue to be employed. The listeners, if they are treated with a modicum of respect, do actually listen, which means they can learn. They are the people who talk to other people whom you may never be able to reach directly.

How do you play? You call the number they keep announcing, give your name (maybe only your first), get put on hold for what seems like forever, finally are told "O.K., you're on," then you are on your own. Fred or Jane or whoever will ask you what you think about the subject (or if it is an open microphone, you pick the topic).

Talk show hosts specialize in knowing a little bit about a lot of things, but chances are they will know very little about your area. So you educate them along with their listeners. Many also specialize in being provocative or argumentative, which is what makes them so popular. Regardless of the host's behavior, you should model good behavior. Always remember that you are selling yourself–even in the anonymity of two-way radio–as well as your views.

In this kind of setting it would be particularly important to talk in concrete examples rather than abstractions. The case of Mary X will continue to bounce around the discussion after you have gone off the line. Stick to your position–agree to disagree if necessary. Do not give in to the temptation to tell the host off. They are past masters at turning put-downs around and making you look dumb.

Even if you decide not to play, it would be worth listening in once in a while. It is an opportunity to see another part of the forest.

Many of those people vote and a few work for candidates on election day.

Mike Fright

It can happen to anybody. There are veteran performers who go into a panic just before going on air. They have learned to manage it. Most important, they know that it passes virtually as soon as they begin talking. Practice will help, but obviously cannot eliminate mike fright. If you happen to have this reaction, be sure to alert your interviewer or host, who is as anxious as you are for a smooth performance. They know techniques for putting a guest at ease. Just the act of admitting the truth to the host will be a step in conquering the problem.

TAMING THE ONE-EYED MONSTER

What words are to radio, pictures are to television. Theories differ as to why Richard Nixon lost the important first debate to John Kennedy and possibly the 1960 election. The most striking thing about that television confrontation is that Nixon *won* overwhelmingly among those who heard it on the radio. It was the visuals that licked him.

Is it, as the late Marshall McLuhan (1964) said, that Nixon's persona was just the wrong one for the tube? Or was it the fact that Nixon looked pasty because he had just gotten over a bout with the flu while Kennedy was tanning off the Florida Keys? Or that Nixon's gray suit blended in with the background while Kennedy's navy blue one stood out?

It does not matter. What matters is that in television, what the eye sees is what stays in the mind. Think back to the 1988 presidential campaign. When you think of Michael Dukakis, what image jumps into your head? Grim face at the microphone? Not much else, probably. George Bush? George Bush standing in front of Boston Harbor or the Statue of Liberty or talking with workers in a steel mill. They always had Bush *doing* something. Then there was the picture of Willie Horton. He did not have to say anything to damage Dukakis's chances.

What do you remember about Ollie North in the Iran-Contra hearings during the summer of 1987? His boyish face and cowlick and cracking voice and uniform with the decorations? What do you remember about the senators who interrogated him? North had the visual advantage and that made all the difference as far as the public was concerned.

We hear a lot about sound bites–short quips that get picked up on the evening news. Sound bites are essentially captions for the visuals they accompany. Television news is basically picture news, not word news. If television has to explain a change in the economy it does it with colorful graphs.

What is the lesson for the social policy advocate? Never forget the visuals. More positively, make them work for you. You will find television people delighted to cooperate, because they need what you need: good visuals. There are endless opportunities to get images of children using services, homeless people struggling to keep warm, ex-mental patients working or lobbying their legislators, pregnant women running the gauntlet to enter an abortion clinic.

The *kind* of image is important. Who is it we want to reach and what will make them identify with our position? Street demonstrations that seem to be getting out of hand, speakers reading from a script, slouching posture instead of visible confidence–these are the visuals that hurt the cause.

Words are not unimportant. They coach the viewer how to respond to the visual image. Television writing is like radio writing except that it works around the picture, supplements it, instead of being the central carrier of information. Much is made of the effectiveness of former President Reagan's one-liners. But more powerful than what he said was the style with which he delivered it, that and the rugged good looks that belied a man in his seventies.

Interviews on TV

As a Guest on an Interview Program

If you are asked to participate in such an interview, try to schedule it when you are not under excessive time pressure, so you can come across as relaxed and confident. If this is a feature program, not a straight newscast, plan to watch one or two broadcasts to learn the interviewer's style. Find out the color of the backdrop so you can dress appropriately. More than in other kinds of interviews, it is desirable to do dry runs with friends, having them lob the kinds of questions you think might be asked.

In all likelihood the person who will arrange the interview will not be the interviewer but the producer. Find out as much as you can from the producer about what they are looking for.

Unless the interviewer is coming to your home or office, arrive early enough to reconnoiter the physical layout. If you can bring a friend along, that is desirable, because you can take up the position you will occupy in the interview and have the friend see how it looks. If the lighting works against you or there is a busy background that will distract attention from you, do not feel bashful about asking for a change. The worst they can do is say they cannot change it. At the least, you will have established yourself as somebody who knows what he or she wants, a healthy climate to set at the outset.

If possible, you should meet the interviewer before the actual broadcast and go over what will be discussed in general terms. If that is not possible, then corner the producer and get a final briefing. They will not be offended. They want a good interview as much as you do.

In the interview itself, look at the interviewer when answering, not at the camera or the light fixtures. Refer to the interviewer by name a few times, but do not overdo it–that sounds amateurish. Be sure you know what is being asked before answering. Do not be afraid to elaborate. If you are going on too long, the interviewer will cut in.

Audiences like humor, so interviewers like humor. Try to work some in if you can do so without making it seem forced. Self-deprecation is effective as long as it is not overdone. You want to come out looking as if you know what you are talking about.

Remember that you are in a visual medium. Help the viewer picture what you are talking about. If you are discussing economic hardship, give an example of Fred or Mary or Sam, with enough concrete detail for the visual image to be formed in the viewer's mind. If you are talking about environmental pollution, bring along a prop, such as a bottle of sludge. If that is not feasible, at least ask the interviewer to suppose, "What would it be like if you found the ugly black stuff in *your* basement?" Viewers will be picturing their own basements, of course.

You should be polite but not subservient. And of course when it is all over, thank your host for the invitation, even if the person has been rude to you in the interview. You may well have the audience on your side.

A follow-up note, with an offer to come back some time, will help to set you and your cause apart from the steady stream of visitors to the program. It can never hurt to enlist the good will of a television personality.

Such programs are always on the lookout for good interviewees. You and your group might send out the word to producers that you have something worth listening to and are available. You should not, however, be indiscriminate about which interview shows to appear on. There are a few whose main purpose is to use guests as punching bags. On-camera mayhem and goon squads in the guise of studio audiences can do nothing to advance your cause. It is a no-win situation. The appeal is the same as that of television wrestling; ditto the potential educational value.

The News Interview

The news department of a television station is working on a documentary that concerns your area of interest. You are contacted for an interview. If there are good potential visuals, be sure to suggest them. These might range from shots of children in a day care center to a background for the interview itself. As for the latter, it should be relevant to the story; otherwise it is a distraction. The time constraints may not allow the same kind of preparation as in the case of the interview show, but you should try to approximate it.

Breaking news events do not allow for much preparation, but you should not hesitate to seize opportunities to be interviewed. The reporter is bent on finding *somebody* to question, and you and your slant on things might as well be it. As you establish yourself as a good information source, you will be more likely to be sought out when they need an on-the-spot reaction. All of the caveats regarding radio interviews apply here.

The Panel Discussion

This is like the solo appearance on an interview show in many respects, but the presence of other participants adds new opportunities and new risks. Some such shows deliberately seek opposing views and provoke a confrontation among panelists. Others also use diverse opinions, but are more interested in enlightenment than heat. Still others will put together a like-minded panel to delve into a particular viewpoint in greater depth.

You should research the program carefully to find out its agenda and the style of the host. You also need to know who else is going to be on the panel and know what to expect from them.

I once walked into a show without sufficient advance preparation. The topic was welfare reform. The other panelist was an attorney in the administration pushing the bill I was opposing. I had in mind a genteel discussion of the issues in which each side listens to the other's arguments and responds in a thoughtful manner. The other panelist had something else in mind. The first question was to me, and I started to give a stock response. The co-panelist suddenly broke in with a sharp attack on my position and for several seconds I just sat there and listened. Then I noticed the interviewer motioning me to jump in, and I realized that I had been operating under the wrong ground rules. I was able to pick up the beat and we ended in one of those impasses in which each side can take something away.

Advocates need to know themselves and environments in which they operate best. Some people relish shouting matches. I do better where people listen to each other.

Television Coverage of Events

In the late 1960s, many activists operated on a simple rule of thumb: the more media exposure the better. They quickly discovered how to increase the amount of time on the video screen: provoke confrontation; dress and speak in outlandish ways. Television news departments loved them for it, even though their commentaries would castigate the performers. Since then, activists have become more sophisticated.

It is clear that the quality of exposure is at least as important as the quantity. In some cases, legislators make it a point to vote for or against a measure, not because of strong feelings about the content of the legislation but to teach obstreperous advocates a lesson. There are times when a quiet corridor conversation or a phone call can yield far more than a widely publicized event. With that in mind, let us consider how to milk a public event for maximum television coverage.

Put yourself in the place of the assignment editor (the one who decides who will cover a story), the reporter, and the camera operator–the three standard actors. Advance notice explaining why the news department should want to cover the event is of course essential. A news release followed by a telephone call will help get the staff there in the first place.

Having the name of a person for the television crew to connect with when they arrive is helpful. The offer of a cup of coffee can only help. Be ready to give background information, on the spot.

A Program with a Presentation

If the event is a scheduled program with a guest speaker, a brief written biographical statement would be useful. Media people pay more attention to organizational affiliations than credentials, which the viewing audience is less likely to be familiar with. Be sure to include a brief description of the sponsoring organization–emphasis on *brief,* less than one page in any case. If an advance copy of the speech is available, give that to the reporter. *Do not* try to edit or underscore; it makes it look as if you are dictating what is to be covered. It may be wise to point up a highlight or two orally.

Facilitate the work of the television crew to the extent feasible. If more than one station is represented, try to keep everybody happy. You also have to keep your members and speakers happy. Having the roving camera operator come up behind them in the middle of a presentation and shine a light into the eyes of the audience may lose you more than it gains in rapport with the news people. It would be best to establish some ground rules with them before they start.

Have somebody monitor the station afterward to see what is shown. Do not expect a lot. A public meeting with a guest speaker at best rates a brief shot of the speaker, audience, then back to speaker, while the newscaster gives the bare essence of the message, ending with a few seconds of the speaker's own voice mouthing a particularly punchy line.

Invitational Events and Visits to Agencies

If the event is an open house or the opening of a facility such as a golden age center, the television crew will be most interested in seeing the clientele using the facility, secondly any prominent public figures who are on the board of directors. Try to set up interviews with the clients themselves or their families. You should also keep in mind local politicians who might like to be shown shaking hands with the clients.

Public demonstrations, picketing of a facility, people boarding buses to visit the state capital to lobby, and the like are all naturals for television. Used wisely they can yield big dividends. Facilitating the work of the reporter and camera operator and making people available to be interviewed are especially important. Just keep in mind that you do not control the kind of coverage you will get, and be sure you want this type of exposure.

Camera Shyness

Like mike fright, discussed earlier, it can happen to the bravest among us. Its origin may be different–for example, self-consciousness about one's height or complexion. Again, experience in front of the camera can help to erase it, but that may all leave you when you are about to be interviewed. In addition to warning the interviewer or host, try to focus on the people you are trying to reach and why you want to reach them. Visualize *a* person and talk to that person. You will be so busy trying to convince this person that you will have less time to be frightened.

LOVE CANAL AND THE MASS MEDIA

The powerful role of the mass media in shaping policy can be seen in the case of Love Canal. Events and the media treatment of those events interacted to turn a local calamity into a national issue. We will see how three parties–a giant corporation, a local citizens group living on a shoestring, and public officials–tried to use the media, either to minimize damage or maximize the response to their plight. However, the media representatives were by no means passive tools as they sought to promote what they perceived to be the public interest.

A Distant Hoofbeat on the Horizon

In October 1976, while the nation was preoccupied with the presidential election campaign, a daily paper in Niagara Falls, New York, *The Niagara Gazette,* carried a number of stories about chemical pollution of fish in Lake Ontario and state investigation of several dump sites used by the Hooker Chemical Company, including the Love Canal. By November, the Buffalo papers were running articles on the subject, stirring state environmental officials into action (Swan, 1979:46-48).

But there the matter seemed to die. The danger, if there was any real danger, was localized. City and county officials, no doubt sensitive to the area's two economic bases, tourism and the chemical industry,–sought to downplay the whole thing (Levine, 1982:16). For the next five-and-a-half months there were no stories on Love Canal.

Then came a public hearing at which residents told of the ground giving way, kids' feet and dogs' noses being mysteriously singed, and rocks exploding when they were thrown against a wall. Michael Brown, who had joined the staff of the *Gazette* in February, became interested. He began writing stories about the unfolding situation at Love Canal. When local officials and industry spokespersons said he was overreacting, Brown's city editor backed him up (Swan, 1979:49).

Still, nobody was panicking. Lois Gibbs recalls reading newspaper articles in *The Niagara Gazette* in the summer of 1978–about the discovery of deadly PCBs in the Love Canal area and laboratory monkeys having miscarriages and a school being built right on top of the toxic stew. "I thought it was terrible," she says, "but I lived on the other side of Pine Avenue." Then it dawned on her that the school they were writing about was the one where her seven-year-old was enrolled in kindergarten. The child's seizures, noticed since he started school, suddenly had a new and more ominous meaning (Gibbs, 1982:9-10).

The Power of the Press

A reporter, newly arrived on a local daily, writes a series of articles about a toxic dump. Its main effect is to stir up the opposition of local public officials, concerned about preserving the image of the honeymoon capital of the United States, and a chemical company that employs 3,200 residents of the area. It galvanizes residents of the affected neighborhood into action, but up to this point it is still a local issue.

In August, a state official makes a public statement that appears to confirm the residents' worst fears. It also gets the attention of *The New York Times.* This newspaper is one of a handful of giant publications that dominate the national news media. Wire services and other big city newspapers, lacking the mammoth resources of these behemoths, rely on them not only for much of their coverage of events outside of the metropolitan area, but often for their interpretation of what is significant news. Television news departments, under much greater time pressure, tend to take their cue from the print media.

So the decision by the *Times* to run front-page stories on Love Canal on August 2, 3, and 5, 1978, together with an editorial on August 5, transformed this local disaster into a national crisis. We should understand that there was nothing automatic about this process. The *Times* editorial staff has access to the papers from upstate New York. For some reason the early revelations did not translate into page one news in 1976 and 1977. Once the genie was out of the bottle, however, there was no containing it.

The August 14 issue of *Time* magazine described the "Nightmare in Niagara." On August 28, *Business Week* said hundreds of companies throughout the country could be affected by the lawsuits arising out of the Love Canal incident. *Newsweek*'s December 11 issue spoke of a "witch's brew of 82 chemical compounds" at Love Canal and warned of more than 100 other hazardous sites across the United States.

In the next year, hundreds of newspaper articles and television and radio newscasts, together with dozens of pieces in periodicals ranging from *The Atlantic* to *Business Week,* kept Love Canal on the front burner. It was the subject of an article by Michael Brown in *The New York Times Magazine* and a documentary, "The Killing

Ground,'' on ABC-TV. It was featured on the *Donahue* show. Jane Fonda held a news conference at the Love Canal site. With every set of revelations, the public controversy was quickly rekindled. ''Love Canal'' became a national synonym for environmental pollution, corporate neglect, and government ineptness. It was a story that fueled itself, new developments automatically vested with a certain presumed significance.

Keeping the Pot Boiling

The greatest ally of the Love Canal Homeowners' Association was media attention, the greatest enemy public apathy. Given the nature of the problem, the residents had little trouble in arousing a sympathetic response over the short run. Leaders such as Lois Gibbs, whose personal plight was easy to identify with, made good copy. The media coverage of her as an individual helped personalize Love Canal for people in other parts of the country. She and her neighbors stood out in sharp contrast to the faceless bureaucrats and corporate officials who were ranged against them.

But public interest erodes rapidly without fresh material. Among other things, Love Canal was competing with a more compelling human crisis: the American hostages in Iran. *Science,* the publication that devoted perhaps more space to the issue than any other, has a specialized readership, and on balance its writers tended to be skeptical of the residents' case.

Sustaining public interest in one's issue is necessary not only for external support but also for internal morale. A group with limited resources can become discouraged and begin to fall apart if it feels its cause has been forgotten by the rest of the world. Public officials, well aware of how fragile citizen movements of this kind are, can deflect the pressure on them merely by dragging things out endlessly.

How does one deal with bureaucratic procrastination? Letters to the editor are one means. On August 9, 1979, just a year after Love Canal first emerged as an issue, a letter by Lois Gibbs, head of the Love Canal Homeowners' Association, appeared in *The New York Times.* In it she attacked federal and state officials for their handling of the problem.

> When President Carter came to Buffalo last October in support of Governor Carey's re-election campaign, he told the Love Canal residents that he would pray for them. That is about all we received from the Federal Government thus far.
>
> Since then, Federal and State bureaucrats have been arguing about how to solve financially the chemical contamination in the area–while hundreds of residents of the Love Canal neighborhood are faced with the choice of staying and risking illness or abandoning their homes and going bankrupt.
>
> On February 9, the New York State Health Department ordered pregnant women and families with children younger than two years of age evacuated from the area where over 200 identified chemicals–many known carcinogens and mutagens–leached into residential regions and the Niagara River. Answers to the following questions would go a long way toward alleviating the crisis of confidence felt by the 1,000 families still living there. . . .
>
> [Six questions with explanatory material are listed.]
>
> We were a proud neighborhood of working people who paid their taxes, paid their bills, served their country in war and raised their children to respect the flag, the country, government and basic values. President Carter and Governor Carey, what can I tell my children to give them confidence in government when they ask me, "Mommy, why do we have to live here with the chemicals?"

Such "open letters" are directed more to the general public than to the officials to whom the questions have been posed. They are a way of embarrassing the bureaucracy into action. One assumes they will be viewed as a hostile act by the bureaucracy, so they are not a way to win its friendship. Such tactics are best used when private communication has failed to get a response.

Occasionally, other people–for example, elected officials or political candidates–will want to gain publicity through going public with an issue. Before you enlist such help, consider whether it is worth losing the goodwill of the objects of the criticism. You bring in a Jane Fonda when you have as much to gain in becoming a political issue as you have to lose in rapport with the opposition.

The citizens' group kept its focus on its own plight, the level of engagement where its credibility was highest. Others sought to draw out the larger lessons. One of these was Ralph Nader, who co-authored an article on Love Canal that appeared in *The Progressive* (Nader & Brownstein, 1980). Another was Michael Brown, the *Niagara Gazette* reporter who had first "discovered" Love Canal.

Brown had already written one book when he returned to Niagara Falls in 1977 to join the staff of the *Gazette*. At first he was reluctant to believe that the Hooker Company and public officials could show such disregard for residents' welfare.

> . . . [A] woman of about twenty got up before the microphone to argue against allowing the waste plant to remain. I watched perplexedly as she began to cry upon mentioning a similar chemical dumpsite in the city of Niagara Falls which, she said, was damaging her neighborhood. She referred to the dump as the "Love Canal". . . . I learned that the "Love Canal" was an old chemical depository located in a residential part of town and once owned by a huge local chemical firm, the Hooker Chemical Company. It was now leaking. The issue, however, appeared to be well in the hands of the authorities, and I decided that the woman's reaction had been based more on emotion than on facts. (Brown, 1980:xii)

As Brown probed further into the situation in 1977 and 1978, his initial perception changed radically. His first attempt to cast the problem of Love Canal in broader terms was an article in *The New York Times Magazine* (1979). He followed this with a book entitled *Laying Waste: The Poisoning of America by Toxic Chemicals* (1980). While it is national in scope, nearly a third of its 336 pages is devoted to a searing indictment of Hooker, a story of corporate irresponsibility, and of failure of public officials to deal with it effectively. Brown's conversion from initial skepticism adds to the impact of his critique; he is, in effect, a "reluctant witness." (See Chapter 6.)

Damage Control: Image-Building

Initially the Hooker Company sought to keep a low profile, as local, state, and federal officials took the brunt of citizen anger. One advantage for the company was the fact that it sold to other companies instead of to the public, so it could afford to be less concerned about its image. There were millions of dollars in lawsuits in relation to Love Canal, and the implications in terms of other chemical dumpsites across the country were staggering. Yet lawsuits are settled in court, not in the arena of public opinion. Far more critical in political terms was the proposed Superfund legislation working its way through Congress. An outraged citizenry would insist not just on protecting itself but on making companies like Hooker pay dearly. Even pro-industry publications like *Business Week* were sounding critical.

There were two sides to the defense: (1) a counterattack against the criticism and (2) positive image building. Hooker left the first of these to others and concentrated on its image in its public presentments. One theme was that "Hooker cares"; as a responsible citizen of the region, the company could be trusted to have the best interests of the community at heart. The other theme was aimed directly at economic self-interest: Hooker is providing jobs for over 3,100 residents of the area.

On March 15, 1979, company officials held a news conference in Buffalo. Lest the news media put the wrong spin on the event, it was described in a full-page newspaper advertisement a few days later. Over the next nine months more ads appeared. The first, which appeared in the *Buffalo Evening News* on May 29, features Bruce Davis, a senior official of the company. The message is clear: Hooker cares, Hooker has spent millions of dollars on pollution control, Hooker has invested heavily in the region's economy, and Hooker employs 3,100 residents of Niagara Falls and neighboring towns.

In the second ad, which ran in the *Buffalo Evening News* and the *Courier Express* on July 13, four employees of the company are shown. Again, Hooker cares. The workers are a cross-section of the people whose jobs depend on Hooker. One, who drives a bulldozer, says, "When I hear people talking about shutting down the chemical companies, it infuriates me. You might as well shut down everything else too." This introduces a threat not being sounded by the Love Canal residents: that the company might have to close down its operations and lay off its employees.

Both ads carry the tag line, "Listen to the people who know." Implication: Do not listen to the critics, who do not know what they are talking about.

The Counterattack

By and large, the Hooker Chemical Company and its parent firm, Occidental Petroleum, took the high road in their response to criticism. It was for others to challenge the credibility of the Love Canal residents and the seriousness of the health effects of the pollution. Another issue, especially important in the court cases, was Hooker's culpability.

There was no question that the company had dumped toxic chemicals in the Love Canal from 1942 to 1953, nor that it had then conveyed the property to the Niagara Falls Board of Education for a token payment of one dollar. Had the company successfully unloaded the pollution problem as well, or was it still legally liable? Had Hooker intentionally misled school officials to get out from under a nasty situation? *Laying Waste* gave one answer to those questions.

> The Hooker Company refused to comment on their chemicals, claiming only that they had no records of the burials and that the problem was not their responsibility. In fact, Hooker had deeded the land to the Niagara Falls Board of Education in 1953 for a token $1. At the time the company issued no detailed warnings about the chemicals; a brief paragraph in the quitclaim document disclaimed company liability for any injuries or deaths that might occur at the site. Ralph Boniello, the board's attorney, said he had never received any phone calls or letters specifically describing the exact nature of the refuse and its potential effects, nor was there, as the company was later to claim, any threat of property condemnation by the board in order to secure the land. (Brown, 1980:8-10)

Laying Waste struck a telling blow. It was being celebrated as an important warning by such guardians of the environment as Jessica Mitford, Ralph Nader, Paul Erlich, Jane Fonda, and Senators Daniel Moynihan and Bill Bradley. The conclusion seemed inescapable:

Love Canal had caused untold damage to innocent victims and it was the result of corporate irresponsibility. But as one learns in policy advocacy, there is no such thing as an inescapable conclusion. There is always a rebuttal. Hooker laid out its basic case in the summer of 1980, in a booklet entitled *Love Canal: The Facts*, but the tone was essentially defensive. The counterattack would come from elsewhere.

The February 1981 issue of *Reason Magazine* carried an article entitled, "Love Canal: The Truth Seeps Out." It was written by Eric Zuesse, a freelance writer and head of a New York-based organization called the Consumer's Alliance. *Reason Magazine* is "a monthly magazine for a readership interested in individual liberty, economic freedom, private enterprise alternatives to government services. . . . " (*The Writer's Market,* 1987:431)

The article takes special aim at Michael Brown's book, and in particular the charge that Hooker knowingly pushed its pollution problem off on an unsuspecting school board. It begins,

> You're about to be untricked. If you believe that the guilty party in the Love Canal tragedy is the Hooker Chemicals & Plastics Corporation, which the Justice Department is suing, rather than the Niagara Falls Board of Education, which bought the dump from Hooker in 1953; or if you believe that Michael Brown's famous book that has become the popular authority on the whole mess . . . , sets out the truth, the whole truth, and nothing but the truth about Love Canal, then you've been snookered. . . . (pp. 16-17)

Zuesse engages three issues: Did the transaction end Hooker's legal liability for later damages? Did Hooker forewarn school officials of the dangerous contents of the pit? And, did the company willingly turn the property over to the government or was it acting under duress? Then he systematically answers his own questions. In doing this he cites evidence Michael Brown omitted. Second, he goes after the credibility of the opposition. In particular, he takes on the nearly sacrosanct image of the embattled housewife, Lois Gibbs.

> . . . [A]s it turned out, Ms. Gibbs knew practically nothing about the Canal itself, although she has said a great deal about the dump.
>
> This is a matter of some consequence, because Lois Gibbs has . . . been one of the chief sources for Mr. and Mrs. America's idea about what went wrong at Love Canal. Apparently, however, no interviewer or reporter has ever checked her facts; nor has she, so far as I am aware, ever been asked probing questions. . . .
>
> * * *
>
> Ms. Gibbs, I soon learned, is fond of snowing the listener with technical terminology that she herself, as it turns out, doesn't understand. (Zuesse, 1981:30)

Zuesse also challenges the credibility of Dr. Beverly Paigen, the chief consultant to Gibbs's group, by citing a review of her work by a five-member panel organized by the New York State Department of Health. According to Zuesse, the panel "concluded that [Paigen's study] is 'literally impossible to interpret' and 'cannot be taken seriously as a piece of sound epidemiological evidence.'" (p. 31)

Reason magazine, with a circulation of 22,000 and a distinct viewpoint, could have only a limited direct impact on public opinion. Yet, published articles can be reprinted and circulated and quoted elsewhere. A Hooker Company ad based on the Zuesse article appeared in the May 29, 1981, issue of the Buffalo *Courier-Express*. But in general the company continued to steer clear of the in-fighting, possibly in an attempt to avoid raising the issue's visibility. The Zuesse piece was cited as an authoritative source in a July 1981 article in *Fortune* (Seligman, 1981), which defended Hooker's role in the land transfer.

Arguments in the mass media, while persuasive, are not legal arguments. Eric Zuesse (1981:18) claimed that by the insertion of language in the quitclaim deed, the Hooker Company was absolved of any future liability for damages suffered at Love Canal. A federal district court ruled otherwise in 1988. The company, said Justice John Curtin of New York's Western District, is "strictly, jointly, and severally liable . . . " (*United States et al. v. Hooker,* 1988).

Public Officials and Public Debates

Elected officials know how to use the mass media to maximum advantage. Not only do they need constant exposure to stay in business, it has been my experience that most of them have a natural craving for it as well. Appointed officials, on the other hand, very often avoid the media. While one should also be sensitive to that need, it is important not to play into it. The advocate has a crucial role in exposing to the public what does and does not happen inside government. But this is always done in relation to one's priorities. Embarrassing a government official has its price in reduced access to information and possible retaliation against both the advocate and the people he or she wants to help.

When using the mass media, persons in government offices have a distinct advantage and several disadvantages. On the plus side, they are automatically news. When I worked in a radio newsroom years ago, it struck me that most of the national stories were datelined Washington, many of them statements of some kind from one or another government agency. It is the same at the state and local levels. For all their complaining about government incompetence, reporters listen when a public official speaks, and there is a built-in tendency to accept what is said as fact. Recall Michael Brown's initial reaction to the woman's testimony about conditions at Love Canal: local officials must know what they are doing.

On the negative side, officers of government lack the freedom, the single-cause focus, and the popular appeal of an embattled grassroots movement of ordinary people. Nor do they have the huge financial resources which a giant corporation can throw into a public relations battle. It makes sense, then, for officials to pick the occasions for public statements, choose their words carefully, and exploit presentations for maximum positive impact.

It appears that this was not the case with the local, state, and federal officials involved in the Love Canal controversy. By sending out shock waves they could not control, issuing statements that added to residents' confusion and sense of panic, relying on rushed, poorly done research and at times seeming to contradict one another, they sent all the wrong messages. As a result, they may have needlessly taken on the brunt of the early criticism, while the Hooker Company sat on the sidelines watching the drama unfold.

ADJUSTING ONE'S MEDIA STRATEGY TO THE CIRCUMSTANCES

The mass media are like any other tool of advocacy. If you learn their potentials and their pitfalls, you can multiply your effectiveness. Blunder in without sufficient care and you can quickly undermine your cause. The policy issue itself dictates certain approaches. In the case of abortion the critical factor of media interest and public attention is built in. The raging controversy which follows this issue will magnify the impact of anything you put forth. Conversely, it is a veritable minefield.

Mental health has media appeal, but often it is the wrong end of the issue that gets the most attention: dangerous weirdos threatening their families and aggressive panhandlers on downtown streets. There is a great deal of public fear of persons labeled "mentally ill," and any discussion of services to that population will unleash some of these sentiments.

As with mental health, media exposure of welfare reform issues will trigger reactions that are already well established, so much attention must be paid to dealing with the image of the recipient population. Unlike mental health, welfare comes and goes as a public concern. As a result, one may decide not to stir a dormant debate, but prepare for future ones which will inevitably occur.

Toxic waste has a major advantage over the other three issues, in that it is everybody's concern, and the public tends to identify with the proponent of effective public policies. The advocate has a natural, built-in audience, particularly at the local level where a specific hazard is concerned. The problem here is the nature of the potential opposition. Large corporations, especially those providing the livelihood of many families, often allied with powerful unions, play rough, and have the resources to demand wide coverage over the long haul.

Assiduous monitoring of the media, both for what the professionals are saying about you and your cause and for what the opposition is doing, pays off handsomely. When any material offers you a hook to hang your story on, take advantage of it. That way you let the opposition work for you. Full-page ads are expensive, so you may not be able to compete in that field, but you can write a letter to the editor, using the ad as a hook.

Is your group the subject of negative news or commentary on television or radio? If it is an expression of opinion, ask for equal time. That way an opponent may give you access to the airwaves you might not be able to obtain in any other way. And, resist being relegated to 2:00 a.m. Sunday. Your response should have a comparable time slot. If the one-sidedness is extreme, you might consider complaining to the Federal Communications Commission. But weigh first whether you gain more as a friend or adversary.

There are exceptions to this general principle. A particularly devastating attack, especially one going to a limited audience, may be better left alone. But it is a tough judgment call to make. A thoroughly researched and well-written piece in a relatively obscure magazine such as Eric Zuesse's polemic in *Reason Magazine* might be better left to die a natural death. Conversely, silence may imply acquiescence. An alternative to firing back, and in so doing giving such an attack increased visibility, is to plan your rebuttal and then sit on it and see if others quote from the offending article. By that time it is second-hand material, and you can come back and tell what the original writer was *really* saying. It is then your interpretation against the quoter's.

POINTS TO REMEMBER

1. You must first decide what audience you want to reach with what message. Once you "go public" you have only limited control over how your words are used.
2. You must catch the attention of the people who prepare the news and convince them their audience will be interested in what you have to say.
3. Newswriting must be concise and understandable to the average reader. The lead sentence must pull the reader in.
4. Keep in mind opportunities for photos.

5. Letters to the editor are most effective when done as an organized effort rather than as an opportunity to see your name and your opinion in print.

6. Even though you use a previous letter as a hook, keep the focus where you want it, rather than reminding people of your opponent's arguments.

7. Writing for radio demands strong attention-getters at the beginning, ideas reduced to short takes, and overall brevity.

8. When interviewed live or on tape, formulate your own "sound bites" in advance. Be sure you understand the question before trying to answer it.

9. Avoidance of jargon and alphabetese is especially important on the radio.

10. Visual images are the key to television. They should always be paramount in your thinking.

11. Prepare thoroughly for participation in an interview or panel program. Research not only the subject matter but all the key actors as well.

12. If you are planning a special event, consider the possibilities for television coverage, especially of activities other than formal speeches. Always keep in mind the messages, intentional and unintentional, you may be sending.

Appendix

The Policymaking Machinery

You already have a general idea of how policymaking takes place in the United States government. The administration, a congressional committee, or an individual senator or representative puts forth a new proposal. It goes into the legislative hopper, setting the process in motion. Both houses of Congress must pass the identical bill and the president must sign it to make it part of the law. If the president vetoes the bill, it can still be enacted by a two-thirds override vote in both houses.

Once the policy change is enacted, an agency within the executive branch implements it, either directly or by developing regulations and guidelines for implementation by the states. The states have a legislative structure which roughly parallels that of the national government. To implement a federal government policy, the relevant agency within the state administration develops policies and programs in compliance with the federal regulations. Enabling legislation may be necessary, in which case the administration requests action by the legislature, whose two houses then engage in the same kind of process as Congress, with the governor's signature making the policy official. The relevant agency then implements the program directly, or by writing regulations and guidelines for local governments and private sector organizations.

At any point along the way the policy may be challenged, in whole or in part, in the courts. The policy may be found to violate the federal or state constitution, in which case it is overturned and its architects go back to the drawing board or give up and go on to other things.

Chances are you knew that already. The purpose of this section is to go beyond the basics and see how policies work their way through that machinery. As we shall see, the reality is not always the way the civics books picture it. What follows is not a detailed treatise on government, but it should help you understand what is going on enough to keep from needlessly wasting a lot of time and energy. We will begin by looking at the executive and legislative branches of the federal government and their respective roles in policymaking. Next, the same branches in state government and how the states interact with Washington. Finally, we will consider the role of the courts in changing policy.

THE PRESIDENT AND THE POWER TO SHAPE THE AGENDA

New policy may originate in many different places: the administration, Congress, or an outside pressure group. But as the machinery of government comes into play, certain roles become crucial. For several reasons, U.S. presidents have a great deal of power. One major source of leverage for the chief executive is the ability to decide what is to be argued about. That can be as important as winning the ensuing contest.

The formal rules and tradition give him a built-in platform from which to present his program. It starts with his inaugural speech, though that tends to consist of platitudes rather than specific policy ideas, and may be more concerned with the sins of his predecessor than his own plans. The annual State of the Union message to both houses of Congress (and the rest of us via television) is listened to carefully to see where the administration is headed in the coming 12 months. The budget message, which comes a few weeks later, also focuses the nation's attention where the president wants it to be.

Aside from these standard occasions, the president is almost always free to take over the television networks during prime time for a major address to the nation. Franklin D. Roosevelt was the first president to discover the power of radio to take him inside people's homes with his periodic fireside chats. He also invented the weekly news conference. Since then, every president has taken full advantage of the mass media's potential.

Still, as heads of government go, the U.S. president is relatively weak, structurally speaking, because of his dependence on an independent legislative branch in enacting policy. A prominent senator, for instance, can set the agenda regarding a particular policy. Especially when the opposition party controls one or both houses, the initiative is as likely to emanate from Capitol Hill as the White House. This is more apt to be so in relation to domestic than foreign policy.

Community mental health services were not a national issue until President John F. Kennedy made them one in a special message to Congress. He could have ignored the report of the Joint Commission on Mental Illness and Health and focused on other things. Or he could have bought the Commission's emphasis on state hospital reform instead of community-based services. Congress might have acted on the issue anyway, although without the support of this high-profile, high-initiative president it is not likely to have happened.

Presidents Kennedy, Nixon, Carter, and Reagan each decided to move welfare reform to the front burner. They not only thereby focused the attention of Congress, the news media, and the country on the issue, but each put his particular stamp on the problem. Because key persons in the Kennedy administration saw individualized social services as an effective way to integrate the welfare poor into the mainstream, that became the thrust of the policy Congress reacted to, and the shape of the scheme that was finally enacted.

The call for a liberal-appearing "guaranteed minimum income," coming from the Republican conservative Nixon, gave his welfare reform proposal extra shock value. If Nixon had called instead for turning welfare over to the states to administer as they saw fit under a block grant system, the debate in Congress would have been different. Chances are, the notion of a standardized national public assistance system for the blind, disabled, and elderly–Supplemental Security Income (SSI)–would never have happened.

In contrast, in 1988 the welfare reform proposals of a highly popular president, Ronald Reagan, went nowhere, and it was Senator Daniel Moynihan's bill that became the vehicle for policy change. One reason was Moynihan's formidable reputation in the area of welfare policy. Another was the fact that the Democrats in Congress had the votes to counter Reagan's influence.

Getting the President's Ear: The Insiders

Presidents cannot afford to become bogged down in every detail of government policy. For guidance on policy they rely heavily on the advice of their inside circle of advisers; in particular White House staff. Certain cabinet members also wield great influence. Being keenly aware of this fact, the advisers actively try to make their own agenda the president's. Needless to say, the president knows people are trying to use him for their own purposes–always, of course, in the name of the national interest.

Even before he entered the White House in 1969, President-elect Richard Nixon appointed a task force on welfare and poverty. He had campaigned against Johnson's Great Society and the "welfare mess," and this was his way of showing that he was ready to act on his rhetoric. Heading the task force was Richard Nathan of the liberal think tank, the Brookings Institution (Nixon, 1978:425-426). It was this task force that came up with the Family Assistance Plan proposal. Upon assuming office, Nixon named Daniel P. Moynihan, a former assistant secretary of labor under Lyndon Johnson, as his urban affairs adviser. Against the opposition of other Nixon advisers, Moynihan was able to convince the president to accept the task force proposal (Lynn & Whitman, 1981:18-19). Without Moynihan's pushing, Nixon might well have been persuaded by members of his cabinet to come out for a punitive welfare scheme, and this would have been what Congress debated in the ensuing months.

During World War II, the United States Public Health Service (USPHS), an established and respected agency, had responsibility for mental health policy. Its director, Dr. Thomas Parran, named a prominent psychiatrist, Robert Felix, to head USPHS's Division of Mental Hygiene. Parran and Felix lobbied within the Truman administration for establishment of the National Institute of Mental Health (Levine, 1981:42-43). Set up under the 1946 National Mental Health Act, NIMH became the architect of administration mental health policy in that and subsequent presidencies. It played a central role in shaping the community-based approach which John F. Kennedy presented to Congress in 1963 (Levine, 1981:42-44, 50-52).

Congressional Initiative

Senate and House committees play a pivotal role in policymaking. A committee chair can simply refuse to bring a bill up for consideration, although there are ways of forcing him to do so. The committee may fail to report a bill out for further action, send it forward in modified form, or do a basic rewrite–essentially creating a new bill under the original title. The House or Senate leadership may be able to exercise discretion as to which committees get to work on a particular bill, though tradition determines this in most cases.

The Senate and House pass different versions of a bill, but a single version must go to the president for his signature. The differences are ironed out in a conference committee, appointed for that purpose. The conference committee is supposed to try to reflect the common thinking in the two bills, but in some cases the committee has written an entirely new bill. This is not as arbitrary as it may sound, because the final version of the bill must be ratified by the membership of both houses.

One way for a committee to influence policy is to hold public hearings. Committee hearings are ostensibly a means by which Congress can gather information as a basis for legislating, but public hearings also serve to generate public support and place an issue at center stage for congressional action. For example, Senator Edward Kennedy has used hearings to put on pressure for health insurance and other social programs when such initiatives were not coming from the White House.

Most individual senators and representatives introduce bills of their own, often to show the voters back in the district that they are hard at work, but it is rare for major policy proposals to begin this way. There are exceptions, of course. Senator Moynihan's welfare reform proposal is an example.

The Power of the Purse

In just about any social policy deliberations, cost is a primary consideration. The taxing and spending powers of government are thus crucial factors in determining the shape of policy. So one's role in the budget-making process helps determine one's impact on policy.

The fiscal year is different from the calendar year. For the federal government it starts on October 1 of the preceding year and ends on September 30. The process of putting together the budget begins almost two years before that, when the federal agencies formulate their requests. These go to the Office of Management and Budget (OMB), which does the actual work of fashioning the president's budget proposal. That places a lot of power in the hands of the director of OMB.

David Stockman, the first person to head OMB under Ronald Reagan, deliberately made himself a lightning rod in the president's campaign to slash spending for social programs. Though others in that post have been less flamboyant, they have wielded tremendous influence over spending decisions. They can serve a useful function for a president who wants to cut costs but does not want to take the heat from interest groups whose funding is cut.

The administration's budget for fiscal year 1980 was already in rough form by the fall of 1988. The president made whatever changes he and his advisers felt were needed, then presented it to Congress in February 1989.

Six congressional committees–three in each house–have the key responsibility in the budget making process. If your U.S. representative or senator sits on one of these, that increases *your* influence on federal policy. If you are a constituent of the chairperson of one of these committees, your potential influence is multiplied. The *House and Senate Budget Committees* are responsible for developing budget estimates, outer limits for spending in certain general categories. The *House and Senate Appropriations Committees* deal with specific spending items within those categories. The *Senate Finance Committee* and the *House Ways and Means Committee* are responsible for tax legislation. They also are the committees dealing with legislation which comes under the Social Security Act (for example, public assistance reform).

Spending proposals are a major battleground between the administration and Congress, particularly when one or both houses are under control of the other party. The administration has the advantage of making up the initial budget proposal. Since 1973, Congress has had its own weapon: a budget resolution setting spending limits in several broad categories that cannot be vetoed by the president. Moreover, the Congressional Budget Office provides an independent source of technical information on budgetary issues. Congress can appropriate more funds for certain programs than the president asks for. He can veto a spending bill if it is too high. Congress can then override the veto if it can muster a two-thirds majority in both houses.

Ronald Reagan sought but did not get line-item veto power. This would have allowed him to strike out any specific item within a larger spending bill. Presidents are thus still forced to agree to expenditures they do not want in order not to jeopardize those they do want.

Some Fiscal Terminology

It will be useful to be familiar with a few basic concepts in financing of government programs. The following list includes only the most essential terms. (For a more detailed discussion of fiscal policy, see Richan, 1988:71-86.)

Appropriations are actual allocations of funds for programs. They are different from *authorizations*, which merely say a program should exist and set a ceiling on expenditures but do not provide the money to make it happen.

Block grants (special revenue sharing) allocate funds for clusters of programs falling under broad categories. They are intended to give states leeway in allocating funds among several specialized programs, designing specific services and setting up eligibility requirements. They are different from *categorical funding*, which sets a fixed rate of federal funding as well as detailed regulations to be followed by states and other recipients in each specialized program.

To make use of federal funds, a state may have to enact *enabling legislation,* which meets the requirements spelled out in the federal regulations. Typically, such federal funding is done through a *grant-in-aid.* The state or other recipient agency may have to put up *matching funds,* based on a designated ratio.

Open-ended appropriations guarantee funds to all recipients (states, agencies, or individuals) meeting certain criteria. This applies to *entitlement* programs, in which recipients are entitled to benefits by law. Since the government has no control over how many will qualify, such appropriations are sometimes called *uncontrollable*. Strictly speaking, the government can control how much it spends in virtually any category by changing the criteria. The exceptions are interest on the public debt, which is owed to financial institutions and individuals outside the government, and long-term contracts under which there is a legal obligation to make payments.

FISCAL POLICY AND COMMUNITY MENTAL HEALTH

John F. Kennedy brought into being federal support of community mental health services, but the actual dollar outlay was limited to start-up costs. The much bigger item of salaries of professional staff in the centers received no federal support in the original legislation. Lyndon Johnson was able to include money for professional salaries in the centers as part of his Great Society push. Community mental health was not the main focus of that program, so this expenditure slid through without serious opposition.

President Richard Nixon had no use for community mental health centers. Not only did they represent the kind of welfare state spending binge that he had vowed to fight during his campaign, but he saw the kind of "social psychiatry" being practiced in the centers as a way of pampering the criminal element (Brown, 1985:54). Over his objections, Congress continued to fund the program. When he tried to impound the money–refuse to spend what was allocated–he was taken to court by mental health advocacy groups and forced to release the funds. Nixon's successor, Gerald Ford, vetoed a 1974 bill to extend the life of the community mental health centers program, but the veto was overridden.

Ronald Reagan got a compliant Congress to go along with legislation lumping the state allocations for community mental health and drug and alcohol abuse programs into a block grant. This gave states considerable leeway in deciding how to allocate the money among these programs. At the same time, total spending for these purposes was cut back sharply. The block grant system severely reduced the National Institute of Mental Health's (NIMH) influence over community mental health services. Up to that time, NIMH had dealt directly with local sponsors of the centers, bypassing the state mental health authorities. Federal versus state control of policy in health and welfare services has always been a bone of contention.

THE ROLE OF THE STATES IN SETTING THE AGENDA

The "Reagan revolution" in 1981 shifted considerable initiative in the making of social policy to state governments. A major argument for this move was that decisions should be closer to the people–thus would democracy be restored by giving the citizenry more control over policy. In one sense there is greater access to the policymaking process at the state level. The initiative and referendum–ways for private citizens to bypass state legislatures and enact new laws directly or require popular ratification of legislative action–are to all intents non-existent in national government. By garnering enough signatures on petitions, a group can have a proposal placed on the ballot and voted on at a regular election. In the 1970s, voters in California and Massachusetts enacted drastic cuts in state taxes in this way.

In another sense, state government is even more remote than the federal. People have to understand a political system to wield effective influence over it, and this is the layer of government least understood by the majority of citizens. The news media give better coverage to the high drama in Washington and controversies in the local school board than they do to what happens in the state capital. Aside from the governor, most policymakers in the state administration are relatively unknown, as are state legislators. Most people can tell you their U.S. senators and House member but have trouble remembering the names of their state senator and representative.

State governments generally parallel the structure at the federal level. Virtually all states are bicameral–have an upper and lower house in the legislature. They are called different names in some cases. Legislative committees play a major role in determining the fate of policy proposals, as they do in Congress. Political parties play a more dominant role in state than in federal policymaking. The budget making process is similar at the state and national levels: typically the state agencies send up their estimates to be melded into the governor's budget, which is then worked over by legislative committees and acted upon by the respective houses. Differences between the versions passed by the upper and lower houses must be ironed out in conference. The governor may sign the resulting bill into law or veto it, requiring further action by the legislature. Unlike the president, many governors have the line-item veto. In these states, programs the governor wants cannot be held hostage to ones he does not. The administrative agencies implement the final spending and other policy decisions.

The dependence of the states on the federal government changes the nature of the power relationships within the state. For one thing, the governor's power is much more limited than that of the president, both in his dealings with the legislature and within the administration itself. The main reason for this is that, despite the changes in the role of states in recent decades, federal policy still dictates much of the agenda at the state level. Certain department heads within the state administration are actually more significant than the governor on some policy issues because they have ties with the corresponding federal agencies and congressional committees. Thus, they can provide access to federal funds. It is they who know the federal requirements the state must meet to draw the money down from Washington. In some cases, they can virtually dictate the policy language to the governor and the legislature.

The Governors wield more power in state-initiated policy. Because of his forceful personality and public support, Governor Ronald Reagan was able to carry much weight in California state affairs. This can be seen in relation to both abortion and welfare reform policies. The question of abortion law reform had always focused on the danger to the woman in completing her pregnancy. But in the early 1960s a new issue arose: the condition of the fetus. This was prompted by the celebrated case of a woman who had unknowingly consumed a drug associated with severe birth defects, and by the discovery that rubella in pregnant women could damage the fetus. It was on this point that Governor Reagan drew the line. If the condition of the fetus was included as grounds for abortion, he would veto the legislation. Not having the votes to override a veto, the proponents struck the offending section from the bill. In New York state in 1972, Governor Nelson Rockefeller vetoed a bill that had passed both houses of the legislature repealing the state's liberal abortion statute.

In the abortion reform fight, Governor Reagan used his power to stop action. In the case of welfare reform, he used his influence to promote a course of action. Reagan had campaigned against "welfare cheats" since the days of his national radio broadcasts, long before his entry into politics, so it came as no surprise when, as governor, he urged a tough welfare reform package, including workfare. The policy was enacted, leading to a program which Reagan claimed afterward knocked thousands of people off the welfare rolls. No matter that later assessments found the claims of success to be exaggerated. (See Evans, 1972.) Reagan had demonstrated another kind of success: the ability of a governor to push through a major change in policy. This has not typically been the case with federally-aided welfare programs. Ordinarily, states stick closely to the federal guidelines to extract the maximum amount of dollars from the U.S. government.

California has a reputation for volatile politics and a penchant for innovative policies. Pennsylvania is at the opposite end of the spectrum, politically as well as geographically. Among the large states, it has the distinction of never having produced a president, nor much in the way of policy innovation in at least the last century. It also has had a tradition of liberal public assistance policies under Republican as well as Democratic administrations. So when its Republican governor, Dick Thornburgh, proposed in 1979 to limit general assistance (no federal support or regulations) for able-bodied persons to one month a year, it set off a major legislative battle lasting more than two years. In the end, Thornburgh got a modified version of the policy he had sought: an assistance cut-off after three months instead of one. Since the average time on general assistance in the Keystone State was less than eight months, this was a major concession (Richan, 1983).

The role of states in pioneering new policies that get picked up nationally is seen in Massachusetts's ET (Employment and Training) initiative. A program emphasizing assistance to welfare recipients in becoming self-supporting, ET was used as a model of a successful welfare innovation, even though it had its share of detractors who asserted that its success depended heavily on the state's surging economy.

State legislators are among the most accessible actors in the policy chain but also among the least powerful. Your congressperson gets back to the district periodically, more so during election season than other times, but often you find yourself dealing with a legislative aide. Your state representative, on the other hand, may spend more time back home than in the state capital. You can quickly get to know this individual on a first-name basis. If the representative chairs a major committee, of course, he or she will have more power, as in the case of congressional committees.

Freshman (first-term) legislators are particularly interested in linking their names with an issue that will play well back home, in order to establish a can-do reputation. (See Bardach, 1971.) It is useful to keep in mind that first-term legislators may go on to become committee chairs, speakers of the House or Senate, governors, U.S. senators, etc. However, they *may* serve out their time in relative obscurity or leave politics after a brief stint. The uncertainty helps to make politics an interesting field.

THE COURTS AS INNOVATORS

Earlier, we saw how President Nixon's effort to impound funds for community health centers was overruled by the U.S. Supreme Court. We think of courts as where the action stops, or at least slows to a snail's pace, but the courts are also capable of breaking new ground in the name of consistency with past principles. One reason courts can take this role is that they are relatively insulated from political pressure. While, structurally, a decision by the U.S. Supreme Court would seem to settle an issue once and for all, it can also precipitate a new round of policy action, as the *Roe v. Wade* case illustrates so well.

Given the alignment of the right-to-life movement with the ultra right and Christian fundamentalists, and feminists with liberal causes, *Roe v. Wade* sounds like something liberals under the leadership of Chief Justice Earl Warren might produce. But the chief justice was Nixon appointee Warren Burger, who joined the seven-to-two majority in declaring that women had a right to an abortion. The majority opinion was written by another Nixon appointee, Harry Blackmun. For that matter, the liberal Warren, who had left the court by that time, was appointed by Republican centrist Dwight Eisenhower.

These seeming paradoxes underscore an important fact about the Supreme Court: its unpredictability. Another thing to note about Supreme Court decisions is that, once a decision has been made, it is rarely reversed outright, though its full application may be trimmed back substantially–as has happened in the case of *Roe v. Wade.*

Failing to achieve their first goal, a Constitutional amendment declaring the fetus a person from conception onward, the anti-abortionists sought to bar use of federal Medicaid funds for abortions. In 1977, Representative Henry Hyde of Illinois was able to tack an amendment with this language onto an appropriation bill. Pro-choice advocates immediately challenged the Hyde Amendment in court, setting the stage for a new policy decision by the Supreme Court. In this case the court upheld the abortion restriction. While the action did not nullify *Roe v. Wade,* it sharply limited its application to low-income women. But as subsequent events have clearly demonstrated, this action did not end the controversy.

Federal district courts play a role similar to that of the U.S. Supreme Court in deciding on the constitutionality of a law. Proceedings at the district level frequently pave the way for consideration by the Supreme Court. State high courts may pass on whether a law accords with the state constitution.

ADMINISTRATIVE POLICY

There is a widely held belief that when the president's or governor's signature goes on a bill that ends the issue–unless of course there is a court challenge. The real formulation of policy continues after that. It is then that persons unknown to the public flesh out the details. These are the "faceless bureaucrats" who oppress us or dedicated public servants who make the system work, depending on one's perspective.

The first task of the administrative agency, once a law is enacted, is to figure out what Congress or the state legislature had in mind, as a basis for crafting program regulations and guidelines. These are human beings working for other human beings, aware that what they produce must pass the scrutiny of not only their bosses and legislative leaders but external interests as well. The most vocal and influential interests will be paid particularly close attention.

This same spirit of wanting to stay out of trouble pervades every stage of implementation, down to the way local agencies interpret the interpretation of legislative intent by federal and state officials. But the interpreters also have their own agenda. They *are* dedicated, in the sense that most of them have a viewpoint as to how things ought to work and some degree of commitment to making policy reflect that vision.

After the *Roe v. Wade* decision by the Supreme Court, pro-choice advocates accused the U.S. Department of Health, Education, and Welfare of failing to do enough to inform women of their newly won right to abortion. At the time, the Department was rigorously enforcing the Hyde Amendment, which barred the use of Medicaid funds for low-income women seeking to end their pregnancies (Jaffe, Lindheim, & Lee, 1981:57-58). In like manner, critics charged the Reagan administration with using policy guidelines to deny thousands of disabled persons benefits to which they were entitled (*The New York Times,* 1982).

There are several ways in which policy regulations have affected the funding of community mental health services contrary to the apparent intent of policy. Despite the emphasis on getting the mentally ill out of hospital settings and into community-based programs, federal rules governing Medicaid reimbursement for health care expenditures have favored inpatient over outpatient care. Medicaid, a major source of federal funds for services to the chronically mentally ill, thus pushes toward custodial care in nursing and boarding homes, as opposed to services in mental health outpatient clinics. SSI regulations, according to Brown (1985:101-102), have helped to eliminate halfway houses and therapeutic group living arrangements and discouraged care of the mentally ill by their relatives.

Sometimes administrative agencies make rule changes as a way of heading off legislative action. In 1984, health there was a bipartisan effort to liberalize Pennsylvania's welfare reform law limiting general assistance for able-bodied persons to three months. Several categories of persons were added to those exempted from the restriction, in a bill passed by both houses of the legislature. Governor Thornburgh vetoed this bill. To avert the possibility of a vote by the legislature to override the veto, the secretary of welfare developed rule changes making many of the revisions contained in the scuttled legislation (Roche, 1984). This points up certain advantages and disadvantages of making policy via administrative regulations. It is fast and bypasses protracted debate in the legislature and in the courts, but it creates no statutory precedent and is vulnerable to reversal by a subsequent regime with a different philosophy.

In the end, it is the application of policy by administrative agencies that determines its true impact on people. The Love Canal incident involved bureaucracies all the way from the local school district to the U.S. Environmental Protection Agency (EPA). All parties were aware that there were huge sums of money at stake—not only in that case but in the precedents which would emanate from it for potentially hundreds of other Love Canals across the country.

When Lois Gibbs became concerned about her child's health, she asked school officials to transfer him to another school. The school superintendent said she needed statements by two doctors certifying the need for a transfer. She got two physicians to write letters. The superintendent avoided answering her phone calls for two weeks, then said the letters had not been received, which was not true. The superintendent was aware that if Gibbs's claim was true, all the children would have to be removed from the school, causing a major disruption. There was a bigger issue involved: the school board had built the school knowing it was sitting on top of a potentially hazardous chemical dump. So the initial response to this rather simple request for a transfer of one child was to say no (Gibbs, 1982).

With many citizens, this might have ended the superintendent's problem. The parent would have assumed public officials never lie, that the asthma and convulsions must be psychological, and decided not to make a fuss. But Lois Gibbs was not just any parent. She began to ask questions. From her brother-in-law, a biologist, she learned the effects of the chemicals described in newspaper stories about the Love Canal site.

It turned out that several public agencies were involved in the issue—and all claimed to have the situation well in hand. The Niagara Falls city engineer said he had a plan for handling the toxic chemicals. The administration was concerned about the effects of a scandal about hazardous waste on the city's tourist business. Niagara Falls also relied on the chemical industry as the largest employer in town.

The New York State Department of Health was studying the problem. Implication: do not worry, we are taking care of things. Meanwhile, stay out of your basements and backyards, avoid eating vegetables from your gardens, and do not let children play in the affected area. Implication: if you get sick, it is your fault. One way of "studying the problem" was to send children out to collect specimens of "hot" rocks. In one master blunder, the department issued a report listing names and addresses of residents, and for each the amounts of different chemical compounds (by their technical names) found on their property. Not having any idea of the implications of this information, the residents panicked.

The Environmental Protection Agency was reluctant to be drawn into the controversy but was forced to by the national publicity and congressional pressure. Its initial approach was to "study the problem." The agency contracted with a private consulting firm to examine blood specimens of residents exposed to the Love Canal pollution. The study revealed more than normal damage to chromosome cells, setting off a new panic and new demands for action. Critiques of the study by other researchers led to charges that the whole Love Canal situation was being blown out of proportion (Kolata, 1980).

Public agencies, on the defensive generally, have to be mindful of their image. Refusal to rehouse and recompense the victims of a disaster, especially mainstream families with young children, seems the perfect embodiment of the callous bureaucrat. It is not the agencies themselves but governors and presidents, with tenures directly determined by the voters, who eventually make the critical decisions. In time, the residents of Love Canal were reimbursed by the government agencies, which then turned around and sued Occidental Petroleum, Hooker's parent company, for the catastrophe they had once tried to minimize.

IMPLICATIONS FOR THE POLICY ADVOCATE

Political systems, like other social systems, are made up of interacting and interdependent parts. Push one button and you set off many others. But it matters which buttons you push. Some are more strategic than others. We have looked at the structures through which policy is formulated, enacted, interpreted, and implemented. We can state several general principles regarding potential policy influence.

1. The closer you are to the beginning of the process, when a proposal is first put forth, the greater your influence on policy. While it is possible for a policy proposal to be drastically rewritten during the enactment stage, there is a tendency to debate the issues posed by the original formulation of the policy question. Once a policy has been enacted, that goes a long way toward determining the basic thrust, but as has been seen interpretation of the final product can also have significant consequences for policy in operation.

2. The more power a person has, the more power will be wielded to influence that person. Since other parties have more at stake in the decisions of this person, they are more motivated to try to affect the outcome. And the higher the power, the larger the number of different interests likely to come into play. The upshot for the advocate is that in a high stakes game, there is more competition for access to the power holder.

3. Other things being equal, elected officials are more vulnerable to outside pressure than appointed officials, for the obvious reason that they have to be concerned about pleasing the voters. (The appointees to whom I am referring here are administrators in the executive branch of government, not aides to elected senators and representatives.) You may have trouble getting an appointment with a member of the bureaucracy fairly far down in the hierarchy. Your representative and senator are likely to try to accommodate you, even though they may not see you in person.

4. Among legislators, committee chairs have the most influence, but it matters which committee we are talking about. Those concerned with money–budget, appropriations, and taxes–are among the heavyweights. At the federal level, foreign relations and the military have special clout. Next to the committee chair, the ranking minority party member (the leader of the opposition, in effect) is most powerful. But depending on the committee, rank-and-file members carry considerable weight.

Bibliography

Aberbach, J.D., Putnam, R.D., & Rockman, B.A. 1981. *Bureaucrats and Politicians in Western Democracies.* Cambridge, MA: Harvard University Press.

Abramson, J.B., Arterson, F.C., & Orren, G.R. 1988. *The Electronic Commonwealth: The Impact of New Technologies on Democratic Politics.* New York: Basic Books.

"A Nightmare in Niagara." 1978. *Time* (August 14): 46.

Arnold, R.D. 1979. *Congress and the Bureaucracy: A Theory of Influence.* New Haven: Yale University Press.

Aronson, E. 1980. *The Social Animal.* 3rd ed. San Francisco: Freeman.

Atlas, J. 1955. The Counter Counterculture. *The New York Times Magazine* (February 12), pp. 32-9, 54, 61-62, 65.

Bachrach, P., & Baratz, M.S. 1970. *Power and Poverty: Theory and Practice.* New York: Oxford University Press.

Baker, J.N., & Krieger, J.J. 1978. "Labors of Love." *Newsweek* (December 11): 16.

Bardach, G. 1971. *The Skill Factor in Politics: Repealing the Mental Health Commitment Laws in California.* Berkeley, CA: University of California Press.

Bartlett, D.L., & Steele, J.B. 1992. *America: What Went Wrong?* Kansas City, MO: Andrews & McMeel.

Bartlett, D.L., & Steele, J.B. 1994. *America: Who Really Pays the Taxes?* New York: Touchstone.

Beatty, J. 1994. Who Speaks for the Middle Class? *Atlantic Monthly,* 273(5): 65-6, 68-70, 73, 76, 78.

Berke, R.L. 1994. The 'Contract' Gets New Ally On the Right. *The New York Times* (January 18), p. D14.

Bibby, J.F. Ed. 1983. *Congress Off the Record.* Washington: American Enterprise Institute.

Block, F., Cloward, R.A., Ehrenreich, B. & Piven, F.P. 1987. *The Mean Season: The Attack on the Welfare State.* New York: Pantheon Books.

Blumenthal, S. 1994. Christian Soldiers. *New Yorker,* LXX(21):31-7.

Brown, M.H. 1979. Love Canal, U.S.A. *The New York Times Magazine* (January 21):23, 38.

Brown, M.H. 1980. *Laying Waste: The Poisoning of America by Toxic Chemicals.* New York: Pantheon.

Brown, P. 1985. *The Transfer of Care: Psychiatric Deinstitutionalization and Its Aftermath.* London: Routledge & Kegan Paul.

Buckley, W.F., Jr. 1955. Publisher's Statement. *National Review,* 1(1):5.

Buckley, W.F., Jr. 1959. *Up From Liberalism.* New York: Hillman.

Carson, R. 1962. *Silent Spring.* Boston, MA: Houghton-Mifflin.

Chu, F.D., & Trotter, S. 1974. *The Madness Establishment: Ralph Nader's Study Group Report on the National Institute of Mental Health.* New York: Grossman.

Clausen, R. 1973. *How Congressman Decide: A Policy Focus.* New York: St. Martin's Press.

Compton, B.R., & Galaway, B. 1989. *Social Work Process.* 4th ed. Belmont, CA: Wadsworth.

Deutsch, M., & Gerard, H. 1955. A Study of Normative and Informational Social Influences on Individual Judgment. *Journal of Abnormal and Social Psychology,* 51:629-636.

Dowd, A.R. 1993. How to Get Things Done in Washington. *Fortune,* 128(3):60-2.

Eckholm, E. 1992. Alarmed by Fund-Raiser, the Elderly Give Millions. *The New York Times,* (November 12), pp. A1, B14.

Eisner, R. 1986. *How Real is the Federal Deficit?* New York: Free Press.

Evans, J. 1972. Welfare Reform Revisited. *California Journal.* December.

Faux, M. 1988. *Roe v. Wade: The Untold Story of the Landmark Supreme Court Decision That Made Abortion Legal.* New York: Macmillan.

Festinger, L. 1957. *A Theory of Cognitive Dissonance.* Stanford, CA: Stanford University Press.

Finney, J.W. 1976. Senator's Young Aide Offers an Insight Into Lobbying. *The New York Times* (July 28).

Frankovic, K.A. 1992. Technology and the Changing Landscape in Media Polls. In *Media Polls in American Politics*. Eds. T.E. Mann & G.R. Orren. Washington: Brookings Institution, pp. 32-54.

Freeman, N.B. 1993. Populism + Telecommunication = Global Democracy. *National Review*, XLV(22):50-1.

Friedman, M. 1962. *Capitalism and Freedom*. Chicago: University of Chicago Press.

Gantz, W., & Kowalewski, P. 1979. Religious Broadcasting as an Alternative to TV: An Initial Assessment of Potential Utilization of the Christian Broadcasting Network Alternative. Unpublished paper, Houston, TX.

Germani, G. 1966. Social and Political Consequences of Mobility. In *Social Structure and Mobility in Economic Development*. Chicago: Aldine, pp. 364-94.

Gibbs, L.M. 1982. *Love Canal: My Story*. Albany, NY: SUNY Press.

Gilbert, M.A. 1979. *How to Win an Argument*. New York: McGraw-Hill.

Greenberg, S.B. 1995. *Middle Class Dreams*. New York: Times Books/Random House.

Gruber, J.E. 1987. *Controlling Bureaucracies: Dilemmas in Democratic Government*. Berkeley, CA: University of California Press.

Heilbroner, R.L., & Thurow, L.C. 1975. *The Economic Problem*. 4th ed. Englewood Cliffs, NJ: Prentice-Hall.

Hofstadter, D. 1994. The Soul of the Old Machine. *The New York Times Magazine* (October 16), pp. 52-55.

Holderness, M. 1993. Power to the People by Modem. *World Press Review*, 40:44 (February).

Huntington, D., & Kaplan, R. 1980. *Whose Gold is Behind the Altar? Corporate Ties to Evangelicals*. Berkeley, CA: California Student Christian Movement.

Hurwitz, J. 1986. Issue Perception and Legislative Decision Making. *American Political Science Quarterly*, 14:150-185.

Jaffe, F.S., Lindheim, B.L., & Lee, P.R. 1981. *Abortion Politics: Private Morality and Public Policy*. New York: McGraw-Hill.

Jenkens, I. 1981. On the Writing of Orders and the Implications of Wyatt. In *Wyatt v. Stickney: Retrospect and Prospect.* Ed. L.R. Jones & R.R. Parlour. New York: Grune & Stratton.

Kamel, R. 1990. *The Global Factory: Analysis and Action for a New Economic Era.* Philadelphia, PA: American Friends Service Committee.

Kennedy, J.F. 1963. Message on Mental Illness and Mental Retardation. *Congressional Record,* 88(1) CIX, Part 2 (February 5):1744-1749.

Kingdon, J.W. 1973. *Congressmen's Voting Decisions.* New York: Harper & Row.

Kleinkauf, C. 1981. A Guide to Giving Legislative Testimony. *Social Work*, 26:297-303.

Kolata, G.B. 1980. Love Canal: False Alarm Caused by Botched Study. *Science,* 208:1239-1242.

Krislov, S. 1963. Amicus Curiae Brief: From Friendship to Advocacy. *Yale Law Journal*, 72:694-721.

Kurtz, R.H., ed. 1960. *Social Work Year Book.* New York: National Association of Social Workers.

Lamendola, L. 1977. Welfare: Governor Eager to Sign 'Able-Bodied' Measure. *Newark Star-Ledger* (October 19):13.

Lecky, P. 1961. *Self-Consistency: A Theory of Personality.* 2nd ed. Hamden, CT: Shoe String Press.

Levine, A., & Silverstein, K. 1993. How the Drug Lobby Cut Cost Controls. *The Nation,* 257(20): 713, 730-2.

Levine, A.G. 1982. *Love Canal: Science, Politics, and People.* Lexington, MA: Lexington Books.

Levine, M. 1981. *The History and Politics of Community Mental Health.* New York: Oxford University Press.

Liebman, R.C. 1983. Mobilizing the Moral Majority. In *The New Christian Right: Mobilization and Legitimation.* Eds. R.C. Liebman & R. Wuthnow. New York: Aldine, pp. 49-73.

Lii, J.H. 1995. Week in Sweatshop Reveals Grim Conspiracy of the Poor. *The New York Times* (March 12), pp. 1, 40.

Lipset, S.M., & Bendix, R. 1959. *Social Mobility in Industrial Society.* Berkeley & Los Angeles, CA: University of California Press.

Luker, K. 1984. *Abortion and the Politics of Motherhood.* Berkeley, CA: University of California Press.

Lynn, L.E., Jr., & Whitman, D. deF. 1981. *The President as Policy-maker: Jimmy Carter and Welfare Reform.* Philadelphia, PA: Temple University Press.

Mahaffey, M. 1982. Lobbying and Social Work. In *Practical Politics: Social Work and Political Responsibility.* Ed. M. Mahaffey & J.W. Hanks. Silver Spring, MD: National Association of Social Workers.

McCroskey, J.C. 1968. *An Introduction to Rhetorical Communication: The Theory and Practice of Public Speaking.* Englewood Cliffs, NJ: Prentice-Hall.

McLuhan, M. 1964. *Understanding Media: The Extensions of Man.* New York: McGraw-Hill.

Meyer, J.A. 1988. Don't Risk America's Job Creation Boom. *The New York Times* (August 14):2F.

Mott, P.E. 1976. *Meeting Human Needs: The Social and Political History of Title XX.* Columbus, OH: National Conference on Social Welfare.

Ms Magazine, 5(2). 1994. (Special issue on domestic abuse).

Murray, C. 1984. *Losing Ground: American Social Policy, 1950-1980.* New York: Basic Books.

Nader, R., & Brownstein, R. 1980. Beyond the Love Canal: Bureaucracy Has Compounded the Chemical Mess. *The Progressive,* 44(5):28-31.

Nasar, S. 1994. More Men in Prime of Life Spending Less Time Working. *The New York Times* (December 1), p. A1, D15.

New York Times, The. 1976. Senator's Young Aide Offers an Insight Into Lobbying. (July 28).

New York Times, The. 1979. Letter from Lois M. Gibbs. (August 9):20.

New York Times, The. 1982. Cutoff of Disability Benefits Challenged. (January 31):XXI-6.

New York Times, The. 1988. Make Work Pay More Than Welfare. (August 14):2F.

New York Times, The. 1989. Senators Examine Baker on Tuesday. (January 16):A2.

Nixon, R.M. 1974. *Public Papers of the Presidents: Richard Nixon; Containing the Public Messages, Speeches and Statements of the President.* Washington: U.S. Government Printing Office.

Nixon, R.M. 1978. *The Memoirs of Richard Nixon.* New York: Grosset & Dunlap.

Nozik, R. 1974. *Anarchy, State and Utopia.* New York: Basic Books.

Nussbaum, B. 1992. Downward Mobility: Corporate Castoffs Are Struggling Just to Stay in the Middle Class. *Business Week,* 3257:56-63.

Paige, C. 1983. *The Right to Lifers: Who They Are, How They Operate, Where They Get Their Money.* New York: Summit Books.

Paletz, D.L., & Entman, R.M. 1981. *Media Power Politics.* New York: Free Press.

Pallack, M.S., & Cummings, W. 1976. Commitment and Voluntary Energy Conservation. *Personal and Social Psychology Bulletin,* 2:27-30.

Perelman, C., & Olbrechts-Tyteca, L. 1969. *The New Rhetoric.* Trans. J. Wilkinson & P. Weaver. South Bend, IN: University of Notre Dame Press.

Petras, E.M. 1992. The Shirt on Your Back: Immigrant Workers and the Reorganization of the Garment Industry. *Social Justice,* 19(1):76-114.

Phillips, K. 1993. Down and Out. *The New York Times Magazine* (January 10), pp. 16-8, 20, 32.

Piven, F.F., & Cloward, R.A. 1971. *Regulating the Poor: The Functions of Public Welfare.* New York: Pantheon.

Potter, N. 1987. Personal communication.

Ray, D. 1982. The Sources of Voting Cues in Three State Legislatures. *Journal of Politics,* 44:1074-1087.

Reagan, R.W. 1983. *A Time for Choosing: The Speeches of Ronald Reagan, 1961-1983.* Chicago: Regney Gateway.

Richan, W.C. 1981. *Social Service Politics in the United States and Britain.* Philadelphia, PA: Temple University Press.

Richan, W.C. 1983. Obstructive Politics in an Anti-Welfare Era. In *Social Work in a Turbulent World.* Ed. M. Dinerman. Silver Spring, MD: National Association of Social Workers.

Richan, W.C. 1987. Government Policies and Black Progress: The Role of Social Research in Public Policy Debates. *Social Work,* 32:353-356.

Richan, W.C. 1988. *Beyond Altruism: Social Welfare Policy in American Society.* New York: The Haworth Press.

Rieke, R.D., & Sillars, M.O. 1975. *Argumentation and the Decision Making Process.* New York: John Wiley & Sons.

Roche, W.F., Jr. 1984. Welfare Officials Trying to Ease 1982 Law That Cut Back Benefits. *Philadelphia Inquirer* (November 13):5-B

Schultze, Q.J. 1991. *Televangelism and American Culture: The Business of Popular Religion.* Grand Rapids, MI: Baker Book House.

Secaucus Home News. 1977. It Costs More to Work Welfare Recipients. (March 18):2.

Seelye, K.Q. 1994. All-Out Strategy Hobbled Lobby Bill. *The New York Times* (October 7), p. A22.

Seligman, D. 1981. A Toxic Turnaround. *Fortune* (July 27):30, 32.

Selnow, G.W. 1994. *High-Tech Campaigns: Computer Technology in Political Communication.* Westport, CT: Praeger.

Shapiro, F.C. 1972. 'Right to Life' Has a Message for New York State Legislators. *New York Times Magazine,* (August 20):10+.

Sharwell, G.R. 1978. How to Testify Before a Legislative Committee. In *Toward Human Dignity.* Ed. J.W. Hanks. New York: National Association of Social Workers.

Shupe, A., & Stacey, W. 1983. The Moral Majority Constituency. In *The New Christian Right: Mobilization and Legitimation.* Eds. R.C. Liebman & R. Wuthnow. New York: Aldine, pp. 103-16.

Smelser, N.J., & Lipset, S.M., eds. 1966. *Social Structure and Mobility in Economic Development.* Chicago: Aldine.

Snider, J.H. 1994. Democracy On-Line: Tomorrow's Electronic Electorate. *Futurist,* 28:15-9 (Sept/Oct).

Songer, D.R., Underwood, J.M., Dillon, S.G., Jameson, P.E., and Kite, D.W. 1985. Voting Cues in Two State Legislatures: A Further Application of the Kingdon Model. *Social Science Quarterly,* 66:983-990.

State of New York, Court of Appeals. 1988. *Brief Amicus Curiae of the Coalition for the Fundamental Rights and Equality of Ex-Patients in Support of Petitioner-Appellant.* In *Anonymous v. New*

York City. Appeal by the petitioner-appellant from a decision of the Supreme Court, Appellate Division, First Department, entered on December 18, 1987.

Stein, I. 1975. *Industry Effects of Government Expenditures: An Input-Output Study.* Washington: U.S. Department of Commerce, Bureau of Economics. COM-75-11157.

Sternberg, W. 1993. Housebreaker. *Atlantic* (June), pp. 26-8, 37-42.

Swan, J. 1979. Uncovering Love Canal. *Columbia Journalism Review,* 17:46-51.

Tallmer, M. 1981. Hooker's Other Love Canals: Chemical Dumping as a Corporate Way of Life. *The Progressive,* 45(11):35-42.

Tedeschi, J., Schlenker, B., & Bonoma, T.V. 1971. Cognitive Dissonance: Private Ratiocination or Public Spectacle? *American Psychologist,* 26:685-695.

Thomma, S. 1995. Religious Right Feels Betrayed by GOP. *Philadelphia Inquirer* (March 24), p. A10.

Tropman, J.E. 1989. *American Values and Social Welfare: Cultural Contradictions in the Welfare State.* Englewood Cliffs, NJ: Prentice-Hall.

United States of America, the State of New York, and UDC–Love Canal v. Hooker Chemicals and Plastics Corporation. 1988. 680 F. Suppl. 546, W.D.N.Y.

U.S. Bureau of Census. *Statistical Abstract of the United States.* Annual. Washington: U.S. Government Printing Office.

U.S. House of Representatives, Committee on Ways and Means, Subcommittee on Public Assistance and Unemployment Compensation. 1987. *Hearings to Examine Proposals to Reform the Federal-State Welfare System.* January 28, February 19, and March 4, 6, 10, 11, and 13. 100th Congress, 1st Session. Washington, DC: U.S. Government Printing Office.

U.S. Senate, Committee on Environment and Public Works, Subcommittees on Environmental Pollution and Resource Protection. 1979. *Hazardous and Toxic Waste Disposal Field Hearings.* May 18, Niagara Falls, NY, and June 29, San Francisco, CA. 96th Congress, lst Session. Washington, DC: U.S. Government Printing Office.

U.S. Senate, Special Committee on Aging, Subcommittee on Long-Term Care. 1976. The Role of Nursing Homes in Caring for

Discharged Mental Patients (And the Birth of a For-Profit Boarding Home Industry). Supporting Paper No. 7; series, *Nursing Home Care in the United States: Failure in Public Policy.* Washington, DC: U.S. Government Printing Office.

Vigoda, R. 1995. Campus Lessons in Downsizing. *Philadelphia Inquirer* (March 12), pp. 1,15.

Viguerie, R.A. 1980. *The New Right: We're Ready to Lead.* Falls Church, VA: The Viguerie Co.

Whiteman, D. 1985. The Fate of Policy Analysis in Congressional Decision Making: Three Types of Use in Committees. *Western Political Quarterly,* 38:294-311.

"Who Will Be Liable for Toxic Dumping?" 1978. *Business Week* (August 26):32.

Wilkerson, I. 1994. As Rostenkowski's Challenger Shows a Surge, A Sleepy Campaign Stirs. *The New York Times* (November 7), p. B11.

The Writer's Market 1988. 1987. Ed. G.T. Neff. Cincinnati, OH: Writer's Digest Books.

Wuthnow, R. 1983. The Political Rebirth of American Evangelicals. In *The New Christian Right: Mobilization and Legitimation.* Eds. R.C. Liebman & R. Wuthnow. New York: Aldine, pp. 167-85.

Wyman v. James. 1971. 400 US 309 (January 12).

Yorke, I. 1978. *The Technique of Television News.* London: Focal Press.

Zeigler, H., & Baer, M.A. 1969. *Lobbying: Interaction and Influence in American State Legislatures.* Belmont, CA: Wadsworth.

Zuckerman, M.B. 1994. Who Does Feel Your Pain? *U.S. News and World Report,* 117:126 (December 26).

Zuesse, E. 1981. Love Canal: The Truth Seeps Out. *Reason* (February):16-33.

Index